The Colors of Zion

The Colors of Zion

BLACKS, JEWS, AND IRISH FROM
1845 TO 1945

George Bornstein

HARVARD UNIVERSITY PRESS

Cambridge, Massachusetts, and London, England · 2011

Library of Congress Cataloging-in-Publication Data
Bornstein, George.
    The colors of Zion : blacks, Jews, and Irish from 1845 to 1945 /
George Bornstein.
        p.   cm.
    Includes bibliographical references and index.
    ISBN 978-0-674-05701-2 (alk. paper)
    1. Racism—History.   2. Racism—United States—History.   3. Ethnic relations—
History.   4. United States—Ethnic relations—History.   5. Jews—Ethnic identity.
6. Blacks—Race identity.   7. Irish—Ethnic identity.   8. Race relations in literature.
9. American literature—African American authors—History and criticism.
10. American literature—Jewish authors—History and criticism.   11. Irish literature—
History and criticism.   I. Title.
HT1507.B67   2011
305.8009—dc22   2010013801

To my wife, Jane, and to Ben, Rebecca, Joshua, Melissa, and all Righteous Gentiles of whatever group

Contents

Illustrations

Preface

The Colors of Zion grows out of a career devoted to teaching and writing about Irish, Jewish, and African-American literature and their many and fascinating interconnections. That experience as scholar and teacher increasingly convinced me that projecting our current conceptions of race and ethnic groups back onto the past results in misreadings of literature, culture, and our own history. That is particularly true of the United States, the spectrum of whose categories differs from that of every other country in the world now and in the past, as Chapter 1 explains in regard particularly to races. Chapters 2 and 3 then explore the twin themes of nationalisms and melting pots, two categories whose seeming opposition represents opposite sides of the same coin. Chapters 4 and 5 extend such lost connections first into the realm of popular culture and its institutions and then into the cauldron of the 1930s and war. The study thus spans the period from the mid-nineteenth century to the mid-twentieth. It ends with the concept of the Righteous Gentile commemorated at the Israeli Holocaust Memorial, Yad Vashem, which has a special section honoring non-Jews who risked their own lives to rescue Jews from the horror of the Holocaust. I expand the term in this study to include all those Irish, Jewish, or African-American figures who fought against narrow identification only with their own group and instead championed a wider and more humane vision of a shared humanity that sees hybridity rather than purity and love rather than resentment. During the heyday of the identity politics of the 1980s and 1990s, recognizing those positive qualities became problematic, especially within academia. But with the election of a mixed-race president who himself embodies mixture and mutual respect (and who famously described himself as a "mutt"), the shallow and arbitrary nature of narrow identity politics becomes evident, along with the outmoded historical contingency of some of our own categories. This study readily acknowledges the tension, exploitation, and sheer horror that are one part of the history of intergroup relations, but it resolutely highlights the neglected aspects of cooperation, sympathy, and support. To that end, I have tried to recuperate strong voices from the past of all three groups in order to let them speak for themselves and their age rather than ventriloquizing them in the terms of our own. They have more to teach us than we have to teach them.

A wide-ranging study such as this one acquires many debts. I have tried to acknowledge all specific ones to literature on the various subjects in the notes for each chapter, though of course I have read more widely than simply the works cited. Earlier versions of sections of Chapter 2 first appeared in 2005 in *Modernism/modernity,* published by Johns Hopkins University Press, and in the *Times Literary Supplement.* I also owe special thanks to Eric Sundquist and Elizabeth Butler Cullingford, both for the pervasive influence of their pioneering scholarship and for serving as careful readers of the entire manuscript. My colleague Gregg Crane read several chapters in typescript and offered unfailing support and useful criticism with each. I could not ask for a more supportive or skillful editor than John Kulka. Others who helped in particular ways include David Bohigian, David Cohen, Matt Cohen, Todd Endelman, Michael Galchinsky, Henry Louis Gates Jr., Lawrence Goldstein, Lorna Goodison, Meg Harper, Robert Hill, David Hollinger, Karen Humes, George Hutchinson, the late Lemuel Johnson, Jonathan Karp, John Knott, Cassandra Laity, Mary Lefkowitz, Julian Levinson, Julie Liss, Elizabeth Loizeaux, Tricia Lootens, Frances Malino, Doug Mao, Peter Mark, Deborah Dash Moore, Maureen Murphy, Edna Nashon, Ifeoma Nwonkwo, Catherine Paul, Jonathan Price, Maris Vinovskis, Maurice Walsh, James West, John Whittier-Ferguson, Hana Wirth-Nesher, John Young, and the librarians at the British Library, the Central Zionist Archive, the Jabotinsky Institute, the Library of Congress, the National Library of Ireland, the New York Public Library, the University of Texas, and especially the University of Michigan. Olivia Bustion, Bill Hogan, Alice Keane, Brian Matzke, Russ McDonald, Nate Mills, Jessica Morton, and Jamie Olson served as capable and helpful graduate research assistants, as did Nicolas Curdumi, Sarah Duffy, and Elizabeth Mann as undergraduate ones. For material support I am pleased to acknowledge the University of Michigan, especially the

College of Literature, Science, and the Arts and the Office of the Vice President for Research, and the Mellon Foundation for an Emeritus Fellowship that enabled me to complete this project over the final two years. I appreciate the loving and unwavering emotional support of my wife, Jane, and of my children, Ben, Rebecca, Josh, and now Melissa. And finally, I acknowledge all those Righteous Gentiles of whatever group who taught me how to love and how to praise.

The Colors of Zion

Introduction

My title may invoke curiosity and perhaps skepticism. At the turn of our current century, most of us neglect what these three groups—which our current culture encourages us to see as separate products of different and often conflicting historical contingencies—might have had in common at the turn of the previous century and perhaps still do. When our present historical memory includes contact at all, it usually stresses tension rather than cooperation. Whether in the Black-Irish confrontation of the movie *Gangs of New York*, the poetry of Amiri Baraka libeling Jews as absent from the World Trade Center on September 11, or the tendency of the Irish nationalist movement to align itself with the Palestine Liberation Organization or Hamas rather than with the Zionist movement it once invoked, the images of the past few years feature antagonism between separate groups. Yet as the novelist L. P. Hartley famously remarked in the prologue to his novel *The Go-Between* (1953), "The past is a foreign country; they do things differently there."[1] The past, of course, pertains not only to an actual past but to a knowable past, which is to say our constructions of the past. And the way we now construct the past of group relations differs so markedly from the way that the groups themselves previously constructed such relations that it calls into question the adequacy of what we think we know as a basis for present understanding and future action. Indeed, the way that we construct the groups themselves has changed dramatically over the past century or even half century. Those categories continue to morph at a surprising rate even while they appear to us as either natural or always existing, in the way that Benedict Anderson posits for nations as imagined communities.[2] I recognize the very real tensions that have existed among these groups, but maintain here that that part of the story has been stressed and even overstressed recently and that it is time to recuperate the network of lost intergroup connections. Sensitized to past exploitation and conflict, we can now use those linkages to imagine and perhaps construct a more hopeful future. The election of Barack Obama as president signifies many things, one of them that it may be time to adjust our paradigms once again. This work argues for that change.

One road into what we have forgotten begins with Frederick Douglass's tour of Famine Ireland. So thoroughly has this episode been erased from current consciousness that it has only recently begun to reemerge from obscurity. In years of lectures and discussions in the classroom and at scholarly conferences, I have only in the past few met rising numbers in North America (and only some in Ireland) who even knew that Douglass made such a tour. Certainly, no one would learn of it from such now canonical sources as the *Norton Anthology of American Literature* or the *Norton Anthology of Afro-American Literature,* the first of which fails to mention Douglass's trip altogether and the second of which misdescribes it as a tour of England. Nor does either reprint Douglass's moving accounts of his experiences there. Yet in late 1845 and early 1846 Douglass did make an anti-slavery lecture tour of what was then Britain, building momentum as he moved from four months in Ireland and five in Scotland to his culminating smash success in England. Along the way he contributed regular accounts of the tour to William Lloyd Garrison's fiery abolitionist journal *The Liberator,* which carried on its masthead at the time the motto "Our Country Is The World—Our Countrymen Are All Mankind."

What Douglass said on the tour sounds even more surprising to us now, conditioned by expectations of separateness and resentment, than the fact that he barnstormed through the then British Isles at all. In one article the degradation of Irish oppression astonished him into a new outlook on the anti-slavery struggle:

I had heard much of the misery and wretchedness of the Irish people. . . . But I must confess, my experience has convinced me that the half has not been told. . . . During my stay in Dublin, I took occasion to visit the huts of the poor in its vicinity—and of all places to witness human misery, ignorance, degradation, filth and wretchedness, an Irish hut is pre-eminent. . . . Four mud walls about six feet high, occupying a space of ground about ten feet square, covered or thatched with straw . . . without floor, without windows, and sometimes without a chimney . . . a piece of pine board . . . a pile of straw . . . a picture representing the crucifixion of Christ . . . a little peat in the fireplace . . . a man and his wife and five children, and a pig. In front of the door-way, and within a step of it, is a hole . . . into [which] all the filth and dirt of the hut are put . . . frequently covered with a green scum, which at times stands in bubbles, as decomposition goes on. Here you have an Irish hut or cabin, such as millions of the people of Ireland live in . . . in much the same degradation as the American [Negro] slaves. I see much here to remind me of my former condition, and I confess I should be ashamed to lift my voice against American slavery, but that I know the cause of humanity is one the world over. He who really and truly feels for the American slave, cannot steel his heart to the woes of others; and he who thinks himself an abolitionist, yet cannot enter into the wrongs of others, has yet to find a true foundation for his anti-slavery faith.[3]

Such a declaration startles us today, so foreign is it to both our justified view of the evils of American slavery and our less justified ignorance or silence about other oppressions. Most of us just do not expect an African-American ex-slave to say what Douglass says. Yet the fact that Douglass does say that, and many similar things, shows how closely Irish and Black causes could be linked in the nineteenth century. Nor did Douglass link American slavery and Irish oppression only in that speech. In his great midcentury *Narrative of the Life of Frederick Douglass, an American Slave,* for example, he expressed his feeling about arriving in Baltimore with the proverb that "being hanged in England is preferable to dying a natural death in Ireland," and he cited the Irish playwright and orator Richard Brinsley Sheridan's "mighty speeches on and in behalf of Catholic emancipation" as "choice documents" to him.[4] And in the crucial scene on the wharf where the two White workers encourage him to run away from slavery to the North, Douglass carefully marks their ethnicity as Irish. Indeed, Douglass's trip to Ireland coincided with publication of the Irish edition of his autobiography, for which demand required a second edition the following year.

Douglass connected his own experiences with Jewish ones as well. A poem in his appendix to the *Narrative* itself compared Christian clergy who championed slavery to those who sacrilegiously lay hands on "Israel's ark of light." More extendedly and memorably, Douglass cited Psalm 137 in his searing 1852 speech "The Meaning of July Fourth for the Negro" to invoke parallels between Black and Jewish diaspora and enslavement:

> By the rivers of Babylon, there we sat down. Yea! We wept when we re-
> membered Zion. We hanged our harps upon the willows in the midst
> thereof. For there, they that carried us away captive, required of us a
> song; and they who wasted us required of us mirth, saying, Sing us one
> of the songs of Zion. How can we sing the Lord's song in a strange land?
> If I forget thee, O Jerusalem, let my right hand forget her cunning. If I
> do not remember thee, let my tongue cleave to the roof of my mouth.[5]

In linking Black, Jewish, and Irish suffering and oppression, Douglass was more normative than exceptional for his age. The analogy between Black and Jewish exile and burden has a long and moving history invoked throughout this study.

The sentiments of Douglass reciprocated those of the Irish leader Daniel O'Connell, who had noted that the Catholic Emancipation bill passed only with strong support from anti-slavery Members of Parliament and who then marshaled Irish votes for the 1833 Emancipation Act that began the aboli-tion of slavery in the British West Indies. Not all Irish patriots agreed (John Mitchel, for example, managed to be both pro-slavery and anti-Semitic), but O'Connell pressed on to denounce slaveholders at the Great Anti-Colonization Meeting in London in 1833, where he intoned, "I would adopt the language of the poet [Milton], but reverse the imagery, and say 'In the deepest hell, there is a depth still more profound,' and that is to be found in the conduct of the American slave holders. They are the basest of the base— the most execrable of the execrable." That remark so struck Douglass when he read it that he echoed it in his own anti-slavery address in Cork on 14 October 1845, where he announced that "I am determined wherever I go, and whatever position I may fill, to speak with grateful emotions of Mr. O'Connell's labours."[6] Earlier he had asked to give his first speech in Dublin in the very jail where O'Connell had been confined, and he was delighted later to deliver a few remarks at one of O'Connell's rallies for the Repeal of the Act of Union between Great Britain and Ireland. No wonder, then, that in his preface to the *Narrative* William Lloyd Garrison had praised O'Connell as "the distinguished advocate of universal emancipation, and the mightiest champion of prostrate but not conquered Ireland." Garrison quoted there, too, phrases from O'Connell's burning denunciation of the brutalizing effects of slavery.

Douglass's association of Black, Jewish, and Irish issues uncannily anticipates those of W. E. B. Du Bois and Marcus Garvey two generations later. As Du Bois acknowledged repeatedly, his early study in Germany had widened his perceptions, much as Douglass's trip to Ireland had expanded his. In the memorable formulation of "The Negro and the Warsaw Ghetto" (1948), Du Bois recalls a trip to Poland and Germany fifty-nine years earlier, when he discovered widespread discrimination against both Poles and Jews. "The race problem in which I was interested cut across lines of color and physique and belief and status and was a matter of cultural patterns, perverted teaching and human hate and prejudice, which reached all sorts of people and caused endless evil to all men," recalled Du Bois. "So that the ghetto of Warsaw helped me to emerge from a certain social provincialism into a broader conception of what the fight against race segregation, religious discrimination and the oppression by wealth had to become if civilization was going to triumph and broaden in the world."[7] Indeed, with the exception of a few early remarks like those in the first edition of *The Souls of Black Folk* and which he later revised, throughout over half a century of articulating his views Du Bois regularly embraced Jewish causes, ranging from including Jews among the "Darker Races" referred to in the subtitle of *The Crisis*, attacking Adolf Hitler's increasingly horrifying anti-Semitic policies, and supporting both Zionism and the establishment of the state of Israel. In that he was at one with his rival Marcus Garvey, who despite his own anti-Semitism (Garvey blamed his 1923 conviction for mail fraud on a Jewish judge, a Jewish prosecutor, and two Jewish jurors) repeatedly aligned Black, Jewish, and Irish nationalisms. At the first mass congress of his Universal Negro Improvement Association (UNIA) in Madison Square Garden in 1920, for example, Garvey first read to the large crowd a telegram of congratulations to UNIA from an American Zionist leader and then read one that he himself was sending to Irish revolutionary leader Eamon de Valera on the success of the Irish revolution.

Such sentiments surprise most readers other than specialists because our schools and public discourse say so much more about tensions than about positive connections among the three groups. The largely Irish anti-Black draft riots in New York City during July 1863 and the participation of Southern Jews in slavery loom large in our consciousness. More people know of the Limerick "pogrom" of January 1904 in Ireland than of the Land Leaguer Michael Davitt's book-length denunciation of the Kishineff pogrom in Russia, and the refusal of Ireland to admit Jewish refugees from Germany during the Holocaust makes it hard to remember the Irish birth of the early president of the state of Israel, Chaim Herzog. Likewise, the fracturing of the long-term Black-Jewish alliance by the Ocean Hill–Brownsville school tensions of 1968 combined with the anti-Israel sentiments of the Black Power movement displace memory of half the lawyers of the civil rights movement in the South being Jewish or the sympathy of virtually all major African-American figures a century ago for Zionism. I readily acknowledge the fissures as an important part of the historical record. But they are not the only part, and they have become so prominent that they too often crowd out the more cooperative efforts among the three groups over a far longer period. *The Colors of Zion* aims to recuperate that network of lost connections and to do so largely by letting the principals speak for themselves. If what they say surprises us, that is because our current constructions of interracial and interethnic relations have been so one-sided as to block not only accurate understanding of the past but also, and perhaps more importantly, diagnosis of our present problems. The project insists on recovering a broad and actual historical record of what Blacks, Jews, and Irish themselves said and did rather than to imagine their reactions and then project them back from the present onto the past. In so doing, this book ranges widely over examples not usually brought together in a comparative perspective. Those include the deliberate invocation of the Irish Renaissance of W. B. Yeats and John Synge as a model for the Harlem Renaissance of Alain Locke and James Weldon Johnson, the association of all three groups with each other by hostile race theorists of the turn of the previous century and the attacks by the racist right on notions of the melting pot, the support of Pan-African liberation movements for Jewish ones, the publication by the same largely new and Jewish New York publishing houses of literature by all three groups, the cross-cultural fertilization by which they performed and enriched each other's music, and a common opposition of Jews and most African Americans (like Langston Hughes or Du Bois himself, among many others) to the rise of Hitler in the 1930s. Here I want first to articulate the principles informing this study and then to sketch each of its main areas of inquiry in a chapter-by-chapter overview.

Most prominently, *The Colors of Zion* takes a comparative stance toward individual groups and their interrelations. I have chosen Blacks, Jews, and Irish both because of the congruencies among them and because current and past tensions dominate our contemporary view. The three constitute tough cases, and an argument that succeeds with them can be extended more easily to others. For example, each group experienced exodus, oppression, and diaspora, with the Holocaust, Middle Passage, and Irish Famine as catastrophic events that changed each group's subsequent history and created common sympathies with each other. "I suffer with the Irish. I think I understand the Irish," wrote the militant Jamaican Claude McKay of a Sinn Fein demonstration in Trafalgar Square. "My belonging to a subject race entitles me to some understanding of them."[8] Similarly, musing in the Roman forum on the frieze of the Arch of Titus depicting the Roman sack of Jerusalem, Frederick Douglass labeled that monument "a painful one to every Jew" and felt that his suffering as an African American had prepared him for empathy with the enslaved and dispersed Jews: "None who have never suffered a like scorn can adequately feel for their humiliation."[9] Numerous fine studies of individual groups, or of two of them (particularly Blacks and Jews), abound, but no previous extended work examines the three groups so extensively. For Ireland, I have found Elizabeth Cullingford's *Ireland's Others* provocative both for its treatment of different ethnic groups and for its ease of movement between "high" and "popular" cultures.[10] The far larger literature devoted to African Americans and Jews amounts to a tidal wave of helpful studies, among which Eric Sundquist's *Strangers in the Land: Blacks, Jews, Post-Holocaust America* superbly synthesizes a wide historical sweep with a continuous argument for interconnection.[11] Keeping Blacks, Jews, and Irish in mind has proved strenuous enough for me, but were I to have expanded the grouping, two obvious candidates are Italians and Native Americans. Italians often aroused similar antipathies to those that greeted Jews and Irish Catholics, and the restrictive immigration acts of the early 1920s aimed at them as much as at the influx from Eastern Europe or the Emerald Isle. Native Americans provided another racial other, often with a repressed guilt at their displacement. I hope in the future to develop the occasional passing references in this study into a fuller investigation.

The comparative approach leads to a transatlantic focus. While paying the most attention to encounters in the United States, I have cited materials from Ireland and from England as well, and occasionally from the European continent. For instance, I draw on English cartoons as much as American ones and discuss novels like George Eliot's *Middlemarch* or James Joyce's *Ulysses* at the same length as Zora Neale Hurston's *Moses, Man of the Mountain* or the early film *The Jazz Singer*. Throughout I focus on Anglophone sources, although I have absorbed important insights from historians and critics mining Gaelic, Yiddish, or African languages. Paul Gilroy's *Black Atlantic* has proved seminal for me, both in its transatlantic span and in its generosity of linkages.[12] The famous remark "England and America are two countries divided by a common language" (most often ascribed to the Irish author George Bernard Shaw, with the Irish Oscar Wilde and half-American Winston Churchill as leading runners-up) has kept me attentive to difference as well as similarity, even while the resultant jostle of cultures and dialects has itself provided a paradigm for cultural interactions.

The Colors of Zion adopts a resolutely hybrid approach to cultural materials. Like a range of theorists, including Declan Kiberd, Anthony Appiah, Henry Louis Gates Jr., and Ross Posnock, I find culture fluid and mixed rather than encapsulated and fixed. In the words of Cornel West, "From the very beginning we must call into question any notions of pure traditions or pristine heritages, or any civilization or culture having a monopoly on virtue or insight. Ambiguous legacies, hybrid cultures. By hybrid, of course, we mean cross-cultural fertilizations. Every culture that we know of is a result of the weaving of antecedent cultures."[13]

The notion of hybridity surfaces repeatedly in the pages that follow, whether in the contending dialects of Henry Roth's novel *Call It Sleep,* the persistent analogies in Douglas Hyde's speech "The Necessity of De-Anglicizing Ireland," or Louis Armstrong playing his composition "Irish Black Bottom" while wearing a Star of David around his neck. While profiting from the work of the "whiteness historians,"[14] particularly Matthew Frye Jacobson, I have resisted their rhetoric of "appropriation" and instead favor a more mingling and mutually enriching view of cultural interaction.

Finally, my approach here grows out of my own expertise in literary and cultural studies and conviction that culture is fluid and hybrid rather than fixed or pure. Indeed, fantasies of racial and cultural "purity" inspired some of the worst and most murderous regimes of the twentieth century. While making forays into history, sociology, and other fields, I ground my argument in examples from literary and popular culture and in works like speeches and essays plausibly considered as literature. Comparative studies like George M. Fredrickson's *Racism: A Short History* and David Hollinger's *Postethnic America* have caused me to think about those texts in different ways, as have a variety of historians on more specialized subjects.[15] My own inquiry closes with World War II, the cataclysm that transformed the way we frame so many issues of race, ethnicity, and culture. I gesture occasionally toward subsequent events and works, and hope that the reader will see clear implications of this study for our current cultural and social debates. But I have generally remained within the hundred-year span from mid-nineteenth to mid-twentieth century in the hope of recuperating its best insights for our contemporary use.

Races

People in the past conceptualized and enacted race and ethnicity differently from us. I accept the constructed aspect of both terms, with "race" tending toward a real or imagined biological component and "ethnicity" toward a more purely socially constructed one, yet distinguishing them in practice is difficult, and I often use the more inclusive and capacious term "groups" instead. It is important to recognize that social construction applies not only to identities within our familiar categories today—like those of the pentagonal division of the United States census into White, African American, Hispanic, Asian, and Native American—but also to the choice of the categories themselves. In the period covered by this project, most people saw the ethnicities now grouped under "White" as comprising a variety of races, including the Irish and Jewish ones. Conversely, many saw the category of "Black" or African American as itself multiple, as the use in past censuses of terms like "mulatto" or "quadroon" attest. The logical extension of a mania for classification led to such absurdities as the "one-drop" rule of the slave and Jim Crow South whereby someone of overwhelmingly White ancestry could still be classified as Black, as they still can today.[16]

The term "race" applied to all three of the groups in this study. Writers across the spectrum used the term that way, including W. E. B. Du Bois,

Theodore Herzl, and James Joyce. Joyce, for example, described his Irish masterpiece *Ulysses* with its Jewish hero Bloom as an "epic of two races (Israel-Ireland)" and carefully mapped the homologies between what he considered two races and what we today might consider two groups of White ethnics. Less positively, the African-American author John Matheus in a piece that unfortunately won first prize in the *Opportunity* magazine contest of 1925 depicted Jews as "enveloped in a racial consciousness unerringly fixed on control and domination of money."[17] So, too, did the creators of the racialist science that arose in the late nineteenth and early twentieth centuries see separate races where we often do not. Robert Knox's *Races of Man* (1850) and William Ripley's *Races of Europe* (1899) proved especially influential, as did John Beddoe's *The Races of Britain* (1885) with its "Index of Nigrescence" purporting to show the degree of African or Negroid blood in the population as one moved westward from first London and then Dublin. The popular conception of Black, Irish, or Jewish races as lower on the scale than Anglo-Saxons or Aryans resulted in their simianization, as the apelike features of a "scientific" frontispiece from H. Strickland Constable's *Ireland from One or Two Neglected Points of View* (1899) makes clear (see Figure 1). On the left side the head of an Irish peasant shows the same receding jaw and cranial shape as that of the African native on the right, both in contrast to the firmer jaw, more aquiline nose, and more vertical skull shape of the Anglo-Saxon (here called Anglo-Teutonic) profile in the center. The now-bizarre caption explains that the Iberians were "originally an African race" who migrated to Spain and then Ireland, where they mixed with the natives, who were "of low type and descendants of savages of the Stone Age"; the descendants were then "out-competed in the healthy struggle of life" by "superior races."[18]

In the United States after the turn of the century, the racialists' heirs, like Madison Grant in *The Passing of the Great Race* (1918) and his disciple Lothrop Stoddard in *The Rising Tide of Color* (1920), proved successful enough to influence the Immigration Act of 1924; the act cut off the stream of immigrants from eastern and southern Europe that along with the northern migration of African Americans so alarmed Grant and Stoddard. They pervaded the culture sufficiently for Stoddard to turn up in Fitzgerald's *The Great Gatsby*, where the bigoted Tom Buchanan tells his guests, in a deliberate garbling by Fitzgerald of Stoddard's *The Rising Tide of Color*, about "'The

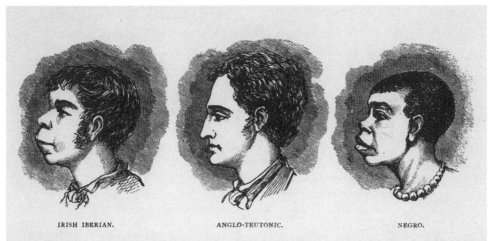

IRISH IBERIAN.   ANGLO-TEUTONIC.   NEGRO.

The Iberians are believed to have been originally an African race, who thousands of years ago spread themselves through Spain over Western Europe. Their remains are found in the barrows, or burying places, in sundry parts of these countries. The skulls are of low, prognathous type. They came to Ireland, and mixed with the natives of the South and West, who themselves are supposed to have been of low type and descendants of savages of the Stone Age, who, in consequence of isolation from the rest of the world, had never been out-competed in the healthy struggle of life, and thus made way, according to the laws of nature, for superior races.

Figure 1. "Irish, Anglo-Teutonic, and Negro Heads," from H. Strickland Constable, 1899. (Courtesy, National Library of Ireland.)

Rise of the Coloured Empires' by this man Goddard. . . . It's all scientific stuff; it's been proved." Stoddard's book, like Grant's volume, had been published by Fitzgerald's own publisher, Scribner, a few years earlier; Stoddard would extend his ideas to immigration and the ethnic makeup of the United States in *Re-forging America* (1927). An even more vulgar form of such ideas animated the Ku Klux Klan in its postwar resurgence, when it targeted African Americans, Jews, and Irish Catholics alike. The once well-known cartoonist Alfred Frueh satirized the Klan's triple animosity in a cartoon for the third issue of the *New Yorker* magazine for 7 March 1925 (see Figure 2). There Frueh took aim at the Klan's controversial applications for major parades by drawing them striding along first on Emancipation Day, then on Yom Kippur, and last on St. Patrick's Day. In each case the police hold back a crowd of the pertinent minority while the Klan marches by holding stereotyped symbols of each group: dice and chains for Blacks; signs in Yiddish and Hebrew for Jews (the Hebrew one says "Kosher"); and a harp, shamrock,

Let the Ku Klux Do It

Figure 2. "Let the Ku Klux Do It," *New Yorker,* 7 March 1925. (© The New Yorker Collection, Alfred Frueh, 1925, from cartoonbank.com. All rights reserved.)

and nationalist slogan for the Irish. Importantly for our argument, Frueh opposes the Klan to all three groups in the same cartoon. The racists and their theorists found an ideological nemesis in the leading anti-racist anthropologist of the time, Franz Boas of Columbia University, who first introduced Du Bois to African history and who mentored Zora Neale Hurston, among others. The triangle of Boas, Du Bois, and Hurston becomes important both here and in my final chapter, on the troubled 1930s.

Grasping the way in which concepts of race and race relations a century ago differ from our own can transform the way that we think of modernist cultural products. The film *The Jazz Singer,* often regarded as the first "talkie," provides a particularly complex case because of its now-controversial short sequence of Al Jolson blacking up for the stage. Unlike predominantly sympathetic earlier takes on the film, which largely explore the tensions involved in melting-pot adaptations, recent scholarship on minstrelsy has taken a negative view of the short blackface sequences and, indeed, of the entire film, seeing it as an example of either appropriation on the one hand or of becoming White by not being Black on the other. Yet such back-projections from the present contradict the film's original reception by both White and African-American audiences. African-American newspapers in fact gave the film glowing reviews, and it played to packed houses in what they termed colored neighborhoods. The New York *Amsterdam News,* for example, labeled *The Jazz Singer* "one of the greatest films ever produced" and in a second notice two years later called Jolson "the one white man who performs 'blackface' in such a manner that every colored performer is proud of him."[19] Jolson himself was on friendly terms with numerous African-American musicians and singers, such as Eubie Blake, Ethel Waters, Cab Calloway, and Noble Sissle, and he wrote an article distinguishing the modern, more sophisticated use of blackface from its earlier derogatory stereotypes. The Negro Actors' Guild sent its president (Sissle) to represent it at Jolson's funeral. Such facts suggest that we need to complicate our attitude to blackface and that Jolson's singing songs like "Mammy" might mirror aspects of, say, Paul Robeson's singing "Kaddish" and other Jewish cantorial works along with African-American songs and Irish ballads like "Danny Boy" in his own concerts.

Diasporas and Nationalisms

The concept of diaspora creates links among the three groups that lead to notions of nationalism as possible solutions. Like "ghetto," the term "diaspora" itself originally applied only to Jews: it derives from the Greek word *diaspora* in the Greek Septuagint translation of the Bible used for the dispersion of the Jews, particularly Deuteronomy 28.25 ("and shalt be removed into all the kingdoms of the earth") and John 7.35, and the only examples given in the *Oxford English Dictionary* (2nd ed., 1989) all concern Jews. But after that, as George Shepperson and Paul Gilroy have pointed out, in the past thirty years the term has come to apply to the dispersion of any racial or ethnic group, particularly the African diaspora and the Irish one.[20] All three deployments involve concepts of dispersal, of a lost homeland, and of the exilic condition in art. Hence the literature of all three groups valorizes and draws upon Psalm 137, particularly the opening verses that so attracted Frederick Douglass ("By the waters of Babylon we sat down . . ."). Those words and cadences recur in such disparate works as Douglass's oration "What to the Slave Is the Fourth of July," Emma Lazarus's poetic sequence "By the Waters of Babylon," and the third chapter of Joyce's *Ulysses*. They continue to permeate reggae music even today, as in the much-recorded "Rivers of Babylon."

One reaction to the common oppression of Blacks, Jews, and Irish was nationalism. That could easily turn separatist, yet even so leaders of each of these groups regularly invoked the others in analogy, support, and empathy. We can see that clearly in the work of Edward Blyden, whom the *Oxford Companion to African American Literature* calls "the most important African thinker of the nineteenth century." In his pamphlet *The Jewish Question* Blyden invoked "that marvelous movement called Zionism" as a model for his own views of African liberation. By dedicating that work to a Jewish friend, Liverpool merchant Lewis Solomon, Blyden expressed his hope that "members of the two suffering races—Africans and Jews—who read these pages, may have a somewhat clearer understanding and a deeper sympathy with each other." That linkage of Black and Jewish liberation movements echoes in a host of later Black thinkers, including W. E. B. Du Bois and Marcus Garvey, among others. It was reciprocated in the work of the founder of

Zionism, Theodore Herzl. In his visionary novel *AltNeuland* (OldNewland) Herzl has his hero Professor Steineck avow: "There is still one problem of racial misfortune unsolved. The depths of that problem in all their horror, only a Jew can fathom. I mean the Negro problem ... now that I have lived to see the restoration of the Jews, I should like to pave the way for the restoration of the Negroes."[21]

Both groups connected their libratory enterprise to Irish experience, too, in terms of both nation and culture. Herzl, for example, recorded in his diary his wish to "be the Parnell of the Jews," and a future prime minister of Israel, Yitzhak Shamir, took the code name "Michael" in homage to the Irish guerilla leader Michael Collins. The musical director of the historically Black Hampton Institute, R. Nathaniel Dett, identified the importance of overcoming cultural stereotypes that supported oppression for all three components of the triad. "The stage character of the Irishman and the Jew ... never existed in real life," he wrote. "Neither did, or does, the Negro character as embodied in the familiar and conventional stage 'darkey.' " Irish nationalists forged reciprocal links to Jewish and Black movements, as we saw with Daniel O'Connell and Frederick Douglass. In a key speech of the nationalist movement, "The Necessity for De-Anglicising Ireland," the future Irish president Douglas Hyde ringingly concluded with the hope that a revival of the Irish language would make ignorance of the national tongue "at least as disgraceful as for an educated Jew to be quite ignorant of Hebrew." And in another famous speech, J. F. Taylor's 1901 oration, which Joyce inscribed in *Ulysses,* Taylor invoked at length the tropes of Moses and Exodus that loom so large throughout Irish, Jewish, and Black nationalisms. No wonder, then, that George Eliot limned those linkages in her proto-Zionist novel *Daniel Deronda,* as in the debate between Daniel himself and Henleigh Grancourt over Governor Eyre's suppression of the 1865 slave rebellion or in Eliot's agreement with a Scotch reader about "the analogy you find between the Celt and the Hebrew" in the novel.[22] Such textual connections could have practical consequences, too. When Ze'ev Jabotinsky wanted to organize his Revisionist Zionist guerillas into Irgun in the 1930s to combat the British in Palestine, he went to Ireland to learn firsthand from Eamon de Valera and Robert Briscoe how the Irish Republican Army had fought the British in Ireland.

Melting Pots

The opposite of nationalism and separatism is the melting pot, with its connotation of assimilation. Yet unlike present misrepresentations, the original idea of the melting pot did not mean simple assimilation of minorities to a dominant culture. Hence the same figure could embrace both nationalism and the melting pot. One writer and activist who did that prominently was the English Zionist Israel Zangwill, whose play *The Melting Pot* (1908) popularized the term. Its premier performance in Washington, D.C., included President Theodore Roosevelt in the audience. At the play's end, Roosevelt leapt to his feet and called out across the theater, "That's a great play, Mr. Zangwill!" Zangwill's play began with a scene of hostility between a Jewish immigrant grandmother and an Irish maid, who despite their differences become fast friends by the end of the play. During the course of the drama, he took care to insert examples of anti-Negro prejudice on the part of the two greatest bigots in it, the American aristocrat Quincy Davenport and the Russian Baron Revendal. In his afterword, Zangwill both highlighted Jews as "the toughest of all the white elements that have been poured into the crucible" and devoted an entire section to the problem of "Negrophobia," which he saw as "barbarous . . . America's nemesis for her ancient slave-raiding" but which he believed would eventually melt in the cauldron, too. Zangwill's conception diverged in two crucial respects from recent critiques of the melting pot. First, he set the goal of a "coming brotherhood" firmly in the future, to be realized by future generations. And second, he argued that "The process of American amalgamation is not assimilation or simple surrender to the dominant type, as is popularly supposed, but an all-round give-and-take by which the final type may be enriched or impoverished." In short, he foresaw a process and mutual influence, not a product and one-way assimilation—a melt*ing* pot, not a melt*ed* pot, that boiled with stress and energy.[23]

Attacks on melting pot theory in its own day came less often from progressives than from racist reactionaries, like the prominent sociologist Henry Pratt Fairchild in *The Melting Pot Mistake* (1926). Fairchild fervently opposed immigration of foreign "stocks" and held that "the qualities of race are carried in the germ plasm." In that he echoed Lothrop Stoddard, who had declared that "there is no more absurd fallacy than that shibboleth of the 'melting pot.' . . . The melting-pot may mix but does not melt." Conversely, progressives like Franz Boas welcomed the new conception. In a *New York Times* review entitled "The Great Melting Pot and Its Problem," Boas tilted explicitly at Stoddard and his mentor Madison Grant. "Race mixture is the rule, not the exception," he wrote. "Assimilation is thus as inevitable as it is desirable."[24] The melting pot appealed to writers of fiction and poetry, too. In key ways Henry Roth's novel *Call It Sleep* not only dramatizes that theme as it affects the interaction of Lower East Side Jews with other ethnic groups in New York, including Irish and African Americans, but also enacts that theme on the linguistic level. There Roth stages in the very language itself the melting-pot theme, using a flowing and lyrical English to represent Yiddish speech and thought, a broken English to mimic the flawed speech of his characters in that language, and a host of other ethnic accents. Correspondingly, the title sequence of African-American poet Melvin Tolson's wartime book *Rendezvous with America* (1944) recalls that

Into the arteries of the Republic poured
 The babels of bloods,
 The omegas of peoples,
 The moods of continents,
 The melting-pots of seas,
 The flotsams of isms

and maintains its vision in the face of hatreds exemplified in the vile words "kikes," "dagos," "chinks," "bohunks," and "niggers." Later the Curator, narrator of Tolson's masterpiece *Harlem Gallery,* would invoke his "Afro-irishjewish Grandpa."[25] He was not the only prominent African American with Irish blood, of course: Martin Luther King Jr., Muhammad Ali, Alex Haley, and Barack Obama all had Irish ancestors as well as African-American ones.

Popular and Institutional Cultures

The spirit of the melting pot pervades popular culture, especially music. Even jazz, an art form mostly created by African Americans, shows a hybridity that the best Black musicians welcomed. As Cornel West reminds us in his argument for cultural hybridity, "There is no jazz without European instruments." More than that, there is no jazz without Louis Armstrong with his Irish and Jewish affinities, or without Miles Davis's attitude to White musicians. "Many blacks felt that since I had the top small group in jazz and was paying the most money that I should have a black piano player," wrote Davis in his autobiography about his White piano player, Bill Evans. "Now, I don't go for that kind of shit; I have always just wanted the best players in my group and I don't care about whether they're black, white, blue, red, or yellow. As long as they can play what I want that's it."[26] Conversely, White musicians contributed to the rise of jazz, among them Bix Beiderbecke, Dave Brubeck, Benny Goodman (who led the first integrated band), and George Gershwin, whose chord changes to "I Got Rhythm" still provide one standard for jazz musicianship. So many of the White minority of jazzmen were Jewish, along with Jewish promoters, that Hitler and others concluded that jazz was an Afro-Jewish plot to subvert Aryan culture, as the cover illustration to the Nazis' notorious *Entartete Kunst* (Degenerate Art) exhibit of 1937 shows (see Figure 3). There a Black man with exaggerated and stereotyped features sports a Star of David rather than a carnation in his dinner jacket lapel as he plays the saxophone.

That hybridity also permeated popular song and stage, going back in America at least to the late nineteenth-century Mulligan Guards routines in New York with their send-up of various ethnic groups. It reached one high point in early twentieth-century songs produced by Tin Pan Alley and elsewhere, which often made Jewish-Irish connections, as in the then popular "If It Wasn't for the Irish and the Jews." The linkage carried over onto the stage and, later, to cinema as well, particularly with the unparalleled long-term run in the 1920s of *Abie's Irish Rose,* featuring a comic treatment of cross-ethnic lovers, the Jewish Abraham Levy and the Irish Rosemary Murphy. First a play (1923), then a novel (1927), and finally a movie (1928), that work spawned numerous imitators, such as the movie *The Cohens and the Kellys* with its numerous sequels, of which *The Cohens and the Kellys in Africa* (1931) speaks most directly to the concerns of *The Colors of Zion.*

Neither popular nor high culture evolved in a vacuum. The material networks that published the literature, staged vaudeville or drama, recorded and distributed the records, or produced the films entangled these three groups in interesting ways. The publishing industry offers a good example of masking connections now but making them then. That is largely because

Figure 3. "Entartete Musik," *Entartete Kunst Exhibition*, 1937.

now-mainstream publishing houses like Knopf or Simon and Schuster operated more marginally when they were founded at the turn of the century. They were largely begun by the first generation of Jews to force their way into the previously closed world of Anglo-Saxon publishing, many of whom found their way upward blocked in the traditional houses. While struggling to establish their own ventures, they ran into the race problem again in scouting for writers to publish. Many mainline authors preferred the mainline houses. As a result, Irish, African-American, and Jewish writers often ended up being published by the same marginal, Jewish-run houses, as did some modernist writers. For example, Knopf published Langston Hughes, James Weldon Johnson, and Nella Larsen as well as Willa Cather and Wallace Stevens; Boni and Liveright published Jean Toomer, Jessie Fauset, and Mike Gold as well as Ezra Pound, T. S. Eliot, and W. B. Yeats, and its successor firm, A. and C. Boni, published the signature anthology of the Harlem Renaissance, Alain Locke's *The New Negro: An Interpretation.* One of the first new Jewish publishers, B. W. Huebsch, published James Joyce and brought Joyce's works with him when he joined Viking, where he also published James Weldon Johnson's *God's Trombones* and other African-American works. Not all modernists stayed with the new Jewish publishing houses who first published them. William Faulkner was happy to place his first two novels with the Jewish Liveright but even happier to move to the more established (and Protestant) Harcourt, Brace. "I'm going to be published by white folks now," he told his great-aunt Alabama. Such views pervaded the magazine and music industries as well. Even with the influential patronage of William Dean Howells, for example, the Jewish writer Abraham Cahan had difficulty placing his work. The editor of *Harper's Weekly* rejected one of Cahan's manuscripts with the explanation that "the life of the Jewish East Side would not interest the American reader."[27]

The Gathering Storm: The 1930s and World War II

Similar connections mark the history of education and civil rights from the turn of the century onward and would intensify in the thirties and the war years. Colleges and universities offer a ready example. England did not allow Jews to enter universities in England or Ireland until 1871. In America different forms of discrimination against all three groups kept their numbers down until after World War II, especially at elite schools, though outright quotas arose mainly to reduce the large number of qualified Jewish applicants. Dean Jones of Yale, for example, anxiously asked the compiler of a report on minorities at Yale: "*Too many Freshmen!* How many Jews among them? And are there any *Coons?* Pennypacker is here & much disturbed over the Jew Problem at Harvard. *Don't let any colored* transfers get *rooms* in the college."[28] As late as World War II, a poll of American high school students identified Negroes, Jews, and Catholics (in that order) as the groups that would be their last choice for roommates. The same discrimination held at the faculty level, where even distinguished academics like Richard Ellmann were turned down for appointments. Many Jewish academics fleeing Nazi Germany, for example, could find work only at historically Black colleges in the American South, as the PBS documentary *From Swastika to Jim Crow* recorded a few years ago. Yet such collaboration at the college level pales alongside the creation of over 3,500 Rosenwald schools for African Americans in the Jim Crow South by the Sears Roebuck magnate Julius Rosenwald. Jews and Blacks campaigned together in the National Association for the Advancement of Colored People, making common cause on issues ranging from education to voting to campaigning against lynching.

With the rise of Nazi Germany, the Black-Jewish bond intensified even as Ireland drifted toward wartime neutrality. Despite some African Americans using the anti-Jewish racial policies of Nazi Germany to fuel their own anti-Semitism, most Blacks both sympathized with the plight of the Jews and stressed parallels to their own experience. Even in 1934, for example, Paul Robeson invoked "the parallel case of the Jews" to talk about Negro progress. And toward the end of World War II Langston Hughes, in an article for the *Chicago Defender* titled "Nazi and Dixie Nordics," wrote of White Southerners that "as the Hitlerites treat the Jews, so they treat the Negroes, in varying degrees of viciousness. . . . The Jewish people and the Negro people both know the meaning of Nordic supremacy. We have both looked into the eyes of terror. Klansmen and Storm Troopers are brothers under the skin."[29] Similarly, Jews like Franz Boas connected opposition to the Nazis with opposition to American racism, as did Du Bois in another of their joint causes. The linkages with the Irish are weaker in the thirties, as American airwaves spread the anti-Semitic screeds of Father Charles Coughlin and Ireland itself moved toward its neutral stance during World War II. Samuel Beckett, for example, pointedly dissented from fascism in his unpublished writings but did not publish his most direct critiques. Author Francis Stuart's disconcerting sympathy with fascism led him to live in Berlin during the war and even to broadcast to Ireland from Nazi Germany, experiences adapted for his retrospective "fictional memoir" *Black List, Section H.* In contrast, two essays in the most important Irish literary journal of the time, Sean O'Faolain's *The Bell,* spoke up for traditional linkages. Harry Craig's "Irish versus Jew in America," for instance, deplored Irish-Jewish tensions in the United States, noted the Ku Klux Klan's extension of enmity from Blacks to "Rome and Israel," and argued instead for "the common interest of Jew and Irishman."[30]

Two American literary works displaying lost connections in this chapter are Zora Neale Hurston's retelling of the Exodus story in her *Moses, Man of the Mountain* (1939) and Arthur Miller's postwar dramatization of tension in a railroad station in Vichy France set during 1942. Hurston's novel draws an extended parallel between Jews in ancient Egypt, African Americans in the slave and Jim Crow South, and Jews in Nazi Germany. She strengthens the point with deliberate anachronisms like the references to Pharaoh's "secret police" as well as by probing issues of racial purity, "mixed people," and even eugenics. Hurston thus daringly takes a theme in which African Americans traditionally apply Jewish tradition to their own experience and reinscribes the plight of modern Jews within it. Reciprocally, Miller carefully includes the situation of African Americans within his only overtly Jewish play, as in the arrested actor Monceau's assertion that "every nation has condemned somebody because of his race, including the Americans and what they do to Negroes." Miller also limns an indictment of Nazi racial science and through it of the racialist science and pseudoscience that surfaced throughout this study (Hitler praised Madison Grant's work as his "Bible"), particularly its emphasis on measuring physical features, such as noses and skull size. Equally important for my argument, he features the importance of the Righteous Gentiles, those non-Jews who risked their own lives to help Jews escape the Holocaust. At the Yad Vashem Holocaust museum in Jerusalem, the State of Israel recognizes over 20,000 Righteous Among the Nations not only out of justice or memory but also as an "ethical obligation" to avoid demonizing the Other. In Miller's play the Austrian aristocrat von Berg embodies that position when he gives up his escape pass to the Jewish resistance leader LeDuc. "Jew is only the name we give to that stranger. . . . Each man has his Jew; it is the other," LeDuc has just told him. "And the Jews have their Jews." The large-mindedness that informs Miller's play also animates this entire study, from Frederick Douglass's sympathy with the starving Irish masses in the mid-nineteenth century through a myriad of examples up to World War II in the mid-twentieth. We badly need that large-mindedness in our society and world today, and awareness of its deep roots in the past can help inspire us to keep striving for it in the present and future. As my late friend Robert Hayden, the first African American to serve as Consultant in Poetry to the Library of Congress (a post that later became Poet Laureate), urged in mourning the deaths of Martin Luther King Jr. and Robert Kennedy in his elegy "Words in the Mourning Time":

We must not be frightened nor cajoled
into accepting evil as deliverance from evil.
We must go on struggling to be human,
though monsters of abstraction
police us and threaten us.

Reclaim now, now renew the vision of
a human world where godliness
is possible and man
is neither gook nigger honkey wop nor kike

but man
      permitted to be man.[31]

1

Races

Irish, Jews, and Blacks a Century Ago

When James Joyce told his friend and Italian translator Carlo Linati that his modernist masterpiece *Ulysses* was "the epic of two races (Israel-Ireland)," he meant it.[1] Nowadays we ordinarily do not classify Jews and Irish as distinct races. Yet a century ago people of all ethnicities viewed such nomenclature as standard for those groups and a host of others now amalgamated under the White or Caucasian label; correspondingly, other groups that we lump together today, such as African Americans in the United States, also received separate status as mulatto, quadroon, Creole, and other labels. Joyce himself offers a paradigm in regularly using the word "race" that way, especially for Irish and Jews but also more widely. The term appears eleven times in his *A Portrait of the Artist as a Young Man,* all of them pertaining to the Irish and three denouncing them as a "priestridden race."[2] When the novel builds to its ringing conclusion of Stephen's desire "to forge in the smithy of my soul the uncreated conscience of my race," he means the Irish race. Its one plural usage for large geographic scope refers not to origins in different continents, as we expect today, but rather to the "entrenched and marshalled races" of Europe (p. 161). The term appears even more frequently in *Ulysses,* whose central diptych of Stephen Dedalus and Leopold Bloom itself foregrounds the Irish and Jewish strands that Joyce said comprised his epic, especially in the confrontation of Bloom with the anti-Semite in "Cyclops" (chapter 12) and the extended parallel of Hebrew and Irish as both languages and races in "Ithaca" (chapter 17). In the first Bloom declares membership in "a race too that is hated and persecuted," and in the second the temporarily omniscient narrator has Bloom identify the "four separating forces" between himself and his guest Stephen as "Name, age, race, creed."[3]

Joyce's usage followed common practice throughout this period, from the days of Daniel O'Connell and Ralph Waldo Emerson in the mid-nineteenth century through to W. B. Yeats and James Weldon Johnson in the twentieth. Affinities between Jews and Irish as separate races permeated discourse in Ireland and England. When first elected to the House of Commons, the Irish champion of Catholic emancipation Daniel O'Connell told a group of Jewish leaders that "Ireland has claims on your ancient race, as it is the only Christian Country that I know of unsullied by any act of persecution against the Jews." At the turn of the century the Irish nationalist leader Michael Davitt invoked the same association in defending Irish Jews after the Limerick riot against them. "The Jews have never to my knowledge done any injury to Ireland," he argued. "Like our own race, they have endured a persecution."[4] A little later, Yeats, the first Irish Nobel Prize winner, told his friend, the Anglo-Jewish painter William Rothenstein, that "the Irish and the Jews are alike in that they are at their best and most fruitful as a ferment among men of other races."[5] Such usage spanned the political spectrum from conservative to liberal and was as common on the left as on the right. In a Fabian Tract, *The Decline in the Birth-Rate* (1907), for example, the socialist Sidney Webb worried that higher birthrates meant that the country was "gradually falling to the Irish and the Jews" but thought he detected "signs that even these races are becoming influenced" by lower reproductive norms.[6] Those who did not associate the Irish with slums and lower intelligence often invoked the contrasting stereotype of them as unworldly and dreamy. Such talk led the cynical Irishman Larry in George Bernard Shaw's play *John Bull's Other Island* to remark that "When people talk about the Celtic race, I feel as if I could burn down London."[7]

Meanwhile, in America, even while balancing the importance that Robert Knox assigned to race in his book *The Races of Men* (1850) with the "reagent" of culture, Ralph Waldo Emerson still accepted the term. In a key paragraph of his essay "Race," he cites the Celt, the Jew, and the Negro in quick succession. "Race is a controlling influence in the Jew," wrote Emerson. "Race in the negro is of appalling importance."[8] The term "race" appeared whether commentators were hostile or sympathetic to each group. For example, Selah Merrill, who served several terms as American consul in Jerusalem in the late nineteenth century, adamantly opposed both Zionism and Jews, branding the latter "a race of weaklings of whom neither soldiers, colonists nor enterprising citizens can be made." Yet at about the same time

Mark Twain arrived in Europe in the wake of the Dreyfus Affair, in which a French Jewish army captain was framed on charges of treason, and took an entirely different line, especially when the Viennese press attacked the author himself as "*der Jude Mark Twain*." In his stinging retort "Concerning the Jews," Twain labeled Jews "a marvelous race—by long odds the most marvelous the world has produced."[9] Back home the monthly journal *World's Work,* which celebrated the growing power and prosperity of the United States, observed in an article on birthrates published in 1903 that "the Negro and the Jew are sure to gain relatively on the other races of our population."[10]

African Americans saw themselves and Jews as separate but often allied races. In *The Future of the American Negro* Booker T. Washington urged that Blacks take Jews as models: "the Jewish race has had faith in itself. Unless the Negro learns more and more to imitate the Jew in these matters, to have faith in himself, he cannot expect to have any high degree of success."[11] A generation later Paul Robeson argued in his important essay "I Want to Be African" that Blacks should consider the parallel case of Jews as also "a race without a nation."[12] James Weldon Johnson's fantasy of a genie coming to him with the command to "Name any race of which you would like to be made a member, and it shall be done" provides one of the most memorable considerations of African Americans and Jews as races. After Johnson protests that he is content to remain a Negro, he imagines the genie commanding him to pick and concludes that "I should answer, probably, make me a Jew."[13] Almost every major African-American writer before the 1960s detected similar affinities between groups regarded as "races." "*All* of us old-fashioned Negroes are Jews," remarked Ralph Ellison in conversation.[14]

Race: The Etymology of a Word

The *Oxford English Dictionary* amply documents the many and changing uses of the English word "race" over the last few centuries. Its myriad definitions and historical examples make clear that the word itself only came into English in the sixteenth century, from the slightly earlier French *race,* Italian *razza,* and Spanish *raza,* all of obscure origin. Its most pertinent meanings include "a group of persons, animals, or plants, connected by common descent or origin"; "a limited group of persons descended from a common ancestor; a house, family, kindred"; "a tribe, nation, or people"; "mankind . . . the human race"; and, perhaps in despair of finding a more informative definition, "a set or class of persons."[15] Of the remaining definitions, my favorite is "a particular class of wine, or the characteristic flavour of this." For all its wobbly meanings, then, the *Oxford English Dictionary* confirms that race is a relatively modern concept, with us only since the Renaissance. The term "race-hatred" itself (as distinct from its widespread practice) has an even shorter ancestry dating from 1882, though before that Macaulay had come close in declaring that "in no country has the enmity of race been carried further than in England." The modern commentator Raymond Williams observes in his book *Keywords: A Vocabulary of Culture and Society* that such bigotry has been directed particularly against our three groups: "It has been used against groups as different in terms of classification as the Jews (culturally specific Europeans and North Americans, in the most usual context), American Blacks (a mixed minority within the heterogeneous population of the United States) . . . 'Orientals' . . . 'West Indians' (a mixed population identified by geographic origin . . .) . . . and then, in different ways, both Irish and Pakistanis."[16]

The relevant recentness of the word "race" and its definitions finds support from scholars of classical and biblical antiquity. In his standard survey *Race: The History of an Idea in the West,* Ivan Hannaford detects in Greek thought "no word that approximates or resembles 'race' . . . the Greek account of the differences between the peoples of Greece, Asia Minor, and Ethiopia was based upon criteria entirely different from those introduced into Greece by interpreters of the late eighteenth and early nineteenth century." To be sure, Greeks distinguished between themselves as civilized people and "hoi barbaroi" outside Greek culture, but hoi barbaroi could come in any color and their condition was not biologically hereditary. This was true of other ancient peoples, too, so that George M. Fredrickson in his *Racism: A Short History* can declare flatly that "no concept truly equivalent to that of 'race' can be detected in the thought of the Greeks, Romans, and early Christians."[17] Both Hannaford and Fredrickson draw on the pioneering African-American scholar Frank Snowden, whose book title, *Before Color Prejudice: The Ancient View of Blacks,* aptly signals his own argument. "Nothing comparable to the virulent color prejudice of modern times existed in the ancient world," he concludes.[18] Students of biblical tradition have reached similar conclusions, often strengthened even further by the idea of monogenesis, or a common origin for mankind, as opposed to polygenesis, or multiple origins. The *Encyclopedia Judaica,* for examples, observes that "The Jewish tradition, with its majestic story of Adam which furnished all men with a common ancestor, can be considered the first historical example of a fundamentally 'anti-racist' conception. On this subject the Talmud states: 'for the sake of peace among creatures, the descent of all men is traced back to one individual, so that one may not say to his neighbor, my father is greater than yours' (Sanh. 4:5)." The New Testament, of course, took over the account of creation from the Hebrew Bible and proclaimed its implications for human equality. In the King James Version of Acts 17.24–26, for example, Paul observes that the "God that made the world and all things therein . . . made of one blood all nations of men for to dwell on the face of the earth." Nineteenth-century British and American abolitionists would often cite that passage as part of their attack on slavery. Monogenesis thus often if not always led to ideas of racial equality and tended to minimize racial differences, whereas polygenesis tended to promote racial hierarchies and differences. Even so, the leading British polygenist Robert Knox fiercely opposed slavery, considering the different races to still belong to the same human species.

The Rise of Racial Science and Racialism

Modern race thinking properly begins with the rise of racial science in the eighteenth century and its flourishing in the nineteenth and early twentieth centuries. The Swedish scientist Carl Linnaeus (1707–1778), often referred to as the "father of taxonomy," fused earlier strands of thought into the first typology of races. Applying to human beings the same penchant for classification that he displayed throughout the realm of biology, Linnaeus sorted the genus "homo" or man into four basic varieties. They corresponded roughly with a geographic division of the continents—*Americanus, Asiaticus, Africanus,* and *Europaeus.* He considered them all the same species but displaying surface differences resulting from different climates and conditions. The French scientist and supervisor of the Royal Garden Georges-Louis Leclerc de Buffon inaugurated the term "race," but Linnaeus's follower, the German medical professor Johann Friedrich Blumenbach, exerted even more influence by dividing mankind into five races, in anticipation of later pentagonal schemes from his own to those of the U.S. government at the end of the twentieth century. Blumenbach coined the term "Caucasian" to describe the White race and constructed the varieties of mankind as Caucasian, Mongolian, Ethiopian, American, and Malay. Blumenbach himself resisted efforts to rank the races, but other scientists and philosophers were divided throughout the period. For every thinker like Voltaire who supported racial hierarchies, there arose a Kant who did not.[19]

The rise of the polygenists in the nineteenth century tipped the balance toward the racialists and racists for a period extending through World War I and not receiving full repudiation until the watershed of World War II. Polygenists both favored racial rankings and assigned relatively low places to the three groups central to this study. The leading British polygenist was perhaps Robert Knox, a Scots anatomy instructor forced to resign his post at the Royal College of Surgeons because of a scandal over cadavers. The very title of his popular *The Races of Men* (1850) signaled his stance. "Race is everything," he wrote in the preface. "Literature, science, art—in a word, civilization, depends on it."[20] He assigned both Jews and Africans to the "darker races" (as W. E. B. Du Bois would do more benignly later) and associated them with each other partly on account of Jewish slavery in Egypt. In his section "The Coptic, Jewish, and Phoenician Races," Knox called attention to "the African character of the Jew, his muzzle-shaped mouth and face removing him from certain other races" (pp. 198–199; cf. p. 186). For him, neither Jews nor Blacks could ever be European. When a Jewish opponent objected in a letter to the *Manchester Examiner* to Knox's obnoxious views, Knox fumed that it "defies all reasoning" that "This respectable Hebrew person describes himself as an Englishman of the Jewish belief" (p. 149). Such views led Knox, like many polygenists, to oppose racial mixing. "Nature produces no mules; no hybrids, neither in man nor animals," he maintained. "When they accidentally appear they soon cease to be, for they are either non-productive, or one or other of the pure breeds speedily predominates" (pp. 65–66).

However much Knox disliked Jews and Blacks, he saved his full hatred for Irish, or "Celts" as he called them. Averse to the Celts of France, Scotland, and Wales, Knox had a special phobia for the Irish. "The Irish Celt is the most to be dreaded," he shuddered (p. 378). And in a sort of parodic catechism, he

determined that "the source of all evil lies in *the race,* the Celtic Race of Ireland." According to Knox, like all Celts the Irish despised labor, order, and
law and tended instead toward idleness, disorder, and violence. Hence, he
championed a simple solution to the Irish Question: "The race must be
forced from the soil; by fair means, if possible; still they must leave" (p. 379).
Otherwise, they might do to England what the combined onslaught of all
three groups had done to contemporary Greece. In a paroxysm lapsing into
incoherence, Knox denounced the corruption of classical physiognomy due
to racial mixing in postclassical Greece in prose that matched the accompanying diagram: "To the admixture of Celtic blood may be traced her warlike
disposition, energy. . . . The substratum was an Oriental mind, not Coptic,
least of all Jewish; but these latter elements now prevail, I believe. The grand
classic face has all but disappeared, and in its place comes out a people with
a rounded profile; the nose large and running into the cheeks, like the Jew;
the chin receding; the eyebrows arched. Anti-classic in all things, how Greece
has fallen!" (p. 404).

Figure 4 features the simianization of African ancestry that pervaded the
nineteenth century and that became even more widespread with the spread
of evolutionary theory that reached one apex in Darwin's *Origin of Species*
(1859), which racists often misused to see Blacks and other deprecated groups
as somehow closer to apes than White and Christian Europeans were. In
Knox's case, Figure 4 displays the alleged similarity between the Negro and
the orangutan in contrast to the more Nordic European. The lines measuring angles of chin and nose lend a spurious pseudoscientific authority to
such claims that extended through the Nazi period.

If Knox became the leading British polygenist at mid-century, Josiah
Clark Nott was his American counterpart. Nott increasingly collaborated
with the eccentric Englishman George Robert Gliddon, who like Nott was a
disciple of Samuel George Morton, dubbed by the *Journal of the Anthropological Society of London* "the founder of anthropology in the United
States."[21] A Southerner, Nott ceaselessly defended the polygenist notions of
races as separate species and the consequent importance of preserving racial purity. That linkage of racialist "science" and social policy informed his
celebrated article in the *American Journal of Medical Science,* as its title
makes clear: "The Mulatto a Hybrid—probable extermination of the two
races if the Whites and Blacks are allowed to intermarry." There Nott argued

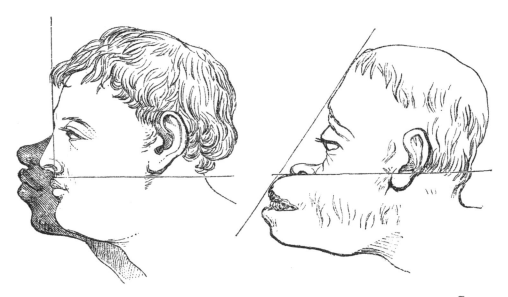

[Profile of Negro, European, and Oran Outan.]

Figure 4. "Profile of Negro, European, and Oran Outan," Robert Knox, 1850. (Courtesy, University of Michigan Library.)

that "mulattoes are intermediate in intelligence between the whites and blacks" and that "the Mulatto is a *Hybrid*" destined to die out.[22] Nott's racial views received full development in his monumental *Types of Mankind* (1854), on which he collaborated with Gliddon and included material by their common mentor, Morton, as well as a dedication to him. The eight-hundred-page tome sold out immediately and went through at least nine editions by the end of the century. *Types of Mankind* allocated separate chapters to Caucasians, to Jews, and to Blacks; the last received two separate chapters—one on "Africans" and the other on "Negro Types." A slaveholder himself, Nott placed Caucasians at the top and Africans at the bottom, with American Negroes "more humanized" because better fed than their African counterparts. Jews continually disrupted Nott's classification system, and he worried repeatedly over where to place them and whether they had any "Negroid" blood. In the end he decided that they were "a primitive stock" and that yet "the race has not entirely escaped adulteration," though he still refused to label groups like the "Black Jews" of Malabar as racially Jewish at all. Following Morton's devotion to craniology (the study of human skulls), Nott included a table arranging races hierarchically according to brain size as allegedly reflected by skull size. "Teutonic" at 92 received the highest score among White groups, with "Semitic" at 89, "Celtic" at 87, and "Negroes (African)" at 83 but still ahead of Hottentots at 75.[23] Underneath the pseudoscientific armature of the volume lurked a deep anxiety about racial purity and fear of hybridity, particularly in regard to infusions of African blood into other populations.

That tension in regard to Irish people underlay the most systematic work of the late nineteenth century on the subject, John Beddoe's *The Races of Britain: A Contribution to the Anthropology of Western Europe* (1885). A medical doctor, Beddoe's illustrious career earned him a host of honors, including stints as president first of the Anthropological Society of London and then of the Royal Anthropological Institute. Of the many pages of charts and statistics that lard his book, the most pertinent is his invention of an "Index of Nigrescence" purporting to measure an African strain in the population of Britain as one moves from east to west. He even constructed a formula for Nigrescence:

$$D + 2N - R - F = \text{Index}.$$

The index stressed particularly hair color and prognatheous jaws. Not surprisingly, Beddoes held that Ireland had the highest proportion, especially in the west. "Most of its lineaments are such as lead us to think of Africa as its possible birthplace; and it may be well, provisionally, to call it Africanoid."[24] Beddoe also supplied two influential maps of the Index of Nigrescence, though they used such complicated symbols that the simplified one circulated in the American ethnologist William Z. Ripley's *Races of Europe* (1899) is easier to grasp (see Figure 5). A Columbia-trained economist and racial theorist who taught successively at Columbia, MIT, and Harvard, Ripley popularized a tripartite scheme for the races of Europe—Teutonic, Alpine, and Mediterranean. The Teutonic (or Nordic to some other theorists) were the tallest and fairest, the Mediterranean the shortest and darkest, and the Alpine came in between. Focusing on the races of Europe, his book included a whole chapter on Jews as well as one on the British Isles, including Ireland. Ripley found Jews to be short, dark in hair and skin, and with

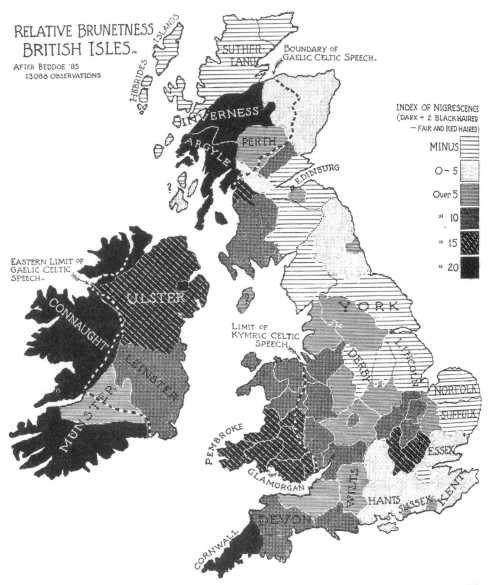

Figure 5. "Relative Brunetness, British Isles," William Z. Ripley, 1899. (Courtesy, University of Michigan Library.)

distinctive noses, but in the end "not a race, but only a people." He judged
the Irish to be a mixture including earlier Celtic and later Teutonic, among
others. His map of "Relative Brunetness British Isles" presented Beddoe's
data and mapping in clearer form. As Figure 5 indicates, Beddoe and Ripley
thought that the population became darker as one proceeded westward and
that this correlated with Gaelic language and blood.[25]

The association of Irish with Blacks carried over into both verbal and visual
representations outside of racialist science itself and often involved portrayals of both as apelike or simian. Two popular American magazines provide
striking examples. On 9 December 1876 *Harper's Weekly* (with uninten-
tional irony subtitled "A Journal of Civilization") devoted its cover to a work
by the most famous political cartoonist of the day, Thomas Nast, on the bitterly disputed 1876 presidential election between the Republican Rutherford
B. Hayes and the Democrat Samuel J. Tilden (see Figure 6). Tilden won the
popular vote, but Hayes won the presidency by a single electoral vote after
a behind-the-scenes deal threw twenty electoral votes from Florida (some
things never change) and two other Southern states to Hayes in exchange for
Republicans then withdrawing federal troops from the South and so effec-
tively ending Reconstruction. The *Harper's* cartoon "The Ignorant Vote"
portrays the election in terms of the allegedly ignorant Irish vote for Democrats in the North balancing the similar Black one for Republicans in the
South. Despite the African American following a more minstrel-like smil-
ing stereotype and the Irishman a more pugnacious Celtic one, both figures
not only match each other but show the simian or apelike characteristics attributed to both groups by race theorists as well. Ironically, northern Irish
themselves often resisted African-American progress as threatening to their
own. Another cartoon for the humor magazine *Puck* six years later, Frederick B. Opper's "The King of A-Shantee" again associates Blacks, Irish, and
apes by depicting a simian-faced Irishman whom a crude pun makes into
both the king of his shanty and the king of the Ghanaian kingdom and tribe
Ashanti (see Figure 7). The poverty and disrepair of the cabin, indulgence of
the alcohol bottle, and violence of the club come together to reinforce popular
stereotypes of the two groups. No wonder that Frederick Douglass wrote in
response to receiving a dignified print of the first African-American senator,
H. R. Revels of Mississippi, that "we colored men so often see ourselves described and painted as monkeys, that we think it a great piece of good fortune

Figure 6. "The Ignorant Vote—Honors Are Easy," *Harper's Weekly,* 9 December 1876.
(Courtesy, University of Michigan Library.)

THE KING OF A-SHANTEE.

Figure 7. "The King of A-Shantee," *Puck,* 15 February 1882. (Courtesy, University of Michigan Library.)

to find an exception to this general rule. . . . Every colored householder in the land should have one of these portraits in his parlor."[26]

Words as well as pictures hammered the association home on both sides of the Atlantic. In 1880, for example, the radical Belgian political thinker and journalist Gustave de Molinari wrote in an article on his visit to Ireland that English newspapers "allow no occasion to escape them of treating the Irish as an inferior race—as a kind of white negroes."[27] The notion of "white negroes," or even more offensively "white niggers," would reappear as an epithet for the Irish in America in the nineteenth century. The English novelist Charles Kingsley used similar but more extended terms in recoiling from starving Irish in the aftermath of the famine but managed to combine anti-Irish feeling with an even deeper if perhaps unconscious anti-Black racism. He interrupted an account of the splendid salmon fishing he enjoyed in County Sligo during a summer tour in 1860 to interject: "I am haunted by the human chimpanzees I saw along that hundred miles of horrible country. I don't believe they are our fault. . . . But to see white chimpanzees is dreadful; if they were black, one would not feel it so much, but their skins, except where tanned by exposure, are as white as ours."[28] Kingsley's "white chimpanzees" find an ironic inversion in the "black Irishmen" of the early African-American historian, pastor, and political figure George Washington Williams, who came to bitterly oppose colonial practices in the Belgian Congo. In his 1890 "Report on the Proposed Congo Railway," Williams described overworked and abused members of the Krooman tribe as "black Irishmen of the West coast" whom misery has taught to boycott working in the Congo.[29] Whether sympathetic or hostile, then, the images and ideas of journalists, cartoonists, and political figures thus accord with those of the racialist scientists of the period.

They also accord with a pervasive streak in "high" culture, for example, in the work of T. S. Eliot. In the first of his University of Virginia lectures collected in *After Strange Gods* (1934), Eliot meditated on what he called "race" and (in a common phrase also used by Joyce in *Ulysses*) "the blood kinship of 'the same people living in the same place.'" Seeing in Jews both a racial and a religious identity, he notoriously proclaimed there that "reasons of race and religion combine to make any large number of free-thinking Jews undesirable."[30] Earlier his presentation of Jews, along with Irish and Blacks, had echoed the language of turn-of-the-century race theorists, especially in the quatrain poems on the Irish Sweeney and Jewish Bleistein printed one after the other in his 1920 *Ara Vos Prec* volume. Named for a legendary Irish king, Sweeney appears in several poems. One of the most famous, "Sweeney among the Nightingales," follows the pervasive simianization of the Irish in introducing the title character as "Apeneck Sweeney." The same poem bestializes Jews as well, referring to "Rachel *née* Rabinovitch" as tearing at grapes "with murderous paws."[31] Other poems continue the animal imagery, particularly of apes and monkeys. "Sweeney Erect" ascribes "Gesture of orang-outang" to Sweeney and the epileptic woman in bed. More extendedly, "Burbank with a Baedeker: Bleistein with a Cigar" associates the Jewish Bleistein with rats, swamps, and most graphically again with apes or monkeys in the quatrain describing Bleistein's manner of walking:

But this or such was Bleistein's way:
A saggy bending of the knees
And elbows, with the palms turned out,
Chicago Semite Viennese.

The lines encapsulate a surprising range of critiques of Jews at the time, including charges of rootless cosmopolitanism, lack of culture, comic names showing degeneracy (here "Bleistein" as "lead-stone" plays off against more expected Jewish names like "Goldstein" or "Silverstein"), and lower status in the evolutionary chain. Henry James, from whose *Aspern Papers* Eliot had quoted in the poem about Bleistein, deployed similar tropes in his account of a 1904 return to the United States in *The American Scene*. Again like Joyce's anti-Semites in *Ulysses,* James used the term "the new Jerusalem," in this case to indicate "the extent of the Hebrew conquest of New York" by what he regarded as an alien "race." Invoking the simianization metaphor yet again, he recoiled from the ghetto of the Lower East Side as a series of cages, a "world of bars and perches and swings for human squirrels and monkeys."[32]

As the inclusion of Jews and Irish as separate races suggests, race theorists and those whom they influenced or drew on had trouble deciding just how many races there were. As is the case up to the present day, differences in methodology led to different conclusions. As Thomas F. Gossett tabulates in his standard *Race: The History of an Idea in America:*

The confusion over methods of determining race differences shows up most sharply in the widespread disagreement over the number of human races. Linnaeus had found four human races; Blumenbach had five; Cuvier had three; John Hunter had seven; Burke had sixty-three; Pickering had eleven; Virey had two "species," each containing three races; Haeckel had thirty-six; Huxley had four; Topinard had nineteen under three headings; Desmoulins had sixteen "species"; Deniker had seventeen races and thirty types. Jean Finot, one of the critics of race theorizing, concluded in 1906 that the methods of classification were so different that "the facility with which human races may be created at will can easily be imagined."[33]

Gossett's catalogue of changing and arbitrary racial classifications in the past should give us scant cause for feelings of superiority in the present, when we continue with our own arbitrary schemes even in the face of research based on DNA and modern genetics that calls into question any rational basis for such distinctions. As the United States Census Bureau cautions even while using its own scheme, "The racial categories included on census questionnaires ... have changed over time ... these categories have reflected social usage and not an attempt to define race biologically or genetically."[34]

Government Classifications and the Shaping of Racial Discourse

Just how much those categories have mutated over time should give us pause both about their validity and about their anachronistic application across periods. Although the idea of a census for tax, military, or other uses goes back to Roman times, its modern use to survey the entire population of a country has existed for only the past two centuries. The United States conducted the first full-scale modern enumeration in 1790, as mandated in Article 1 of the Constitution. Censuses followed in 1791 in France, 1801 in Great Britain, and 1813 in Ireland, among others. Canada and India did so in 1871, Egypt in 1897, and China not until 1953. Although most people think of censuses (if they think of them at all) as simply reflecting already existing realities, the fact is that they create those realities as much as reflect them or even distort them. An obvious example of distortion is the Soviet Union census of 1937, for which Stalin instructed his officials to find a total population of about 170 million people, a figure that hid the many millions who had died by purge, famine, or in the gulag. But even less deliberate fabrications still lead to distortion. As Melissa Nobles argues astutely in her book on race and the census, "censuses help form racial discourse . . . race is not an objective category, which censuses simply count, but a fluid and internally contradicting discourse . . . ideas about race are partly created and enlivened by census bureaus."[35] The history of the U.S. census clearly indicates both the way in which racial categories change and the way in which government agencies like census bureaus help create the very categories in which we think. I want to look at those processes first in the American census and then more briefly in those of other countries, particularly the United Kingdom and the Republic of Ireland.

The American census has been one of the most persistently obsessed with race, but the racial categories it employs have varied enormously over time. The first census, in 1790, listed only free White males, free White females, all other free persons, and slaves. The next several added "Indians not taxed" (eventually just Indian) and several divisions by age. By 1850 African Americans were divided into "Black" and "Mulatto" or mixed race, and by 1870, the race categories included Chinese. The 1890 census added Japanese and now included mixed-race categories—Mulatto, Quadroon, and Octoroon, according to amounts of perceived African blood. By 1920 quadroon and octoroon had disappeared, but Filipino, Hindu, and Korean suddenly sprang up. The mutations continued after World War II, with Hawaiian, Eskimo, and others joining the parade of terms. In short, American racial categories as reflected on the decennial censuses changed over time and showed a particular obsession with issues involving people whom we now call African Americans.

Most Americans are surprised to learn that our current and widely used five-part scheme of Caucasian, African American, American Indian or Alaskan Native, Asian and Pacific Islander, and Hispanic (as an ethnicity, not a race) dates only to 1977. In that year the Office of Management and Budget (OMB) issued its unexpectedly influential Statistical Policy Directive No. 15, setting racial and ethnic standards for federal statistics and administrative reporting. Minor revisions by OMB twenty years later made small adjustments and cleared the way for the category "some other race" on the

2000 census. Never intended to shape thought and society so broadly, the categories of Directive 15 became normative for thinking within government, private enterprise, universities, and other institutions. A steady and increasing resistance to such categorization led the Census Bureau in 2000 to allow respondents to check more than one box. That allows for sixty-three possible combinations—the original categories plus fifty-seven other possible combinations of two, three, four, five, or six races. Individuals can now be counted in multiple categories ("alone or in combination"), but no matter how many boxes they check, according to an OMB guideline on allocation in its Bulletin 00-02, "responses that combine one minority race and white are allocated to the minority race."[36]

Put simply, the OMB mandate means that people can check as many boxes as they want on the census form, but that for practical purposes if they check boxes for White and minority the government will still consider them as only minority. That is a surprising response to the growing demand to recognize racial hybridity, with nearly seven million people identifying themselves as multiracial on the 2000 census. The number of interracial marriages has steadily increased over the last several censuses, now about 13 percent and rising rapidly.[37] Popular culture today features figures like golfer Tiger Woods, who describes his racial identity as "Cabalasian" for Caucasian, African American, and Asian; singer Mariah Carey, who proudly claims Irish, Black, and Hispanic bloodlines; and CNN anchor Soledad O'Brien, who appears repeatedly on *Irish American Magazine*'s list of "Top One Hundred Irish Americans" and also belongs to the National Association of Black Journalists and National Association of Hispanic Journalists. These figures choose to depict themselves more accurately than current census or other racial classifications do. And, of course, the original "racial" categories are themselves already mixed, so that hybridity proliferates all the more. President Obama foregrounds his own mixed-race background in his books and speeches, where he continually salutes White ancestors like his mother and grandmother along with his Black ones.

Other countries' censuses show less preoccupation with race and often use different categories as well, sometimes with dizzying differences. For example, Great Britain held its first census in 1801 but did not use race as a category during the entire nineteenth century. Religion appeared only once, in 1851, although in 1891 and again in 1901 the census included mock-ups in

German and Yiddish for Jewish immigrants. The first question about ethnicity appeared in 1991, when the choices were White, Black-Caribbean, Black-African, Black-Other, Indian, Pakistani, Bangladeshi, Chinese, and Any Other, along with various "mixed" categories. When the form added a religious question in 2001, 390,000 inhabitants registered their resistance by identifying their faith as "Jedi knight." In Palestine, the two censuses during the British Mandate emphasized religion (Muslim, Jewish, Christian, or Other), as have those of subsequent Israeli surveys. Holding its first census in 1871, Canada also did not use race in the nineteenth century, or indeed until the 1980s, when multiple responses to the question of ethnic origin were encouraged. India paid much more attention to caste than to race, including 273 castes on the first general census of 1881. Importantly for our main groups, the Irish censuses (more reliable since 1841) did not include a question about race (labeled as "Ethnicity or Cultural Background") until 2006. Religious categories loomed larger than racial ones there, as often elsewhere, and from 1861 onward census takers asked for religious identification, with the dwindling Jewish category being dropped in favor of the growing Islamic one in 2002. The bewildering array and proliferation of categories shows clearly that those ordinarily used in the United States, and increasingly in Europe, are not the only ones and not always defined in the same way.

For half a century beginning in 1899, the U.S. Immigration Service developed racial categories of its own that confused as many people as the Census Bureau's distinctions did. First came the "List of Races or Peoples" created by Ellis Island immigration officials in 1899, under Terence V. Powderly as commissioner of immigration, which first classified arriving immigrants by race.[38] That list included forty-six categories, including, of course, African (Black), Hebrew, and Irish. More ambitiously, the Immigration Commission published a *Dictionary of Races or Peoples* at the behest of Congress in 1911, a compilation used by the Commission until repeal of racial categories in the early 1950s. Other branches of government used it, too, including the Supreme Court in such high-profile decisions as the internationally famous Bhagat Singh Thind case of 1923, in which a high-caste Hindu from the Punjab was denied naturalization. The authors knew well that the "scientific" literature of the day numbered races differently and noted a range from three, four, or five up to fifteen, twenty-nine, and as high as sixty-three.[39]

That did not stop the *Dictionary* from making its own contribution to the confusion by devising definitions as much linguistic as genetic. "The bureau recognizes 45 races or peoples among immigrants coming to the United States, and of these 36 are indigenous to Europe," it stated.

All three of our groups appeared prominently in the *Dictionary* in ways derived from nineteenth-century racial theory. The Irish, for example, emerged as members of the Celtic group whose ancestral language was Irish. Description of the Irish type cited the same John Beddoe whose *Races of Britain* contained the notorious Index of Nigrescence. Jews appeared under the heading "Hebrew, Jewish, or Israelite," defined as "the race or people that originally spoke the Hebrew language." The "Hebrew" category proved unpopular from the start and drew opposition from Jewish organizations fearful of being classified a separate race elsewhere in society as well, but it embarrassingly persisted until World War II.[40] Unfortunately for its own coherence even at the time, the *Dictionary* further observed that "Physically the Hebrew is a mixed race, like all our immigrant races," a position that undermined its own categories. Why classify people as separate races if the "races" are mixed to begin with? Nonetheless, the *Dictionary* heroically marched on to the category of "Negro, Negroid, African, Black, Ethiopian, or Austafrican," which it considered a "grand division of mankind distinguished by its black color and . . . by its woolly hair" and saw as "belonging to the lowest division of mankind from an evolutionary standpoint" (p. 100). The authors confessed to "a bewildering confusion in the terms used to indicate the different mixtures of white and dark races in America" and spent two paragraphs trying to sort out appropriate terminology before concluding that its own statistics counted as Negro or African "aliens whose appearance indicates an admixture of Negro blood."

Racial Categories: Porous or Pure?

Particular confusion in American categories derives from a unique insistence on the "one-drop" rule for determining who is an African American. Arising from the slave and then Jim Crow South, the rule means that a single drop of African blood makes someone Black. As sociologist F. James Davis explains in his authoritative *Who Is Black? One Nation's Definition,* "not only does the one-drop rule apply to no other group than American blacks, but apparently the rule is unique in that it is found only in the United States and not in any other nation in the world. In fact, definitions of who is black vary quite sharply from country to country."[41] As already indicated, if the rule applied to other groups, then Muhammad Ali, Martin Luther King Jr., and Alex Haley would be considered Irish rather than African American. Henry Louis Gates Jr., chairman of the Department of African and African-American Studies at Harvard for fifteen years, surprisingly found through DNA testing that his ancestry included both Jewish and Irish ancestors as well as African ones, yet the one-drop rule renders him Black rather than Jewish or Irish. President Obama would qualify as Irish, too, given that his great-great-great grandfather Fulmuth Kearney emigrated to America from the obscure Irish village of Moneygall in 1850. And of course Jewish and Irish ancestries themselves feature mixture. As Davis observes, "A person who is half or more white would not be defined as a black in Latin America, the Caribbean, the Republic of South Africa, and other places" (p. 125). That list might include Adam Clayton Powell Jr., Lena Horne, Julian Bond, Whitney Young, and many light-skinned Blacks whom Americans think of as "African American."

Racial categories wobble particularly when they come to Jews. Bryan Cheyette has pointed out for representations principally in England and Ireland "the protean instability of 'the Jew' as a signifier . . . 'the Jew', like all 'doubles', is inherently ambivalent and can represent both the 'best' and the 'worst' of selves."[42] That was true for the United States, too, especially after the Civil War and in the color-conscious South. Jews' primary problem, of course, was that they were not Christian, as a host of newspaper advertisements for jobs and housing made clear ("Christians Only"), as did the clash of Jewish and Christian Sabbaths (Orthodox Jews could not work on the then standard workday Saturday), difficulties of keeping kosher, and the like. Nonetheless, Southern race thinkers after the Alabaman Josiah Nott and Scots-English Knox repeatedly questioned whether Jews were fully White. A peripheral literature sprang up to classify Jews as "negroid." One notorious instance is *The Jew a Negro* (1910) by the North Carolinian Reverend Arthur T. Abernethy, which followed the lead of the Missourian Charles Carroll's even more obnoxious *The Negro a Beast* (1900). "The Jew of today, as well as his ancestors in other times, is the kinsman and descendant of the Negro," wrote the professor and minister Abernethy, who later became Poet

Laureate of North Carolina and under Franklin Roosevelt an "Ambassador of Sunshine."[43] Abernethy drew heavily on the racial theorist William Z. Ripley, who shared Daniel G. Brinton's attribution of an African origin for Semites, regarded Jews as a mixed race, and detected in the Bible "an original dark type."

More genteel than the Jim Crow South, the North, too, sought to erect new barriers against a perceived Jewish racial onslaught. Along with Jewish exclusion from business companies and leisure organizations alike came highly visible discrimination in hotels. Two famous instances took place in Saratoga and Manhattan Beach, both in New York. In 1877 the Grand Hotel in Saratoga excluded upper-class German-Jewish banker Joseph Seligman, who had vacationed there for years. In 1879 the Manhattan Beach resort barred Jews even while featuring the celebrated cornetist Julius Levi as its major entertainment attraction. The owner of the Grand Hotel, Judge Henry Hilton, and of the Manhattan Beach resort, industrialist Austin Corbin, helped found (with a hundred others) in 1879 the American Society for the Suppression of the Jews, which sought to erect barriers in business, literature, and entertainment. The proscription of Jews at both Saratoga and Manhattan Beach drew national attention. A cartoon entitled "Hints for the Jews—Several Ways of Getting to Manhattan Beach" from the popular humor magazine *Puck* in the summer of 1879 evinces the widespread ambivalence (see Figure 8). On the one hand, the cartoon shows some sympathy for the plight of excluded Jews. The bottom of the cartoon even carries a modified inscription from Exodus comparing Corbin to Pharaoh. On the other hand, it sports standard anti-Semitic caricatures. Except for the dignified figure at the right with the cornet under his arm presumably representing the acceptable Julius Levi, the Jews trying unsuccessfully to appear "Christian" display large "parabolic" noses, wear bizarre clothes, have "kinky hair," tote a variety of musical instruments, and even stoop to ordering pork. But their efforts clearly fail, as the insert at the top left of "Corbin's 'White Jew' and Whiter Jewess" makes clear. Apparently, the idea of Jews trying to appear Christian engenders as much panic as their original ethnicity does: it troubles precarious barriers.

Word and image, like North and South or Jew and Gentile, come together in the pamphlet *A Gallery of Jewish Types* with portrait drawings by the Polish-born Jewish artist Lionel Reiss and text by the Brookline-born racial

HINTS FOR THE JEWS.—SEVERAL WAYS OF GETTING TO MANHATTAN BEACH.

"And the Lord hardened Corbin's heart, and he would not let Israel come."—Exodus, x.

theorist Lothrop Stoddard. The full title indicates the pamphlet's racist thrust: *A Gallery of Jewish Types, Indicating "A Negroid Strain Undoubtedly Exists in Jewry," This Explains Why Jews Support and Finance the NAACP,* published by "The Thunderbolt, Inc. A Patriotic Christian Newspaper" operated by Edward R. Fields, a chiropractor who lived in Marietta, Georgia, the town where the Jewish Leo Frank had been lynched. While Fields (whose causes on the racist right included the Ku Klux Klan, the Anti-Jewish Party, and the National States Rights Party) assembled his pamphlet after World War II, the words and pictures originated earlier—Stoddard's text, for example, simply reprints his article "The Pedigree of Judah" from *The Forum* magazine for March 1926. Obsessed with tracing "the racial make-up of the Jews," Stoddard found them a mixed rather than pure group originating in a fusion of Semitic and Hittite peoples with later admixtures. Ominously, one of those was African, which Stoddard thought tinged the Jews during their slavery in Egypt. "It was probably during their Egyptian sojourn that the Jews picked up their first traces of Negro blood," he wrote. "A Negroid strain undoubtedly exists in Jewry; to it the frizzy or woolly hair, thick lips, and prognathous jaws appearing in many Jewish individuals are probably due."[44] Stoddard's alarm at Jewish destabilization of racial purity appears in several of the accompanying portraits by Lionel Reiss, whom editor Fields may not have known was himself a Polish Jewish immigrant. One of them, "Disharmonic Type" (Figure 9), shows a mixture of Black and Jewish stereotypes, as the accompanying caption makes clear: "Note the strongly marked Hamitic features, the apparent negroid traces in lips and prognathous jaw, and the skull formation betraying Alpine or Mongoloid infusion."

Literary Culture: *The Great Gatsby, Ulysses,* and *The New Negro*

Stoddard's influence spilled over from racist corners to mainstream publications and culture. A bestselling work like F. Scott Fitzgerald's novel *The Great Gatsby* (1925) at once critiques the racialist tradition exemplified by Stoddard and yet displays the same nervousness about classification that plagued Stoddard and his predecessors, especially in relation to African

---

Figure 8 *(opposite page).* "Hints for the Jews," *Puck,* 30 July 1879. (Courtesy, University of Michigan Library.)

DISHARMONIC TYPE

An interesting disharmonic combination. Note the strongly marked Hamitic features, the apparent negroid traces in lips and prognathous jaw, and the skull formation betraying Alpine or Mongoloid infusion

Figure 9. "Disharmonic Type," Lothrop Stoddard and Lionel Reiss, circa 1926. (Courtesy, University of Michigan Library.)

Americans, Jews, and Irish. Both the critique and the anxiety erupt into the
first major scene of the novel, when the narrator, Nick Carraway, travels
from upstart West Egg to traditionally moneyed East Egg to visit his cousin
Daisy and her enormously rich husband, Tom Buchanan, whom Nick knew
at Yale and who now has moved east with his string of polo ponies. Before
allowing Tom to speak, Fitzgerald makes sure the reader sees him as
unsympathetic—Tom has "a rather hard mouth and a supercilious manner"
with "arrogant eyes . . . [and] a cruel body."[45] Tom disrupts the four-way
conversation with a racist rant that Daisy tries in vain to puncture:

> "Civilization's going to pieces," broke out Tom violently. "I've gotten to
> be a terrible pessimist about things. Have you read 'The Rise of the
> Coloured Empires' by this man Goddard?"
>
> "Why, no," I answered, rather surprised by his tone.
>
> "Well, it's a fine book and everybody ought to read it. The idea is if
> we don't look out the white race will be—will be utterly submerged. It's
> all scientific stuff; it's been proved."
>
> "Tom's getting very profound," said Daisy with an expression of un-
> thoughtful sadness. He reads deep books with long words in them.
> What was that word we—"
>
> "Well, these books are all scientific," insisted Tom, glancing at her
> impatiently. "This fellow has worked out the whole thing. It's up to us
> who are the dominant race to watch out or these other races will have
> control of things. . . . This idea is that we're Nordics. I am and you are
> and you are and—" After an infinitesimal hesitation he included Daisy
> with a slight nod and she winked at me again, "—and we've produced
> all the things that go to make civilization—oh, science and art and all
> that. Do you see?"

Tom's tirade derives from the same Lothrop Stoddard who supplied the text
for *A Gallery of Jewish Types,* though Tom garbles both his name and his
book title, perhaps signaling his own limits or maybe Fitzgerald's deference
toward his own publisher's sensitivities. Stoddard's *The Rising Tide of Color*
first appeared five years before Fitzgerald's novel from the same publisher,
Scribner. It carried an introduction by Madison Grant, Stoddard's own mentor and president of the New York Zoological Society, whose own racialist

tome, *The Passing of the Great Race, or the Racial Basis of European History*, had appeared four years earlier, also published by Scribner. Fitzgerald could hardly have missed either book; they not only appeared from his own publisher but went through multiple editions and attracted large public attention in the decade leading up to *Gatsby*.

Itself carrying a preface by Henry Fairfield Osborn, president of the American Museum of Natural History and a research professor of zoology at Columbia University, Grant's *The Passing of the Great Race* (1916) steadfastly held (as Osborn put it) that "race has played a far larger part than either language or nationality in moulding the destinies of men" and lent support to the eugenics and anti-immigration movements. Grant unhesitatingly labeled both Blacks and Jews as "inferior races": "it has taken us fifty years to learn that speaking English, wearing good clothes and going to school and to church does not transform a Negro into a white man. . . . Americans will have a similar experience with the Polish Jew, whose dwarf stature, peculiar mentality and ruthless concentration on self-interest are being engrafted upon the stock of the nation."[46] He held an even dimmer view of the Irish, in whom he detected an "unstable temperament and the lack of coordinating and reasoning power" and credulously reported a factual basis for the ape-like stereotype common to all three groups: "ferocious gorilla-like living specimens of Paleolithic man are found not infrequently on the west coast of Ireland and are easily recognized by the great upper lip, bridgeless nose, beetling brow with low growing hair and wild and savage aspect. . . . This is the Irishman of caricature and the type was very frequent in America when the first Irish immigrants came in 1846 and the following years" (pp. 203, 109). As his remark about the "stock of the nation" suggests, Grant saw such aliens as a source of contamination. Hence the prospect of intermarriage or cross-breeding raised anxieties that drove him to the one-drop rule as solution. "The cross between a white man and an Indian is an Indian; the cross between a white man and a Negro is a Negro . . . and the cross between any of the three European races and a Jew is a Jew," he declared flatly (p. 18). Hence Grant favored laws against miscegenation and immigration, regarding the melting pot concept as a heresy that would doom the White race.

A Harvard PhD in history, Stoddard picked up where his mentor Grant ended. For him, too, "the basic factor in human affairs is not politics, but race."[47] Following a century of racial theorists, he saw mankind as divided into five primary races—white, yellow, brown, black, and red. The White race itself contained three main divisions—Mediterranean, Alpine, and, highest of all, the Nordic, to which Tom Buchanan would assign himself and his friends in the opening scene of *Gatsby*. Stoddard, too, feared both racial mixture and the challenge he saw other races posing toward White domination. He worried about "the situation in mongrel-ruled America" and railed in particular against "the shibboleth of the 'melting-pot'" (pp. 123, 165). That led to a generalized opposition to immigration, which threatened White America with hordes of "Asiatic elements like Levantines and Jews" (p. 165). Stoddard noticed with alarm the Pan-African Congress held at Paris in 1919 and repeated his frequent opponent W. E. B. Du Bois's warning that victims of the Color Line would fight back. For a master metaphor he chose that of the oceans, with a rising tide of peoples and nations of color threatening to replace the ebbing one of White domination and to burst through its dikes. External immigration by Irish and Jews or internal movement northward by Blacks from the South all swelled that surge.

Although Fitzgerald took care to have his narrator, Nick, immediately brand Tom Buchanan's intoxication with Stoddard and Grant as "pathetic," *The Great Gatsby* does display a heightened awareness of "non-Nordic" groups like Blacks, Irish, and especially Jews coming onto the American scene and both reflects and propagates an anxiety over issues of group purity and mixed identity. The growing pressure of newer groups on the previous establishment shows up clearly in the list of attendees at Gatsby's party that opens chapter 4. The "old money" East Egg furnishes WASP-sounding surnames like Becker, Bunsen, Hornbeam, and Chrystie and first names like Chester, Webster, Hubert, Ulysses, and Ripley. Yet Fitzgerald has some fun with that part of the list, too, mixing in increasingly outrageous names like Leeches, Blackbuck, Ulysses Swett, and S. B. Whitebait. But unmistakably Jewish and Irish names swell the catalogue from nouveaux riche West Egg— Schoen, Gulick, Cohen, Schwartze (mixing Black and Jewish overtones), Bemberg, and possibly Klipspringer among the Jews, and McCarty, Muldoon, Corrigan, Kelleher, Quinn, McClenahan, and O'Brien among the Irish. Such names do not appear in East Egg, to which they constitute a threat but also a mirror image across the bay.

African Americans and Irish make several guest appearances in the novel. African Americans underlie the recurrent references to jazz, an art form associated at the time with both African Americans and Jews—to the Frisco dances and W. C. Handy's Beale Street Blues, for example. The Frisco dances, including "The Jewish Charleston," were invented by the White entertainer Joe Frisco, who also created the "black bottom" dance. While Frisco used "Darktown Strutters' Ball" as a theme song, Handy was one of the great African-American blues and jazz composers; his works include "St. Louis Blues" and "Memphis Blues," among many others. Indeed, Fitzgerald himself coined the term "the Jazz Age" in the title for his collection of short stories, *Tales of the Jazz Age,* in 1922. And African Americans appear at two crucial junctures of *Gatsby,* both times linked to the fast motor cars that also marked the age. The first one indicates the new era's challenge to the old social order as refracted through Nick's sensibility, which avoids the crassness of Tom's racism but still includes cultural stereotyping. As Gatsby and Nick drive across the Queensboro Bridge into New York, "a limousine passed us, driven by a white chauffeur, in which sat three modish Negroes, two bucks and a girl. I laughed aloud as the yolks of their eyeballs rolled toward us in haughty rivalry. 'Anything can happen now that we've slid over this bridge,' I thought; 'anything at all'" (p. 73). The second encounter lasts longer in its effects: after Daisy hits and kills Tom's mistress, Myrtle Wilson, "a pale, well dressed Negro," himself an obvious racial mixture, identifies the car for the police. The plot has no compelling need for such particular ethnic references: Fitzgerald clearly wants them as part of his portrait of the age. So, too, with the Irish names from West Egg and for the novel's other clear Irish reference, Daisy's casual invocation of Maria Edgeworth's *Castle Rackrent,* an earlier Irish novel of the decline of one class and rise of another. Given that Fitzgerald's own mother, Mollie McQuillan, was the daughter of an Irish-Catholic immigrant and his father came from a longer-settled immigrant family, one might expect more Irish references in the novel, but African Americans and especially Jews feature much more prominently, as though in a more grotesque displacement of some of Fitzgerald's own unease at Princeton and elsewhere.

Jews figure most importantly in the novel through the portrait of the menacing gambler Meyer Wolfshiem, who enters the novel immediately after Nick and Gatsby pass the car with the three modish Negroes on the bridge into New York. Based on the actual gangster and gambler Arnold Rothstein, who also invented the floating craps game made so famous by Nathan Detroit in *Guys and Dolls,* Wolfshiem appears here as the man who fixed the 1919 World Series and "could play with the faith of fifty million people." Fitzgerald omits that Rothstein/Wolfsheim was never convicted or even indicted for the crime, which involved players and gamblers of multiple ethnicities, including the Boston Irish gambler J. J. "Sport" Sullivan; in the novel, a single Jew toys with the faith of a nation. Fitzgerald presents him right after the Negroes in a manner that echoes the prominent nose and vermin-like eyes of centuries of Jewish caricature: "A small flat-nosed Jew raised his large head and regarded me with two fine growths of hair which luxuriated in either nostril. After a moment I discovered his tiny eyes in the half darkness" (pp. 73–74). Wolfshiem consorts with other gamblers like Rosy Rosenthal; sells alcohol illegally from fraudulent drugstores; and has his family take over Gatsby's house at the end. He speaks with a Jewish accent meant to be both comic and overreaching, as when he mispronounces "Oxford" as "Oggsford" and labels it a college rather than a university. And when Wolfshiem tries to hide from Nick to avoid attending Gatsby's funeral, Fitzgerald makes sure to describe his secretary as "a lovely Jewess," which is at least better than Myrtle Wilson labeling her unsuccessful suitor "a little kyke" (pp. 178, 38)—though part of the same binary of attraction and repulsion.

The novel's racialist strain and anxieties over pure lineage and group identification come together most prominently in the character of Gatsby. Without going so far as critics who see Gatsby as Jewish or African American but passing for a White Gentile,[48] I do see his racial and ethnic origins as ambiguous. So does the narrator, Nick, who gestures toward possible Jewish or Negro blood in admitting that "I would have accepted without question the information that Gatsby sprang from the swamps of Louisiana or from the lower East Side of New York" (p. 54). Gatsby favors jazz, hangs out with Jews, and has an original name Gatz that echoes Jewish ones like Katz. He seems to have invented himself without reference to family or origin and made fabulous amounts of money that vanish just as mysteriously. Yet racial ambiguity hangs over other characters, too, as when in the opening scene Tom Buchanan hesitates before including Daisy among the Nordic race. Later, when Tom interrupts his tirade against Gatsby's pursuit of Daisy to denounce "intermarriage between black and white" (p. 137), Jordan murmurs, "We're all white here," an odd remark that itself calls racial purity into question. In *Trimalchio,* the earlier version of *The Great Gatsby,* Jordan's remark does that even more clearly when she adds "except possibly Tom."[49] She may intend simply to goad him or else to imply that the chief racist in the novel may have mixed origin. My point is not the exact racial makeup of any particular character but rather the notions of ambiguity and hybridity that dog any notions of group purity in the novel. Whatever his occasional personal lapses, Nick manages to shout out to Gatsby that "They're a rotten crowd. . . . You're worth the whole damn bunch put together" (p. 162). Fitzgerald as novelist surpasses the anxieties of his age over group purity and ethnic identity even while he renders them. *The Great Gatsby* honors a vision of what is possible in the land of its original title, *Under the Red, White, and Blue.*

Across the Atlantic in the 1920s, James Joyce structured his major novel *Ulysses* around the events of a single day but gave it an encyclopedic scope and situated it firmly in the racial discourse of his time. *Ulysses* articulates and champions the hybridity that *The Great Gatsby* recognizes and edgily accepts. Joyce himself held that view throughout his writing career and saw it as bulwark against the evils to which concepts of racial purity led. "What race, or what language . . . can boast of being pure today?" he asked in his early lecture "Ireland, Island of Saints and Sages" given during his sojourn in Trieste. "And no race has less right to utter such a boast than the race now living in Ireland."[50] The lecture listed Danes, Firbolgs, Milesians from Spain, Norman invaders, and Anglo-Saxons, a catalogue that Joyce would expand in *Ulysses.* And at the other end of his career, in his final and most difficult work, *Finnegans Wake,* published in 1939, he inscribed at the outset, "It is the same told of all. Many. Miscegenations on miscegenations." Familiar with eighteenth- and nineteenth- century racialist theories, Joyce learned about Jews especially from the eminent American anthropologist Maurice Fishberg's *The Jews: A Study of Race and Environment,* which he owned while still in Trieste.[51] After hundreds of pages, Fishberg concluded that "the alleged purity of the Jewish race is visionary and not substantiated by scientific observation." Such multiple origins for Irish on the one hand and Jews on the other became one of the insistent parallels between the two groups in *Ulysses* and one of the myriad ways in which they act as synecdoche for all "races." Joyce not only recognized but celebrated hybridity. "Mixed races and mixed marriage," he has Bloom exclaim in his vision of the "new Bloomusalem."

Ulysses has two main Irish protagonists, the Jewish-named, down-to-earth Leopold Bloom and the Greek-named, hyperesthetic Stephen Dedalus, who meet in the final section. Their coming together marks one of the meanings of the key phrase "Jewgreek is greekjew," which remakes a famous remark of Saint Paul's about the fellowship of Christians ("where there is neither Greek nor Jew, circumcised nor uncircumcised, barbarian, Scythian, slave nor free"; Col. 3.9–10) into an articulation of racial and cultural mixing (p. 411). Part of the novel's brilliance lies in Joyce not simply telling but showing us what such hybridity means, especially in the case of the problematically Jewish Bloom. The son of a Hungarian Jew who converted to Christianity and a Christian mother herself part Jewish, Bloom himself embodies racial mixture as imagined by his time. Further, although he thinks of himself as Jewish and identifies with the Jewish "race" (especially when attacked by anti-Semites), he neither practices Judaism nor has been circumcised but instead has been baptized twice. The anti-Semitic Citizen in the pub resorts to animal imagery when labeling him a "half and half . . . a fellow that's neither fish nor flesh" (p. 263). Yet in line with Madison Grant's contention that "the cross between any of the three European races and a Jew is a Jew," the Citizen goes on first to brand Bloom a Jew and then to persecute him. Bloom's own marriage to Molly continues such crossover, for she is the daughter of Major Brian Cooper Tweedy and the Spanish Jewess Lunita Laredo. Although Molly does not think of herself as Jewish, she can technically claim to be so under Jewish law by having a Jewish mother. Bloom and Molly embody and enact various theories of racial mixing, which racists execrate but Joyce extols.

The parallels between the Jewish and Irish races run right through the novel, from the Englishman Haines's feelings toward Jews and Irish in the opening scene in the Martello Tower to Molly's invocation of Jews twenty-two lines from the end of her closing soliloquy. High (or sometimes low) points along the way include the Anglophile schoolmaster Deasey's anti-Semitism, references to forced conversions, the confrontation with the Citizen and others in the pub in "Cyclops," and the New Bloomusalem of "Circe." Perhaps the most extended treatment comes in the second-to-last chapter, "Ithaca," whose catechistic form presents extended comparisons. While acknowledging "race, creed" among the factors separating Bloom and Stephen, the catechism nonetheless constructs a series of analogies between the

Irish and Jewish experiences and even languages. Here is its extended (and confusing) list of parallels in language and culture going back to biblical times, first in language and books and then in persecution and social conditions up through the present, culminating in the Zionist and Irish Nationalist liberation movements at the turn of the century:

> What points of contact existed between these languages and between the peoples who spoke them?

> The presence of guttural sounds, diacritic aspirations, epenthetic and servile letters in both languages: their antiquity, both having been taught on the plain of Shinar 242 years after the deluge in the seminary instituted by Fenius Farsaigh, descendant of Noah, progenitor of Israel, and ascendant of Heber and Heremon, progenitors of Ireland: their archaeological, genealogical, hagiographical, exegetical, homiletic, toponomastic, historical and religious literatures comprising the works of rabbis and culdees, Torah, Talmud (Mischna and Ghemara), Massor, Pentateuch, Book of the Dun Cow, Book of Ballymote, Garland of Howth, Book of Kells: their dispersal, persecution, survival and revival: the isolation of their synagogical and ecclesiastical rites in ghetto (S. Mary's Abbey) and masshouse (Adam and Eve's tavern): the proscription of their national costumes in penal laws and jewish dress acts: the restoration in Chanah David of Zion and the possibility of Irish political autonomy or devolution. (p. 564)

Joyce derives his extended list partly from a once-powerful Irish historical tradition beginning with Reverend Geoffrey Keating's *History of Ireland* (c. 1629) and continuing onward to the colorful if eventually discredited general and antiquary Charles Vallancey. A cofounder of the Royal Irish Academy in 1782, Vallancey also founded the bizarre Phoenician-Scytho-Celtic school of Irish philology that imagined a kinship of Irish with the languages of the Phoenicians, Hebrews, Scythians, Carthaginians, Celts, and Algonquin Indians. Such theories circulated widely in some intellectual circles despite their lack of scientific support. Joyce invokes them not as history but as yet another tactic to undermine racial chauvinism and prejudice. As Elizabeth Butler Cullingford has astutely observed, "Joyce's absorbent analogies express . . . the formal strategy most consistent with his rejection of what he called 'the old pap of racial hatred.' "[52]

Joyce does not expect such rejection to come lightly, as the recurrent renderings of anti-Semitism in *Ulysses* demonstrate. He follows the catechistic racial analogies with the Hebrew of the thematically appropriate first two lines of the poem "Hatikvah" ("The Hope"), which became the anthem first of the Zionist movement and later of the state of Israel and which we might translate as "So long as a Jewish spirit cannot find rest in the heart." But Joyce follows that with two pages of words and music for the ballad of Little Harry Hughes, one of the many renderings of the canard about Jews murdering Christian children exemplified in the legend of St. Hugh of Lincoln and permeating English literature from Chaucer's "Prioress's Tale" onward. In his most astounding counter to the representations of anti-Semitism dotting *Ulysses*, Joyce toward the end of the chapter inserts a synopsis of the novel's plot that parallels major actions to Jewish ritual and holidays, some well-known and some obscure:

> The preparation of breakfast (burnt offering): intestinal congestion and premeditative defecation (holy of holies): the bath (rite of John): the funeral (rite of Samuel): the advertisement of Alexander Keyes (Urim and Thummim): the unsubstantial lunch (rite of Melchisedek): the visit to museum and national library (holy place): the bookhunt along Bedford row, Merchants' Arch, Wellington Quay (Simchath Torah): the music in the Ormond Hotel (Shira Shirim): the altercation with a truculent troglodyte in Bernard Kiernan's premises (holocaust): a blank period of time including a cardrive, a visit to a house of mourning, a leavetaking (wilderness): the eroticism produced by feminine exhibitionism (rite of Onan): the prolonged delivery of Mrs Mina Purefoy (heave offering): the visit to the disorderly house of Mrs Bella Cohen, 82 Tyrone street, lower, and subsequent brawl and chance medley in Beaver Street (Armageddon): nocturnal perambulation to and from the cabman's shelter, Butt Bridge (atonement). (p. 599)

Placed near the end of chapter 17, with only Molly's long soliloquy to follow it as final chapter, the passage recapitulates in miniature some of the key events of this capacious novel. It also obviously matches the Greek parallels to the *Odyssey* of Joyce's schema for the book and of the chapters themselves. In so doing it provides another instance of jewgreek as greekjew, of the racial and cultural congruencies that Joyce deploys against racism and prejudice, and of the paralleling of both to Irish experience.

While the Jewish-Irish analogies loom largest, Joyce carefully brings Black instances into alignment with Jewish and Irish ones. A short passage when Bloom provokes and then flees the anti-Semitic Citizen epitomizes such associations. At that point the final text reads: "a loafer with a patch over his eye starts singing *If the man in the moon was a jew, jew, jew*" (p. 280). Joyce had originally chosen the song "The Boys of Wexford," an Irish nationalist ballad about the United Irishmen's uprising of 1798 ("We are the boys of Wexford, / Who fought with heart and hand / To burst in twain the galling chain, / And free our native land!"). Changing it to its final form obviously demonstrates a link between Irish and Jewish causes. But the significance cuts even deeper because there was no song called "If the Man in the Moon Was a Jew, Jew, Jew." There was, however, a hit American ditty of the time called "If the Man in the Moon Were a Coon, Coon, Coon," composed in ragtime by the same songwriter, Fred Fischer, who later wrote the popular Irish-American ballad "Peg o' My Heart." Its chorus began, "If the man in the moon were a coon, coon, coon, / What would you do? / He would fade with his shade the silvery moon, moon, moon, / Away from you."[53] In substituting "Jew" for the derogatory "coon" as epithet for an African American, *Ulysses* suggests the interchangeability of the terms, a linkage prepared for by the description of the Jew Bloom several chapters earlier as "a coon like that" (p. 88). Joyce both depicts and resists the portrayal of both groups through caricatures reflecting racial stereotypes of the period. As the submerged connection to the Irish nationalist ballad implies, he connects the Irish with the same treatment.

The Black-Jewish parallels in this Irish setting emerge throughout the novel, as a key scene makes clear in the "Lestrygonians" chapter, where Bloom orders a light lunch in a pub. Like Keats, Joyce revised more by accretion than deletion, and the accretions often intensified lost linkages between races. The revisions to Bloom's thoughts as he orders lunch exemplify that process. Here is the early version of the scene recorded in the Rosenbach manuscript as Bloom's mind bounces between an ad for Plumtrees potted meat and the obituary notice for his friend Paddy Dignam:

Sardines on the shelves. Potted meats. What is home without Plum-trees potted meat? Incomplete. What a stupid ad Right under the obit-uary notices too. Dignam's potted meat. With it abode of bliss. Lord knows what concoction.

And here is the final rendering of the scene, in which allusions to a Black African chief jostle with Jewish dietary laws involving keeping kosher and Yom Kippur:

—Tiptop . . . Let me see. I'll take a glass of burgundy and . . . let me see. Sardines on the shelves. Almost taste them by looking. Sandwich? Ham and his descendants musterred and bred there. Potted meats. What is home without Plumtree's potted meat? Incomplete. What a stupid ad! Under the obituary notices they stuck it. All up a plumtree. Dignam's potted meat. Cannibals would with lemon and rice. White missionary too salty. Like pickled pork. Expect the chief consumes the parts of honour. Ought to be tough from exercise. His wives in a row to watch the effect. *There was a right royal old nigger. Who ate or something the somethings of the reverend Mr MacTrigger.* With it an abode of bliss. Lord knows what concoction. Cauls mouldy tripes windpipes faked and minced up. Puzzle find the meat. Kosher. No meat and milk together. Hygiene that was what they call now. Yom Kippur fast spring cleaning of inside. (pp. 140–141)

The additions clearly parallel the African meal with a Jewish kosher one as Bloom ponders his own forthcoming repast, an association prefigured by the early biblical reference to "Ham and his descendants." Apologists for Black slavery regularly invoked that text to justify viewing Africans as infe-rior and destined for servitude, although the Bible does not explicitly iden-tify Ham's descendants with Africans. Hans Gabler's innovative Synoptic Edition of *Ulysses* reveals a further important point about this scene in that heavily revised novel with its multiple typescripts and seven sets of proof: Joyce added those revisions at the same stage of composition, in typescript (B).[54] He does that time after time in the novel, showing that he not only as-sociated Black and Jewish with each other but that he deliberately con-structed the parallels in his novel between them and the Irish scene, whether through the lunch in Davy Byrne's pub, the song about the man in the moon, or in a host of other places. And just as he balanced positive portrayals of Jews with acknowledgments of anti-Semitism, so did he include anti-Black racism as well, whether by allusions to lynching in a newspaper story titled "Black Beast Burned in Omaha, Ga.," use of the derogatory epithet "nigger," or the milder distortions of minstrelsy, less objectionable then than now. Throughout his work Joyce left no doubt where he himself stood. In his novella *The Dead,* for example, when the talk turns to famous singers, Freddy Malins mentions "a negro chieftain singing in the second part of the Gaiety pantomime who had one of the finest tenor voices he had ever heard." When gently challenged by Browne, Freddy exclaims, "And why couldn't he have a voice too? Is it because he's only a black?"[55]

Joyce's devotion to linkages among Irish, Jews, and Blacks finds a strong counterpart in the signature anthology of the Harlem Renaissance, Alain Locke's *The New Negro,* published in 1925, three years after *Ulysses* and the same year as *The Great Gatsby.* The volume grew out of a special number of *Survey Graphic* magazine, which had previously run special issues on similar cultural nationalisms in Russia, Mexico, and Ireland. "Harlem has the same role to play for the New Negro as Dublin has had for the New Ireland," wrote the editor Alain Locke in his title essay for the volume.[56] That role meant serving as center for African-American cultural revival just as Dublin had for Irish writers, whether they lived in Dublin, like John Synge and Sean O'Casey, or wrote about it from elsewhere, like Joyce. The very title "New Negro" signified a break with stock figures from the past and the creation of a new identity. Jews and Irish were going through the same process at the same time, of course, and *The New Negro* picked up on the links. The novelist Jessie Fauset, for example, emphasized representational ties in sketching the Jamaican-born blackface star Bert Williams's depiction of Black people. "Williams might just as well have portrayed the Irishman, the Jew," she wrote (p. 164). Novelist, poet, and general secretary of the National Association for the Advancement of Colored People (NAACP) James Weldon Johnson began his essay, "Harlem: The Culture Capital," with the blunt geographical and economic statement that "In the history of New York, the significance of the name Harlem has changed from Dutch to Irish to Jewish to Negro" (p. 301). Johnson's assistant at the NAACP was Walter White, who himself would become general secretary of that organization for over a quarter-century. The light-skinned White in his contribution "The Paradox of Color," referred humorously to the role of all three groups in New York in remarking that "It was no idle joke when some forgotten wit remarked, 'The Jews own New York, the Irish run it and the Negroes enjoy it'" (p. 363). It was one thing for hostile bigots to say such things, another for a Negro or Jew or Irishman to do so.

Like most commentaries of the time, the anthology quickly racialized such discussions. On the first page of his introduction to the *Survey Graphic* special issue, Locke had imagined the city of New York watching as "Irish, Jew, Italian, Negro, a score of other races drift in and out of the same color-less tenements."[57] The word "race" occurs throughout the anthology for various groups in line with common usage of the time, even though the book resisted the theories of both pernicious racialists and their simplistic opponents. In "The Negro Digs up His Past," the historian and bibliophile Arthur Schomburg lamented that "The blatant Caucasian racialist with his theories and assumptions of race superiority and dominance has in turn bred his Ethiopian counterpart—the rash and rabid amateur who has glibly tried to prove half of the world's geniuses to have been Negroes and to trace the pedigree of nineteenth century Americans from the Queen of Sheba" (p. 236). As with the Jews and Irish, centuries of caricature had led to a reaction that amounted to little more than putting a minus sign in front of hostile images to turn them unrealistically positive.

The most explicit attack came from the young Jewish anthropologist Melville J. Herskovits, who would go on to a distinguished career and would found at Northwestern University the first major interdisciplinary American program in African studies. He unleashed a two-pronged assault on notions that race determined culture, arguing both for the elusiveness of the term "race" and the hybridity of so-called races anyway: "But what is it that makes cultures different? There are those, of course, who will maintain that it is the racial factor," he wrote. "All this sounds very convincing until one tries to define the term 'race.' . . . The efforts of numerous psychological testers to establish racial norms for intelligence are vitiated by the two facts that first, as many of them will admit, it is doubtful just what it is they are testing, and, in the second place, that races are mixed. . . . The vast majority of Negroes in America are of mixed ancestry" (pp. 357–358). Herskovits's insistence that culture trumps biology echoes throughout the volume and, indeed, provides its underlying rationale. *The New Negro* aimed both to document and to further the creation of a new type of African American through changes in "culture" broadly conceived as a social or anthropological term. And it both explicitly and implicitly saw the hybridity rather than purity of cultures attributed to separate groups, acknowledging African, American, and European elements in African Americans.

The then-novel argument for culture shaping race rather than the other way around stems from Herskovits's mentor, Franz Boas, the German- and Jewish-born anthropologist who became the most important figure in his profession in America. A resolute foe of pseudoscientific racism, Boas heroically led the fight against racial hierarchies and racial determinism, leading historian Thomas F. Gossett in his standard *Race: The History of an Idea in America* to salute the possibility that "Boas did more to combat race prejudice than any other person in history."[58] Boas not only critiqued the hierarchical racial science of the nineteenth century but also combated its twentieth-century avatars, like Madison Grant and his disciple Lothrop Stoddard, who labeled Boas's major early book *The Mind of Primitive Man* as "the desperate attempt of a Jew to pass himself off as white." Yet far from trying to pass, Boas repeatedly drew on his own Jewish sensitivities to make analogies between Blacks and Jews that influenced W. E. B. Du Bois, among many others. Indeed, Du Bois and Boas became allies in twin fights against American and, later, Nazi racism. Du Bois also credited Boas with opening his eyes to the achievements of past African civilizations. In his prominent preface to *Black Folk Then and Now* (1939) Du Bois recalled sharing the then widespread conviction that "the Negro has no history": "I remember my own rather sudden awakening from the paralysis of this judgment. . . . Franz Boas came to Atlanta University where I was teaching history in 1906 and said to a graduating class: You need not be ashamed of your African past; and then he recounted the history of the black kingdoms south of the Sahara for a thousand years. I was too astonished to speak. All of this I had never heard."[59] That recovery of an African past reverberates throughout *The New Negro,* as does the speech's insistence on racial hybridity and on parallels between Jews and Blacks. Boas's influence also shows itself in the presence of two of his prize students, Herskovits and Zora Neale Hurston.

Attention to the original material forms of the text reinforces its hybridity. So-called reprints depart from the original 1925 version in major ways that make it seem more separatist. Most glaringly, the 1925 book proclaims itself *The New Negro: An Interpretation / Edited by Alain Locke / Book Decoration and Portraits by Winold Reiss.*" In contrast, the title page of the only current paperback "reprint" announces itself as *The New Negro / Edited by Alain Locke / With an Introduction by Arnold Rampersad.*[60] In the process, the most obvious interracial feature of the original document disappears, for Winold Reiss was White and his seventeen color drawings along with extensive book decoration comprised the most obvious bibliographic feature of *The New Negro.* A Bavarian-born artist who emigrated to the United States, Reiss became best known for his representation of different ethnic groups, including Blackfeet Indians, Asian Americans, Mexicans, and of course African Americans. At first he himself demurred about doing sketches of Blacks for the *Survey Graphic* and *New Negro,* but Locke persuaded him and allowed him to delegate some of the work to the young Aaron Douglass, who himself praised Reiss's work copiously. "The most cogent single factor that eventually turned my face to New York was the publication of the spectacular issue of 'Survey Graphic' magazine . . . with the splendid portrait of a black man on the front cover drawn by Fritz Winold Reiss."[61]

Fourteen of Reiss's works in *The New Negro* portrayed African-American contributors to the volume and by their very coloring supported Herskovitz's contention that most American Negroes were of mixed race. They ranged from the light-skinned writer Jean Toomer, who like the blond-haired civil rights leader Walter White could pass as White, to the darker tones of actor and singer Paul Robeson or singer Roland Hayes. The portraits of women displayed the same variety, ranging from the light-skinned educator Elise Johnson McDougald to the much darker Mary McLeod Bethune. Even two sketches of types rather than individuals displayed a similar dichotomy, with the relatively light-skinned Librarian followed sixteen pages later by the darker School Teachers. The portraits proved controversial, partly because Reiss was White but even more so because they did not simply exalt their subjects, a charge that reappears in both Irish Renaissance and Jewish contexts of the time. Opposition to the School Teachers sketch boiled up at a noisy meeting in the Harlem branch of the New York Public Library, where a Mr. Williams declared that "Should he meet those two school teachers in the street, he would be afraid of them." In response, Elise McDougald wrote to Locke that one of the teachers portrayed claimed that the portrait was "a pretty good likeness," and Locke himself defended the portrait in "To Certain of Our Philistines" as showing "a professional ideal, that peculiar seriousness, that race redemption spirit, that professional earnestness" representative of teaching at its best.[62] Reiss himself had signaled his own respect for the teachers by displaying Phi Beta Kappa keys dangling from their necklaces. Both the Harlem Renaissance and *The New Negro* continue to attract such criticisms down to our own day. As George Hutchinson shrewdly noted, "Every interpretation of the movement turns upon an attempt to either suppress or scapegoat its interracial qualities" (pp. 25–26). Yet as we move toward what historian David Hollinger calls "post-ethnic America," those very qualities increasingly seem strengths rather than weaknesses. Indeed, *The New Negro* included a sort of reverse Winold Reiss figure in the African-American artist Henry O. Tanner. "Our Negro American painter of outstanding success is Henry O. Tanner," wrote Locke. "Though a professed painter of types, he has devoted his art talent mainly to the portrayal of Jewish Biblical types and subjects" (p. 264). Locke acted according to his own precepts and included two other Whites besides Herskovits and Reiss in his anthology, the *Survey Graphic* editor Paul U. Kellogg and the self-made philanthropist and art devotee Albert Barnes.

The hybridity of the verbal and visual constructions of *The New Negro* comes forth clearly in its use of music and musical analogies, too. For example, in praising Black spirituals as "America's only great music," Albert Barnes wrote that "Idea and emotion are fused in an art which ranks with the Psalms and the songs of Zion in their compelling, universal appeal" (p. 21). Almost 200 pages later Alain Locke devoted an entire article to "The Negro Spirituals," which included words and melody from "Father Abraham" and "Tell It to de Lambs." The African-American Locke made the same comparison that the White Barnes had, deriving the link from another contributor, W. E. B. Du Bois, in his foundational work *The Souls of Black Folk*. Locke emphasized that underneath a deceptively simple surface "lies, as Dr. Du Bois pointed out, an epic intensity and a tragic profundity of emotional experience, for which the only historical analogy is the spiritual experience of the Jews and the only analogue, the Psalms" (p. 200). Its nonverbal nature makes music in some ways the easiest of the arts to understand across cultures and the most likely to cross-fertilize to create new products and linkages. Even songs, which combine music and language, can leap across cultural gaps through both emotional and intellectual responses. That means that music cannot be "appropriated" (what would it mean to "appropriate" a Beethoven quartet or Bob Marley song?) but rather understood, enjoyed, and used to create still more art.

That crossing of cultures around song reaches its crescendo in "Fern," one of the two chapters from Jean Toomer's lyrical novel *Cane* included in *The New Negro*. So light-skinned that he could and sometimes did pass for White, Toomer resisted simplistic racial categorization and insisted on his own mixed origins. "Racially, I seem to have (who knows for sure) seven blood mixtures: French, Dutch, Welsh, Negro, German, Jewish, and Indian," he wrote in a 1922 letter to the *Liberator* magazine. "Because of these, my position in America has been a curious one."[63] For Toomer, the categories used in the America of his day created false divisions among human beings. In a preface to an unpublished autobiography Toomer argued that "If I have to say 'colored,' 'white,' 'jew,' 'gentile,' and so forth, I will unwittingly do my bit toward reinforcing the limited views of mankind which dismember mankind into mutually repellant factions." Accordingly, he resists a simple racial identify for the female Fern, who exercises an almost hypnotic hold over men, a mixture of sexual desire, emotional longing, and even spiritual grace. Instead Toomer paints her hybrid Jewish and Negro ancestry four times in the story's six pages, three of them in terms of analogies to the song of a Jewish cantor. "Her nose was aquiline, Semitic," he writes in the first and longest of such passages. "If you have heard a Jewish cantor sing, if he has touched you and made your own sorrow seem trivial when compared with his, you will know my feeling" (p. 99). Of key importance is who the "you" and "your" are in the passage. The narrator is apparently himself Black and says that "it is black folks whom I have been talking about thus far" before adding, "What white men thought of Fern I can arrive at only by analogy" (p. 100). In the first instance, then, the "you" is African American, though, of course, both novel and anthology aimed at White readers, too, and the "you" carries a secondary sense of White or any other reader. Toomer's assertion that the sorrow in the voice of the Jewish cantor will be deeper than that of the Black or other audience, a common one of the period, seems less important now than their connection in the first place. Toomer invokes that mutual comprehension and recognition of Black and Jew through the sorrow in the voice of a Jewish cantor, singer of traditional hymns and songs in religious services, twice more in his story. But he saves his biggest surprise for last, in fact for the last word of the chapter, when he reveals for the first time Fern's full name—Fernie May Rosen. The Jewish surname clinches his point about the hybrid nature of identity. Yet no one to my knowledge has (or presumably even would) argue that Toomer has somehow "appropriated" the cantor and his song here, and to do so would be a back-projection of our present ways of thinking and categorizing onto a past work that deliberately resists them. As Alain Locke remarked, "Culture-goods, once evolved, are no longer the exclusive property of the race or people that originated them. They belong to all who can use them; and belong most to those who can use them best."[64]

Blackface: Al Jolson and *The Jazz Singer*

Current-scruples opposed to the inclusiveness of Locke have not prevented attacks on another work involving links between African Americans and Jewish cantors, the first feature movie with audible dialogue, *The Jazz Singer* (1927). The film highlights themes common to multiple racial and ethnic groups—particularly the tensions between assimilation and group identity or between Old World parents and New World children. It begins with the boy Jakie Rabinowitz, son of a proud if poor fifth-generation cantor, or singer of Jewish holy songs. While Cantor Rabinowitz prepares his son to succeed him in the synagogue, Jakie has begun singing popular jazz tunes in a neighborhood saloon. Jakie's unmasking by the busybody Yudelson triggers the first of several Oedipal confrontations in the movie, after which Jakie runs off to a catch-as-catch-can career in show business. The rising Gentile star Mary Dale recognizes his talent out West and helps land him a job on Broadway, which leads again to sympathy from his mother and another angry quarrel with his father over the central dilemma of the movie, becoming a cantor or a jazz singer. His change in name from Jakie Rabinowitz to the more Gentile-sounding Jack Robin epitomizes the tensions and indicates which way he will go. Melodramatically, the movie builds to a climax pitting Jack and his new friends' desire for his success on Broadway against his dying father's desire for Jakie/Jack to replace him in synagogue for the Yom Kippur service. In a sleight of hand, the film opts for both, with Jack singing first the Kol Nidre in shul and then a mammy song to his mother in the Broadway review. Despite or perhaps because of its sentimentality, the film became an immediate hit, not only because of it starring the most popular entertainer of his day, Al Jolson, as Jack Robin but also because of its technical innovation. Through a sound system called Vitaphone *The Jazz Singer* could claim to be the first talking movie with dialogue and song as important elements of the plot.

The film grew from first a short story and then a stage play by the young Jewish writer Samson Raphaelson, who had been inspired by the appearance of Al Jolson in Champaign during Raphaelson's final year at the University of Illinois. In a reaction that the Jean Toomer of "Fern" would have understood well, Raphaelson confessed his response to Jolson's performance. "My God, this isn't a jazz singer. This is a cantor!" he exclaimed to his date. "The words didn't matter, the melody didn't matter. It was the emotion—the emotion of a cantor."[65] That emotion dominated the story, called "Day of Atonement" in double homage to the Jewish holiday of Yom Kippur and to Jack Robin's act of atonement in singing the Kol Nidre, a famous chant appropriate to the story both because of its sanctity and because it cancels vows that observant Jews were forced to make to Gentile society in contradiction to their own faith. Minstrelsy plays no role in the tale, except for passing mention of a "blackface comedian." Instead, Raphaelson like Toomer stresses that his character's singing "might have been deep wells of lamentation even one generation ago had his lyric voice been born to cry the sorrows of Israel in a Russian synagogue" (p. 147). Raphaelson goes on to misapply bizarrely to Jews Matthew Arnold's famous line about the monks in the Grand Chartreuse monastery: "Jakie was simply translating the age-old music of the cantors—that vast loneliness of a race wandering 'between two worlds, one dead, the other powerless to be born'—into primitive and passionate Americanese" (p. 151). The identification between Jewish and African-American music carries over into the play as well, where the stage direction to Jack's rendition of "Dixie Mammy" states, "We are listening to a Cantor in blackface" despite "the obvious shoddiness of the words and the music."[66] The play enjoyed a modestly successful Broadway run, drawing mild praise from the *New York Times*, among others. Reviewers who disliked the drama saw it as too Jewish, including the critic for the *American*, who branded it a "garish and tawdry Hebrew play" (Carringer, p. 13). That charge was repeated when Raphaelson tried to shop the manuscript around in Hollywood. Irish characters turn up only peripherally, but they do turn up, first in the Irish boy who taunts Jake with the derogatory term "sheeny" in the story version and then in the Irish doctor O'Shaughnessey in the play and film.

Despite the film's massive focus on a Jewish inflection of issues common to many groups, criticism over the last thirty years has focused on the few minutes of the movie where Jolson blacks up and then sings in blackface. Earlier criticism had viewed such actions positively as showing intergroup identification and sympathy. Irving Howe spoke for that tradition of ethnic pastiche in *World of Our Fathers* (1976) when he wrote that Jolson "brought together—for him, a quite natural thing to do—Yiddish shmaltz and black-face sentiment . . . but it is hard to resist the impression that some deeper affinity was also at work. . . . Black became a mask for Jewish expressiveness, with one woe speaking through the voice of another." He further noted that "Gershwin's biographer, Isaac Goldberg, found a musical kinship between the 'Negro blue note' and the 'blue note' of Hasidic chant. Put Yiddish and Black together, he wrote, 'and they spell Al Jolson.'"[67] Where Howe saw af-finity and common woe, Whiteness historians like Michael Rogin saw ap-propriation and distancing. For Rogin, the jazz singer succeeds "at the ex-pense of blacks" and the move shows not cooperation but "assimilation to old inequalities. . . . Blackface emancipated the jazz singer from Jews and blacks by linking him to the groups he was leaving behind."[68] Recently, Mi-chael Alexander has convincingly argued back that sources from the time speak differently and that "In Jewish-American descriptions of ragtime and minstrelsy, becoming 'Caucasian' does not appear as a need, desire, or even a question."[69] Indeed, Jews stand out from many other groups of the period for identifying downward rather than upward, aligning themselves with the underprivileged even as they rise in the social scale, a trend that persists still today.

Current attacks on *The Jazz Singer* turn out to be largely back-projections of present attitudes onto the foreign country of the past, starting with the meanings of the term "race" itself that we have already seen. Jewish per-formers regularly used that word with no sense of trying to escape from the Jewish race to a putative white race, though sometimes critical of "the stage Jew." On the contrary, they reveled in their status. The early Jewish star Fanny Brice (the model for "Funny Girl") insisted that "In anything Jewish I ever did, I wasn't standing apart, making fun of the race, I *was* the race." Likewise, the Jewish American team of Rodgers and Hart wrote in "Bugle

Blow" from their 1926 show *Betsy* that "We've a race that's het'rogeneous /
With folks from all the earth . . . All were diff'rent when they came, / But
jazz has made them all the same!" (Alexander, pp. 145, 164). In *The Jazz
Singer* itself, after the beseeching visit of his mother and Yudelson, Jack
Robin in blackface describes the tug back to the synagogue in the following
terms: "maybe it's the call of the ages—the cry of my race." He means the
Jewish race, not a hypothetical White one that nowadays embraces a variety
of origins earlier thought of as distinct races.

Whiteness critiques of *The Jazz Singer* run even further afoul in arraign-
ing Al Jolson himself of supposed racism in art and life. On the contrary,
Jolson articulately distinguished his own blackface from earlier demeaning
forms of minstrelsy, and he regularly championed African-American performers as both artists and friends. In his 1918 article "The Art of Minstrelsy," Jolson criticized those who "are confusing the modern minstrel
with the old-time worker in black-face."[70] For Jolson, modern blackface only
suggested Black character and demanded much more sophistication than
the old and often derogatory stereotypes. "The old-fashioned darky was not
a subtle creature—he was simple—almost childish—and I defy any man or
woman to go out on the Winter Garden runway and be simple," he wrote.
"They would not last five minutes." That the Winter Garden was the theater
where Jolson himself starred confirms that he spoke of his own art as well as
that of others of his generation, when many of the best-known blackface
performers were Jews, who replaced the Irish Americans who began the blackface tradition. He called attention, too, to the frequency and importance of
blackface crossings with other groups. "Perhaps the most striking point is
that the negro dialect is seldom used, and it is possible to hear a man in
black-face telling a story in Jewish or Italian dialect," he observed. That is
certainly the case in *The Jazz Singer*, where Jolson speaks his normal accent
and everyone understands that he is Al Jolson the Jewish entertainer in
blackface. Considering the difference in sophistication, racial crossing, and
absence of derogatory intent, Jolson concluded that "The minstrel of 1918 is
a vastly different fellow from his old-time friend." Even more so was the
minstrel of 1927, when *The Jazz Singer* appeared.

Jolson's friendship with African Americans and championing of their opportunities runs throughout his life, beginning with his boyhood friendship
with the African American Bill Johnson, later famous as "Bojangles." In
1910 Jolson covered for *Variety* the racially charged "Great White Hope"

prizefight between the Black Jack Johnson and the White Jim Jeffries, which Jeffries had entered expressly for "proving that a white man is better than a Negro." Jolson was one of the few journalists to report that Johnson won because he fought better, writing that "Johnson is the greatest fighter that ever lived." Jolson had even more influence in the theater, where although he failed to persuade producers to incorporate a Black dance team into his show the year after the Johnson-Jeffries fight, he succeeded a decade later in helping the Black porter Garland Anderson to get his play *Appearances* produced in 1925, two years before *The Jazz Singer*. That was the first drama with an entirely African-American cast ever performed on Broadway. And perhaps most famously, when a Hartford restaurant refused service to the Black jazz musicians Eubie Blake and Noble Sissle, Jolson immediately looked them up and invited them out to dinner, offering to punch anybody who dared to exclude them. Blake and Sissle, of course, wrote *Shuffle Along*, the first Broadway hit musical by and about African Americans. Blake and Sissle never forgot Jolson's actions, and the three remained friends for the rest of Jolson's life. Sissle even served as official representative of the Negro Actor's Union at Jolson's funeral, hardly something that he would have done had he felt that Jolson's roles somehow demeaned Blacks. A prominent African-American architect in Los Angeles, Paul Williams, designed Jolson's elaborate monument, which included a statue of him in the famous pose of "Mammy" from *The Jazz Singer*.[71]

Neglected by hostile later critics, contemporary reviews in the mainstream, Jewish, and African-American press can help to correct modern back-projections further by showing us what actual people of the time said. None saw the blackface as demeaning to any group or even central to the film. The review in *Variety*, for example, opened by calling *The Jazz Singer* "the best thing Vitaphone has ever put on the screen" and praising "the combination of the religious heart interest story and Jolson's singing 'Kol Nidre' in a synagogue while his father is dying and two 'Mammy' lyrics as his mother stands in the wings of the theater and later as she sits in the first row." Nowhere did *Variety* highlight Black racial aspects to the story, and it accurately noted that Jolson sings the mammy songs about his own mother, not a stereotypical Negro one. The only comment on the blackface was to note that it released a spark of Jolson's individuality, as the singer himself had maintained in an article on modern minstrelsy. But the *Variety* review did doubt one racial aspect of the film, its appeal to a wide audience: "It's doubtful if the general public will take to the Jewish boy's problem of becoming a cantor or a stage luminary." The *New York Times* cautiously praised the movie and again led with the Vitaphone aspect. That review devoted only one paragraph to blackface, lauding the "dexterity" of Jack's blacking up and calling attention to the "engaging" scene where he sings to his mother. More enthusiastically, *Moving Picture World* labeled the film "the best show on Broadway" and said that "in every sequence it is effective and affecting." That journal called particular attention to the "sweet, pure" notes of the cantor. In contrast, *Film Daily* dismissed the film curtly as "strictly a Jewish story" but, like the others, did praise the Vitaphone accompaniment. In sum, the mainstream media of the time saw the film as technically innovative, and if they detected racial aspects at all, saw them as overtly Jewish.[72]

For its part the Jewish press waxed even more enthusiastic about *The Jazz Singer*. Hasia Diner has called attention to a long article on Al Jolson in the most influential Yiddish newspaper, New York's *Forward,* in which the reviewer speculated on a Jewish-Black artistic bond that again featured cantorial melancholy. She translates, "Is there any incongruity in this Jewish boy [Jolson] with his face painted like a Southern Negro singing in the Negro dialect? No, there is not. Indeed, I detected again and again the minor key of Jewish music, the wail of the *Chazan,* the cry of anguish of a people who had suffered. The son of a line of rabbis well knows how to sing the songs of the most cruelly wronged people in the world's history."[73] Again, the link with Toomer's Fern comes across clearly, although where the African-American writer made Jews the deeper-suffering people, the Jewish reviewer awards that status to African Americans. The key point is that the connection between the two groups on grounds of suffering and persecution pervades their respective presses and informs reception of the movie there. As Michael Alexander observes in his book *Jazz Age Jews,* "Jewish audiences loved it. . . . Not one Jewish paper in America wrote a bad review." The praise ran across the political spectrum from the socialist *Forward* to the more conservative and Republican *Morgen Zhurnal.* That paper, the only Yiddish morning daily in New York, opined that "It is a curious thing that there are so many points of resemblance between Jews and Negroes" and saw blackface as one validation of that claim (Alexander, pp. 178, 147).

Current detractors of *The Jazz Singer* go farthest astray when they project contemporary racial attitudes back onto the beginning of the last century. Their demeaning views of blackface in the film never cite any actual African

Americans of the time but project onto past ones a fantasy composed of present attitudes. They, and not Jolson, ventriloquize Blacks and often cite a lack of Black response to the film as evidence of hostility. Even Michael Alexander in his otherwise sound argument against such readings states that "no major African-American newspaper even mentioned *The Jazz Singer*" (p. 178). But in fact the film played to sold-out audiences in Black theaters and received glowing reviews in the African-American press, which could excoriate Whites when it wanted to. The *New York Amsterdam News*, arguably the most influential Black newspaper in the country, noticed *The Jazz Singer* not once but twice. Both were raves. "It is one of the greatest pictures ever produced," declared the review of 2 May 1928, which particularly commended Jolson. The review also approved the accompanying presentation at the Lafayette theater of the Black jazzman Willie Jackson and the Jewish cantor Silverbush, in which Jackson sang the popular songs from the picture (including "Mammy") and Silverbush sang "Eli Eli" and "Kol Nidre," both of which the paper judged "increases the beauty of a truly wonderful film."[74] The same paper returned to the film two years later, when it extolled both *The Jazz Singer* as "a tremendous hit" and praised Jolson's new film, *Mammy,* as a "talking, singing, dancing marvel." The column particularly praised Jolson's blackface performances. "He is beyond all doubt one of the world's greatest entertainers," said the review. "He is the one white man who performs 'blackface' in such a manner that every colored performer is proud of him." Not only Eubie Blake and Noble Sissle but a host of other African-American stars like Cab Calloway or Bill Robinson saw it the same way.

So did Black newspapers outside New York. The Baltimore *Afro-American,* for example, enthused about the film in a review headed " 'Jazz Singer' Seen as Gripping Drama" with a subhead "Sings Songs of Israel." It too praised both Jolson's performance and the new Vitaphone technology. "The minstrel man, king of jazz singers and one of the leading entertainers of the world, Jolson, is scoring heavily in this, his first screen attempt. . . . With Jolson's singing accompanying the acting that would have alone made the picture outstanding, the Vitaphone makes the effect more intense," wrote the reviewer, who also quoted the line about cantorial and jazz singing, "he has a cry in his voice," from the film. According to the review, the film "is being acclaimed by throngs of Regent patrons as by theatre-goers in scores of other cities." The *Pittsburgh Courier*'s review again highlighted

Jolson, the "Famous 'Mammy' Star," and Vitaphone. It also explained one reason why Black entertainers supported the film so strongly. "The experiment is looked upon with great interest by the colored performers, insofar as three famous Negro comedians, Bert Williams (deceased); S. H. Dudley and S. T. Whitney would undoubtedly have become factors in the screen world had they been able to register equally as well upon the screen as they have upon the stage." For many Black musical entertainers, when he combined blackface with Vitaphone, Jolson opened a door through which they too could follow, as Duke Ellington and others did during the following decade. Significantly for our purposes, the *Pittsburgh Courier* ran its *Jazz Singer* story right next to one headlined "Race Tenor Sings Old Irish Ballads" in which the Black tenor Charles Willis "created a mild sensation" by singing Irish ballads at the Pantages theater in Los Angeles. Cross-racial masquerade extended to a variety of groups.

The racial and cultural fluidity found in Joyce's *Ulysses,* Locke's *The New Negro,* and Jolson's *The Jazz Singer* finds apt analogy in Paul Robeson's featuring of "The Hassidic Chant" and other Jewish songs in his concerts from the 1930s onward. To my knowledge no one has ever denied Robeson's "right" to sing such songs (whatever that would mean) or suggested that he sang them to somehow separate himself from Jews. On the contrary, everyone understands that in so doing Robeson declares an affinity with Jews and exemplifies the ability of culture to speak across different racial and religious divides. Certainly, that is what Robeson himself thought he was doing. He told friends that he felt "an almost unexplainable rapport with Jews" in both his artistic and his personal life. Indeed, his devoted wife, Eslanda Cardozo Goode Robeson, combined African-American, Jewish, and other Caucasian ancestry, making Robeson's children and grandchildren part Jewish, as he liked to point out.[75] The same year that *The Jazz Singer* appeared, Robeson told the *Jewish Tribune* that the refrain of a Black spiritual like "Rock Me, Rock Me" reminded him of "Jewish synagogue music" and six years later confided to the *New York World-Telegram* that "I know the wail of the Hebrew."[76]

No wonder, then, that as the 1930s progressed he incorporated "The Hassidic Chant of Levi Isaac" into his concerts and kept singing it along with other Jewish songs for the rest of his career. That chant was a version of the Kaddish (memorial prayer for the dead) attributed to Levi Yitzhak of

Berditchev, a Hasidic rabbi who died in 1810. Both political sympathy with the plight of the Jews and personal sympathy with them propelled his choice. Coming close to the "cry in the voice" of Jolson in the film, Robeson told a Yiddish paper that he could sing such songs far more easily than he could European opera or lieder: "I do not understand the psychology of these [French, German, or Italian] people, their history has no parallels with the history of my forbearers who were slaves. The Jewish sigh and tear are close to me. I understand . . . them . . . feel that these people are closer to the traditions of my race."[77] That was particularly true of the "Hassidic Chant." As Robeson wrote, "The Hassidic Chant, for example, has a profound impact on the Negro listener not only for its content—a powerful protest against an age-old persecution—but also because of its form: the phrasing and rhythm have counterparts in traditional Negro sermon-song."[78] For all the differences, Robeson's rendering of the "Hassidic Chant" carries analogies to Jolson's offering of minstrel songs in blackface, all the more so when Robeson wore a yarmulke or skullcap, as he did when he studied biblical Hebrew. No one has ever accused him of Jew-face in doing so. Rather, his performances exemplify the contingency of racial and ethnic identities and of the deep linkages underlying them. Against the deprecatory connections of Jews, Blacks, and Irish by hostile racial theorists or by those who felt threatened by various groups, Robeson—like Fitzgerald, Joyce, Locke, Toomer, and Raphaelson and Jolson—speaks for their positive links. Such connections could lead in two directions, either toward nationalism and separatism or toward a melting pot and assimilation. The next two chapters explore first one and then the other of those mirrored alternatives, and the surprising racial and ethnic reciprocities within them.

2

Diasporas and Nationalisms

Diaspora: A Fluid Term

Writing in anguish after the bloody start of World War I, the anti-racist scientist Franz Boas pondered the relation between racial theory and the rampant nationalism of the times. "It is clear that the term *race* is only a disguise of the idea of *nationality,* which has really very, very little to do with racial descent," he concluded.[1] Tragically, Boas's view of racial mixing and nationality failed to carry the day against a tradition that in modern times went back at least to the German romanticism and national awareness of the philosophers Johann Gottfried von Herder and Johann Gottlieb Fichte and pervaded Western thought until its explosion by Nazi theory and the horror of the Holocaust. Nowadays, nationalism often elicits an even more negative reaction than it did in some quarters after World War I, with a nasty history involving World War II and lesser conflicts up to the present day. Correspondingly, the notion of diaspora or dispersal, traditionally seen as negative ever since the expulsion of the Jews from the holy land in biblical times, often carries a positive valence today, suggesting hybridity and cosmopolitanism. But in the late nineteenth and early twentieth centuries, the valences were reversed. Diaspora seemed a negative condition fraught with dislocation, dispersal, and anxiety, to all of which nationalism seemed one positive alternative (the other was assimilation or at least acculturation, as will be discussed in the next chapter).

The concept of diaspora originally applied only to Jews, as the *Oxford English Dictionary* makes clear. It defines "diaspora" as "The Dispersion; i.e. (among the Hellenistic Jews) the whole body of Jews living dispersed among the Gentiles after the Captivity."[2] That took place after the fall of the

Kingdom of Judah and destruction of the First Temple in 586 B.C., with the resultant captivity in Babylon; a second great diaspora occurred after the destruction of the Second Temple in Roman times. Three of the dictionary's four early examples, all from the late nineteenth century, concern Jews (the other makes an analogy to Moravian evangelizing on the Continent). The term itself derives from the Greek word *diaspora* (or dispersion, literally a sowing or scattering through) used to translate the Hebrew *le-za'ava* (literally "horror") in Deuteronomy 28.25, where Moses prophesies God's punishment if the Hebrews fail to follow God's commandments: "thou shalt be a diaspora (or dispersion) in all the kingdoms of the earth." This usage is echoed by the Greek of the New Testament in John 7.35, where the Jews ask whether Jesus "will go unto the dispersed among the Gentiles." Whether scattered as a Hebrew "horror" or Greek "diaspora," the biblical term obviously brands the condition as negative. And as Michael Galchinsky has pointed out, the very use of a Greek term to describe the condition of the Hebrews enacts the same condition that it describes.[3]

When scholars extended notions of diaspora to other groups in the second half of the twentieth century, first Blacks and then Irish quickly cropped up, usually with an explicit recognition of the Jewish parallel that now sometimes disappears. A pioneering British scholar of the African diaspora, George Shepperson noted that the term "African diaspora" originated in the English-speaking world. Maintaining that "the only people who really have the right to use the word *diaspora* without a qualifying adjective are the Jews," he pointed out that such Black forerunners as Edward Blyden and Alexander Crummell were "conscious of the parallels" even in the nineteenth century. A decade later Paul Gilroy in his influential study *The Black Atlantic: Modernity and Double Consciousness* stressed that "the term 'diaspora' comes into the vocabulary of Black studies and the practice of pan-Africanist politics from Jewish thought. It is used in the Bible but begins to acquire something like its looser contemporary usage during the late nineteenth century—the period which saw the birth of modern Zionism and of the forms of Black nationalist thought which share many of its aspirations and some of its rhetoric." Mary J. Hickman displays a similar awareness in her helpful survey of Irish diaspora when she first invokes "the traditional account, derived from the Jewish diaspora," and then goes on to identify in discussions since the 1960s "the hallmark of diasporic experience [as] a process of unsettling, recombination and hybridisation."[4]

Since then others have stretched the term to cover a bewildering variety of groups and, in the process, evacuated it of any specific meaning other than dispersal, and sometimes not even that. The founding of the journal *Diaspora: A Journal of Transnational Studies* in 1991 provided both a stimulus and a gauge of the new range. Besides Jews, Irish, and Blacks, its pages have covered Native Americans, Cubans, Eritreans, Kurds, Sikhs, Tibetans, Palestinians, Lithuanians, Turks, Indians, Pakistanis, Egyptians, Sri Lankans, Filipinos, and Mexicans, among others. Yet in the very first issue of that journal William Safran provided a taxonomy of diaspora that helps keep the term meaningful and indicates why it applies especially well to our three groups. Safran names as its salient criteria: dispersal from an original center, collective memory about the homeland, alienation from their current host society, a regard for the original homeland as the true home, belief in its maintenance or restoration, and solidarity toward that goal.[5] The catastrophes of the destruction of the Jewish Temple, the Irish Famine, and the transatlantic slave trade all led to forced dispersals that engendered the other terms as well. Not all members of those groups embrace all six items on Safran's list, and even today most Jews remain outside of Israel, most Irish outside of Ireland, and many Blacks outside of Africa. Yet awareness of the diasporic condition runs through all three groups, as a look at their adaptations of the classic diasporic text, Psalm 137, will demonstrate.

Psalm 137 and Its Influence: Lament for the Diasporic Condition

Expressing Jewish anguish after the destruction of the First Temple and the Kingdom of Judah, in order the first seven verses of Psalm 137 mourn the loss of Jerusalem, the giving up of song by hanging harps on the willows, the mocking insistence of their captors upon a song, and the difficulty of singing in a strange land before arriving at the famous pledge of fidelity in both hand and tongue and then ending with the ironic curse upon Edom and Babylon. The paradigmatic expression of diasporic sorrow attracted not just Jews but other groups after them, including Blacks and Irish. Frederick Douglass invokes the first seven verses of the psalm in "The Meaning of the Fourth of July for the Negro" that we noted in the Introduction:

By the rivers of Babylon, there we sat down. Yea! We wept when we remembered Zion. We hanged our harps upon the willows in the midst thereof. For there, they that carried us away captive, required of us a song; and they who wasted us required of us mirth, saying, Sing us one of the songs of Zion. How can we sing the Lord's song in a strange land? If I forget thee, O Jerusalem, let my right hand forget her cunning. If I do not remember thee, let my tongue cleave to the roof of my mouth if I prefer not Jerusalem above my chief joy.[6]

For all three groups, the initial expression of sorrow leads to a pledge of continued fidelity and then an actual making of song, whether in Psalm 137 itself or in the numerous adaptations and invocations of it that stretch to the present day. Even the rarely quoted final two verses find later echoes by engendering a trickster tradition in which the Children of Israel appear to fulfill the demand by their conquerors the Edomites and Babylonians for a song but then give their masters one that they cannot understand (because it is in Hebrew) and that foretells their eventual destruction. But the first seven verses dominate the adaptation by Irish, Black, and Jewish writers of the nineteenth and early twentieth centuries.

Not that they were the only ones to draw upon those verses. Psalm 137 stimulated a host of later applications, perhaps foremost among them the political. The power of the psalm touched a wide range of writers in the period, including Lord Byron, James Greenleaf Whittier, Harriet Beecher Stowe, Abraham Lincoln, Christina Rossetti, Algernon Swinburne, T. S. Eliot, William Faulkner, and Steven Vincent Benet, among others. Byron, for example, turned his version in *Hebrew Melodies* into a typical romantic lament for lost liberty. Its second stanza began, "While sadly we gazed on the river / Which rolled on in freedom below" in accord with the incipient nationalisms of his day. Similarly, Swinburne later adapted the psalm to the political events of the second half of the nineteenth century. His "Super Flumina Babylonis" began with a close adaptation but finished with a lengthy presaging of Italian freedom through the Risorgimento, an event celebrated by other poems in his *Songs before Sunrise* volume of 1871. Lincoln picked up on the political application, too. Stopping at Independence Hall in Philadelphia on his way to Washington to take the oath of office as president, he pledged fidelity to the Constitution drafted there and exclaimed, "May my right hand forget its cunning and my tongue cleave to the roof of my mouth, if ever I prove false to those teachings." In contrast, Christina Rossetti highlighted the religious and Mosaic aspect of divine punishment. Her "By the Waters of Babylon, B.C. 570" begins, "Here where I dwell I waste to skin and bone; / The curse is come upon me, and I waste / In penal torment powerless to atone." In the early twentieth century, Eliot invoked the psalm in *The Waste Land* ("By the waters of Leman I sat down and wept"); Faulkner originally chose *If I Forget Thee, Jerusalem* as title for his novel *The Wild Palms*, a label that the recent Library of America edition restores; and Benet called his 1937 dystopian science fiction tale "By the Waters of Babylon."[7]

The popularity of the psalm throughout Anglophone texts intensified for our three diasporic groups, all of which identified with the ancient Hebrew exile. While there were Gaelic translations of Psalm 137 and invocations of it in English from early times onward, it permeated turn-of-the-century Irish culture. The Irish Catholic writer and cultural naturalist Katharine Tynan, for example, was friendly with Douglas Hyde, George Russell, and especially W. B. Yeats, with whom she was a fellow disciple of the Fenian John O'Leary. In her autobiographical volume *The Wandering Years* (1922), written during the Irish Troubles, she recalled her time in London drumming up support for the Irish cause. "We did our duty to Ireland by the waters of Babylon," she wrote, and added archly: "and we found very few of the Babylonians who were not willing to listen." In his novel *Ulysses,* published the same year, James Joyce had young Stephen Dedalus culminate a string of national references ending in the invocation of the imprisoned Fenian rebel Kevin Egan (based on Joseph Casey) with the thought that "They have forgotten Kevin Egan, not he them. Remembering thee, O Sion." Joyce liked the psalm well enough to return to it at the end of chapter 4 of *Finnegans Wake*. There he puns multiple times: "let naaman laugh at Jordan! For we, we have taken our sheet upon her stones where we have hanged our hearts in her trees; and we list, as she bibs us, by the waters of babalong."[8] More recently, Louis MacNeice included several lines based on Psalm 137 in his 1966 translation of the exiled medieval monk Gottschalk's "Ut Quid Iubes, Pusiole."

Adaptations of Psalm 137 permeate not only high but also popular culture up to our own day. For instance, the Irish pop superstar Sinéad O'Connor recorded her hit "Rivers of Babylon" on both the Dublin and London sessions of her 2007 CD *Theology*. There she mixes biblical lyrics with interpolations of her own and substitutes breaking her "guitar" for the biblical hanging of lyres on trees. O'Connor's use of the biblically derived Rastafarian term "Jah" for God or Jehovah echoes perhaps the best-known contemporary musical adaptation of the psalm, also called "Rivers of Babylon" and recorded first by the Melodians and then by various Rasta singers up through Jimmy Cliff. The Jamaican version invokes God as "King Alpha," urges brothers and sisters to sing a song of freedom, and includes a verse from Psalm 19 as well ("Let the words of my mouth, and the meditation of my heart . . ."). To complete the circle, the Jewish rapper Matisyahu uses two verses from the psalm as chorus to his song "Jerusalem" on the CD *Youth:* "Jerusalem, if I forget you, / fire not gonna come from me tongue. / Jerusalem, if I forget you, / let my right hand forget what it's supposed to do."[9] Even with the establishment of an independent Ireland and Israel along with numerous Black states in the Caribbean and Africa, the adaptations continue strong into the twenty-first century, though more often with overtones of personal artistic creation and less often with nationalist nuances than in earlier times.

The politics and sometimes separatism come through loud and clear in the African-American tradition, of which Frederick Douglass is but one example. Douglass, of course, opposed schemes for colonization of Africa by American Blacks (championed early by Martin Delaney and Henry Highland Garnet, among others) and thus stressed the exilic and sorrowful strains in Psalm 137 more than the nationalist and restorative ones, as in his "Fourth of July" address. In contrast, advocates of Pan-African colonization and independence, including the New York–born Reverend Alexander Crummell (1819–1898), invoked the psalm to support their cause, in Crummell's case particularly for Liberia. Now little known outside of African and African-American studies, Crummell was described by the Black activist John Cromwell in his 1914 book *The Negro in American History* as "easily the ripest literary scholar, the writer of the most graceful and faultless English and the most brilliant conversationalist the race has produced in this country." In his 1863 sermon "Emigration, an Aid to the Evangelization of Africa" Crummell used that text to find biblical sanction for Black colonization of that continent. "We find it here in our Bibles," he intoned. "Many men, women, and children; just touching our shores, singing the 'songs of Zion,' joining in olden Litanies, for the first time, 'in a strange land.'" Crummell liked to point out the parallels with other groups. In his 1888 address at the Episcopal Church Congress in Buffalo, for example, he began with ancient Babylon and repeatedly cited Jewish and Irish (Celtic) experience to support his opening thesis that "the residence of various races of men in the same national community, is a fact which has occurred in every period of time and in every quarter of the globe." Crummell's biblical studies sensitized him particularly to parallels between modern Blacks and ancient Jews, as in his famous sermon "Joseph."[10]

African-American poetic adapters of Psalm 137 tended to follow Douglass more than Crummell, though they often gestured toward a nationalist implication. Albert Allson Whitman, known in his own time as "Poet Laureate of the Negro Race," provides an apt example. His long 1877 poem *Not a Man and Yet a Man* features brave Native Americans and a mulatto hero struggling against treacherous White slavers and their supporters. It contains the lyric "The Lute of Afric's Tribe," which opens with an orthodox rendering of Psalm 137, "When Israel sate by Babel's stream and wept, / The heathen said, 'Sing one of Zion's songs,'" but then segues into first the silencing of Afric's lute when "her iron clutch the Slave power reached, / And sable generations captive held" until its awakening by "Freedom's lispings." Whitman located his poem within the politics of his own day by dedicating it to Dr. J. McSimpson, "a colored Author of Anti-Slavery Ballads," and publishing it first in a newspaper. Twenty years later, the South Carolina educator and poet Mary Weston Fordham included "'By the Rivers of Babylon,'" in her collection *Magnolia Leaves,* which sported an introduction by Booker T. Washington giving the volume his "cordial endorsement." The poem began conventionally enough, "By the Rivers of Babylon we mournfully bent, / With 'harps on the willows' and vesture all rent," but ended with an endorsement of Jewish and implicitly Black nationalist aims of restoration in a native land: "O! soon may the exiles of Israel return, / To sing Zion's songs in their own holy land." By placing those words only two poems after "Song to Erin" in the collection, Fordham gave them an Irish nationalist implication as well. Thirty years on, the California-educated Harlem Renaissance poet Arna Bontemps included an unmistakable reference to Psalm 137 in his "Nocturne at Bethesda," which won the poetry prize of Du Bois's *Crisis* magazine for 1927. In it the narrator urges readers to "mourn / upon the harps still hanging in the trees / near Babylon along the river's edge" but then reminds them that "If you want me you must search for me / beneath the palms of Africa."[11]

However much Irish, Black, or other writers might invoke Psalm 137, it resonated most in the Jewish tradition from which it springs. Even a short list of pertinent Jewish-American works would include several poems by Emma Lazarus, Charles Reznikoff's prose and poetry, and later adaptations like Grace Paley's wonderful "A Warning" and Allen Grossman's near-repudiation in "City of David." Yiddish poems like A. Leyeles's "A Poem under Skyscrapers" and I. J. Schwartz's "Blue Grass" section of his long poem *Kentucky* echo Psalm 137. And Yehuda Amichae provides a stunning Hebrew adaptation in "If I Forget Thee, Jerusalem." The phrase "By the Waters of Manhattan," for example, obsessed the American writer Charles Reznikoff. He used it variously as the title of a novella, a book of prose, and finally his 1962 volume of selected verse. The seventy-sixth section of his 1924 book *Jerusalem the Golden* memorably invoked the biblical original to describe diasporic Jewry: "but these wept beside the waters of Babylon and Rome, / and did not forget Jerusalem, nor the citadel of the Lord."[12] Rather than explore those multiple adaptations and authors further, I focus here on Emma Lazarus, both because of her multiple uses of Psalm 137 and because of the rich matrix of connections between her writings about diaspora and nationalism to those of many other writers, including the non-Jewish George Eliot, whom she admired.

Emma Lazarus came to Jewish themes comparatively late in her short life (1849–1887). The privately educated daughter of a wealthy Sephardic merchant family in Philadelphia, Lazarus began as a protégé of Ralph Waldo Emerson writing highly assimilated nineteenth-century verse. Yet *Admetus and Other Poems* (1871) contained an answer to Henry Wadsworth Longfellow's celebrated "The Jewish Cemetery at Newport" in Lazarus's own "In the Jewish Synagogue at Newport." But where Longfellow saw extinction— "Closed are the portals of their Synagogue, / No psalms of David now the silence break"—Lazarus detected ongoing life. Her own poem constituted a song in a strange land by a dispersed people and explicitly echoed Psalm 137: "Alas! We wake: one scene alone remains,—/ The exiles by the streams of Babylon."[13] A startling awakening to Jewish urgencies and evocation of Jewish themes flooded her Jewish-identified volume *Songs of a Semite* a decade later in 1882. The rash of pogroms in the Jewish Pale of Settlement in Russia, combined with anti-Semitic events at home, such as the barring of the banker Joseph Seligman from a Saratoga resort in 1877, awakened Lazarus's indignation. So, too, did a magazine article, "The Russian Side of the Story," in which the émigré Zenaide Alexeievna Ragozin followed the age-old tactic of blaming anti-Semitism itself on Jews. That evoked Lazarus's stinging response, "Russian Christianity versus Modern Judaism," followed a few months later by a gathering of recent verse whose title left no doubt about its author's Jewish identification; Lazarus called it *Songs of a Semite*.

The last of Lazarus's volumes published in her lifetime, *Songs of a Semite* contained much of her best work on Jewish themes, including "The New Year: Rosh-Hashanah, 5643," "The Crowing of the Red Cock," "In Exile," "The Banner of the Jew," and translations from Jewish poets of medieval Spain like Judah Halevi. She followed it a year later with an ambitious adaptation of Psalm 137, her seven-part "By the Waters of Babylon: Little Poems in Prose." Beginning with the expulsion of the Jews from Spain in 1492 labeled "The Exodus" to invoke biblical parallels, the prose poem asks "Whither shall they turn? For the West hath cast them out, and the East refuseth to receive" (p. 243). That line exemplifies Lazarus's double vision for the fate of modern Jewry, split between the desire for religious freedom in Gentile America and for national liberation in Palestine. At the same time, the title and subtitle enact her dual allegiance toward European and Jewish culture. The title gestures toward Psalm 137 and prefigures the numbering of verses in the biblical manner that marks the poem itself. But the subtitle explicitly evokes Baudelaire's famous prose poem *Petits poèmes en prose*, whose technique Lazarus was one of the first to adapt to English. The struggle of a double consciousness working in two traditions at once emerges over and over in writers from all three of our groups.

Daniel Deronda's Proto-Zionism and Its Affinities

Lazarus particularly admired a work by a non-Jewish author that held out hope for bridging her two traditions. It also had an enormous impact on her conversion to Zionist ideals. The work was George Eliot's proto-Zionist novel *Daniel Deronda* (1876), which like Eliot's friend Harriet Beecher Stowe's *Uncle Tom's Cabin* ends with the minority hero emigrating to an overseas national homeland, in Deronda's case Palestine. Lazarus acknowledged her forerunner in blending Zionism and art by inscribing the longest work in *Songs of a Semite*, the play *The Dance of Death*, to Eliot: "This play is

dedicated in profound veneration and respect to the memory of George Eliot, the illustrious writer, who did most among the artists of our day toward
elevating and ennobling the spirit of Jewish nationality." Lazarus's veneration did not stop there. She kept a photograph of Eliot on her desk and cited
her repeatedly in letters and polemics. In section XII of her long essay *Epis-
tle to the Hebrews,* for example, Lazarus wrote that "'The vision is there—it
will be fulfilled,' said George Eliot." And in her refutation of the anti-Semitic
Madame Ragozin, she quoted at length from the same section of *Daniel
Deronda,* chapter 42.[14] Eliot's novel stimulated the Zionist impulse in other
Jews as well, including the American founder of Hadassah, Henrietta Szold,
and English author and Zionist leader Israel Zangwill, author of *The Melting
Pot.* Its impact even extended to Eastern Europe, where the originator of
modern Hebrew Eliezar Ben Yehuda read *Daniel Deronda* with delight, as
did A. D. Gordon and Peretz Smolenskin, who quoted it in their own polemics. In his memoir *A Dream Come True,* Ben Yehuda credited reading the
novel in Russian translation with pushing him to put his ideas into practice:
"After I had read the story a few times I made up my mind and I acted: I
went to Paris, to the source of light and the center of international politics,
in order to learn and equip myself there with the information needed for my
work in the Land of Israel." The book affected so many Zionist activists that
even the most influential founder of Zionism, Theodor Herzl, recorded in
his diary for June 1895 that "I must read *Daniel Deronda.* Perhaps it contains ideas similar to mine."[15] Other nationalists noticed, too. For example,
Edward Blyden quoted from it in a letter to a friend about his inauguration
as president of Liberia College in 1881. Given the importance of the novel in
multiple traditions, examination of *Daniel Deronda* itself helps us move from
the linkages of Black, Jewish, and Irish suffering and oppression through
Psalm 137 by writers from Frederick Douglass onward to broader nationalist emancipatory projects. I proceed in turn to Irish, Jewish, and Black nationalisms, beginning with their affiliation in Eliot's last major novel, which
foreshadows themes of the following half century.

What was the condition of the Jews of George Eliot's England, numbering
as they did around 40,000 at the time? Nowadays, we forget that England
was the last Western European country except for Spain and Portugal to
grant full civil equality to Jews. Historically, there had been considerable
progress since the slaughter of the Jews of York in 1190 by crusaders, the

execution of eighteen Jews of Lincoln in 1255 on a ritual murder charge deriving from the legend of Little St. Hugh later memorialized by Chaucer,
and the expulsion of all 5,000 English Jews in 1290. Conditions had im-
proved further since the readmission of the Jews in 1660 and the debate
about the so-called Jew Bill in the eighteenth century. Catholics and Jews both
sought emancipation in the early nineteenth century, and passage of the
Catholic Emancipation Act in 1829 stimulated two Jews, Isaac and Frances
Goldsmid, to petition Parliament for similar Jewish relief a year later. Nonetheless, in the nineteenth century Jews still could not serve in Parliament
until 1858, graduate from universities until 1871, or achieve full emancipation until 1890. Well aware of this history, Eliot wrote to her friend
the American novelist Harriet Beecher Stowe shortly after publication of
the novel:

> As to the Jewish element in "Deronda," I expected from first to last in
> writing it, that it would create much stronger resistance and even re-
> pulsion than it has actually met with. But precisely because I felt that
> the usual attitude of Christians towards Jews is—I hardly know
> whether to say more impious or more stupid when viewed in the light
> of their professed principles, I therefore felt urged to treat Jews with
> such sympathy and understanding as my nature and knowledge could
> attain to. Moreover, not only towards the Jews, but towards all oriental
> peoples with whom we English come in contact, a spirit of arrogance
> and contemptuous dictatorialness is observable which has become a
> national disgrace to us.[16]

In the later nineteenth century, solutions to the problem of anti-Semitism
began to oscillate between the same two extremes—assimilation or a national state—that they do today. Both poles appear in Eliot's novel. On one
hand stands the proto-Zionism of Deronda and Mordecai, one more civic
and liberal, the other more mystical and religious. On the other hand stands
the assimilationism of the German-Jewish musician Klesmer, who "has cosmopolitan ideas . . . [and] looks forward to a fusion of races."[17] Eliot's sympathetic depiction of a range of Jewish characters and customs in the half of
the novel centered on the Daniel-Mirah plot made the novel's reception
more problematic and controversial than the intricate psychologizing of the

sections featuring the Gentile Henleigh Grandcourt and Gwendolen Harleth. The book's embrace of a proto-Zionism is well known, but its association of that cause with Black and Irish ones is not.

References to African Americans, especially to the slave plantations of the West Indies and to the Civil War in the United States, dot the novel, though as often overlooked by the characters themselves as by readers. Eliot tells us at the start that Gwendolen "had no notion how her maternal grandfather got the fortune inherited by his two daughters" as a White plantation owner in the West Indies, and a few chapters later reiterates that it had never "occurred to her to inquire into the conditions of colonial property and banking, on which, as she had had many opportunities of knowing, the family fortune was dependent" (pp. 16, 53). These references culminate in the dispute between the Gentile Grandcourt and the Jewish Deronda about the brutal suppression of the Jamaican slave rebellion by Governor Edward Eyre in 1865 that echoed throughout Victorian England: "Grandcourt held that the Jamaican Negro was a beastly sort of Baptist Caliban; Deronda said he had always felt a little with Caliban, who naturally had his own point of view and could sing a good song" (p. 295). Deronda's sly inversion of the Caliban issue eerily prefigures a characteristic move of contemporary postcolonial theory in valorizing the subordinate other; here it tellingly reinforces the Black-Jewish connections of the novel's subtext. As Eliot's friendship with Harriet Beecher Stowe suggests, Eliot also inserted references to the American Civil War into this proto-Zionist novel. They, too, begin early in the novel, with the narrator's invocation of the "universal kinship" inspired by the war. Comparing American women whose men died in that struggle with Englishmen thrown out of work in the cotton mills, the narrator describes the age as one "when women on the other side of the world would not mourn for the husbands and sons who died bravely in a common cause, and men stinted of bread on our side of the world heard of that willing loss and were patient" (p. 108). The analogies reach a crescendo near the end in Deronda's impassioned speech to Gwendolen of his commitment to "restoring a political existence to my people, making them a nation again, giving them a national center, such as the English have." Eliot interrupts that account to invoke "the dire clash of civil war" in the United States as a time when "submission of the soul to the Highest is tested" (p. 730).

Just as *Daniel Deronda* calls up Jewish-Black associations of its time, so does it summon Jewish-Irish ones, even if of an occasionally stereotypical

sort. When the supreme Jewish musician Klesmer reverts to Germanic intonations, the narrator immediately invokes the simile "as Irishmen resume
their strongest brogue when they are fervid or quarrelsome" (p. 39). The
links can be sexual as well as political: Grandcourt's early paramour, Mrs.
Glasher, had eloped with him from her marriage to an Irish army officer.
And they can be national. When Mordecai brings Daniel to the discussion
at his Philosophers' Club, Deronda discovers that most of the members
are Jewish, but that "Croope, the dark-eyed shoemaker, was probably more
Celtic than he knew" (p. 474). In that same discussion, Mordecai makes the
parallels between Jews and Irish explicit when he takes a dim view of intermarriage: "Thousands on thousands of our race have mixed with the Gentile as Celt with Saxon" (p. 478). In each case the victimized race intermar-
ries with the conquering one. But the connections could be positive as well
as negative. A year after publication of the novel, George Eliot made that
clear in a letter. "The analogy you find between the Celt and the Hebrew
seems to me also not fanciful but real," she wrote to the Scots woman of letters and early feminist Charlotte Carmichael (later Stopes). "Both have a
literature which has been a fount of religious feeling and imagination to
other races" (*Letters*, 6:438).

Eliot's linkages mirror those of her friend Harriet Beecher Stowe in the
abolitionist novel *Uncle Tom's Cabin,* which Stowe laced with references to
Jews and Irish. The Jewish connections often spring from the Bible, particularly from the Exodus from Egypt and from the Babylonian exile after the
fall of Jerusalem. References to "Jordan's banks," "Canaan's fields," and the
"New Jerusalem" run right through the story, starting with chapter 4's description of the prayer meeting in Uncle Tom's cabin. When Stowe depicts
the sorrow of the slaves on the steamboat headed south, she invokes the language of Psalm 137's lament by the rivers of Babylon—"they that wasted
them required of them mirth"—as had so many other chroniclers of diaspora. Uncle Tom in St. Clare's house identifies himself with Joseph in Egypt.[18]
The Irish connections also work largely through literary allusions that invoke writers like the poet Thomas Moore or orator and jurist John Philpot
Curran, both of whom opposed slavery and supported Irish independence.
The quotation from Curran beginning "Chapter 37: Liberty" cites Curran's
ringing defense of the Jamaican slave James Somerset, who in 1772 won his
case that upon arrival in England he was a free man. That vision of freedom in a world elsewhere accords with Stowe's showing us little of integrated

society in the United States. Once out of slavery, George and Eliza Harris can only set up their establishment in Canada, and they intend to emigrate back to Africa and join the Liberian venture of Crummell and others, as Eliot's own Daniel and Mirah journey to Palestine at the end of *Daniel Deronda*.

I suggest here not only the separate couplings of any two members of these three groups but the frequency with which both their partisans and their detractors put the three together, as in Stowe's and Eliot's novels. That happens even more concentratedly in George Eliot's great essay on anti-Semitism, "The Modern Hep! Hep! Hep!" published shortly after *Daniel Deronda* in her collection *Impressions of Theophrastus Such*. The title phrase "Hep! Hep! Hep!" comes from the cry of anti-Jewish rioters, as examples from *Penny Cyclopedia* through the *Oxford English Dictionary* make clear. It derives from the initials of "Jerusalema est perdita" ("Jerusalem is lost"), a key condition of diaspora. On one page there Eliot first invokes the Black-Jewish analogy. "Edicts issued to protect 'the King's Jews' equally with the King's game from being harassed and hunted by the commonality were only slight mitigations to the deplorable lot of a race held to be under the divine curse, and had little force after the Crusades began," she wrote.

> As the slave-holders in the United States counted the curse on Ham a justification of negro slavery, so the curse on the Jews was counted a justification for hindering them from pursuing agriculture and handi-crafts; for marking them out as execrable figures by a peculiar dress; for torturing them to make them part with their gains, or for more gratu-itously spitting at them and pelting them; for taking it as certain that they killed and ate babies, poisoned the wells, and took pains to spread the plague; . . . finally, for hounding them by tens on tens of thousands from the homes where they had found shelter for centuries, and inflict-ing on them the horrors of a new exile and a new dispersion.

After that fiery passage, Eliot turns her attention to discrimination against Irish Catholics, too, again invoking a parallel to treatment of the Jews: "All which is mirrored in an analogy, namely, that of the Irish, also a servile race, who have rejected Protestantism though it has been repeatedly urged on them by fire and sword and penal laws, and whose place in the moral scale may be judged by our advertisements, where the clause, 'No Irish need apply,' parallels the sentence which for many polite persons sums up the question of Judaism—'I never *did* like the Jews.'"[19] Eliot connects the dots astutely here, moving easily among complex topics. She does, too, tend to foreground the religious element, just at the moment when European anti-Semitism began to develop a pseudorespectable scientific racial rationale to augment the traditional religious one. Indeed, the very term "anti-Semitism" was invented by the German journalist Wilhelm Marr in the same decade as Eliot's novel and essay to describe that racial orientation as part of his creation of the first Anti-Semitic League, which led to the growth of explicitly anti-Semitic parties throughout Europe. The synchrony of admiration for Jews and the rise of anti-Semitism typifies the ambiguity of the representation of Jews in modern Western culture. Bryan Cheyette, for example, has identified "a semitic discourse which constructed 'the Jew' as both within *and* without; a stranger *and* familiar; an object of esteem *and* odium."[20] But within that duality the religious component of Black, Jewish, and Irish linkages took primacy for a long time and provides a helpful entrance into future developments.

Irish, Jewish, and Black Nationalists

Most important of all was the story of the Exodus from Egypt, which became a foundational trope in the growth of Irish, Black, and of course Jewish nationalisms. The saga of Moses leading the enslaved children of Israel out of bondage in Egypt into freedom in Canaan had for centuries represented liberation of the spirit from things of this world and a turning of the soul from idolatry toward God. In Dante's *Purgatorio*, to take one of myriad examples, the saved souls sing the 114th Psalm ("When Israel came out of Egypt") as their boat reaches the mountain of their salvation. Late nineteenth-century nationalisms favored instead the political allegory, which had of course also been there all along. Comparison of leaders to Moses and the ancient Hebrews to modern Irish, Blacks, and Jews electrified adherents and helped to attract more. In his great novel *Ulysses*, set in 1904, James Joyce inscribes one of the most famous speeches of the modern Irish nationalist movement, the orator John F. Taylor's crucial comparison of the modern Irish and ancient Jewish causes. Despite the overt anti-Semitism of some nationalist leaders (including Sinn Féin founder Arthur Griffith, orator and Daughters of Ireland founder Maud Gonne, and Irish envoy to

Nazi Germany in the 1930s Charles Bewley), Taylor's sympathetic parallel between Jews and Irish struck the more normative note. Ironically, the actual speech was never printed and exists now only in multiple versions, among them those given by Joyce in his novel, by Yeats in his autobiography, and by the newspaper *Freeman's Journal* the day after its delivery in 1901. I abridge Joyce's version here:

> *Great was my admiration in listening to the remarks addressed to the youth of Ireland a moment since by my learned friend. It seemed to me that I had been transported into a country far away from this country, into an age remote from this age, that I stood in ancient Egypt and that I was listening to the speech of some highpriest of that land addressed to the youthful Moses.*
>
> *—And it seemed to me that I heard the voice of that Egyptian highpriest raised in a tone of like haughtiness and like pride. I heard his words and their meaning was revealed to me.*
>
> *—Why will you jews not accept our culture, our religion and our language? You are a tribe of nomad herdsmen: we are a mighty people. . . . You pray to a local and obscure idol: our temples, majestic and mysterious, are the abodes of Isis and Osiris, of Horus and Ammon Ra. . . . Israel is weak and few are her children: Egypt is an host and terrible are her arms. . . .*
>
> *—But, ladies and gentlemen, had the youthful Moses listened and accepted that view of life, had he bowed his head and bowed his will and bowed his spirit before that arrogant admonition he would never have brought the chosen people out of their house of bondage, nor followed the pillar of the cloud by day.*[21]

Taylor's speech touches the key tropes of deliverance from bondage to a mighty enemy, independence for a beleaguered people, and the importance of a charismatic leader that would animate Irish, Black, and Jewish nationalisms and link them to each other. When the great Irish leader Charles Stewart Parnell died in 1891, the young W. B. Yeats immediately vented his grief in a poem called "Mourn—And Then Onward!" which invokes the Mosaic analogy developed more fully by John F. Taylor. The sentiments are impeccable, though not the technique, and Yeats later wisely omitted the lyric from his collected works:

Ye on the broad high mountains of old Eri,
  Mourn all the night and day,
The man is gone who guided ye, unweary,
  Through the long bitter way.

. . .

Mourn—and then onward, there is no returning
  He guides ye from the tomb;
  His memory now is a tall pillar, burning
  Before us in the gloom![22]

Yeats's association of Irish and Jewish themes would shortly blossom into endorsement of the Zionist project, not least because of his indignation at the English historian Arnold Toynbee's famous assignment of the Jewish and Irish national movements to the dust heap of history and description of present members of those groups as fossils. That was enough to get Yeats's back up (not that it always took so much). During an American lecture tour in early 1920 near the height of the Irish struggle against the English, he issued the following statement to the Palestine restoration fund committee. Yeats clearly had one eye on the situation in Ireland, and much of his endorsement transfers readily to his hopes for his own homeland:

Every race should have one spot where its traditions may develop unobstructed. . . .

The establishment of a [Jewish] homeland in Palestine would accentuate the national life of a people the world cannot but admire.

For one thing it would result in a new Jewish literature. The Jews have created a great literature in the past, but more will be achieved by the establishment of a native soil.

A nation must have roots to cling to if it is to produce literature or anything of value. If the English race did not have a country of its own, Shakespeare would never have been produced.

The Palestine restoration movement appeals to me in a broad sense and I heartily endorse the campaign for funds now being conducted to make this dream a possibility.[23]

If John Taylor's speech and Yeats's Parnell poem and Zionist endorsement touch key facets of the Exodus trope, an even more influential one by

Douglas Hyde blazes a trail that colonial liberatory rhetoric of the twentieth century would follow in Irish, Zionist, and Pan-African movements, among others. Hyde's influential and then innovative 1892 discourse, "The Necessity for De-Anglicising Ireland," strikes now familiar notes: the decline of the oppressed race, its glorious past, its ambivalent love-hate relationship with the dominant culture, the necessity of rebirth or renaissance, and the key role of a national language in forging political and cultural identity. Hyde himself practiced what he preached, of course, serving as president of the Gaelic League and eventually of the Republic of Ireland. His oration built to its magnificent last sentence, where he once again invoked a Jewish analogy for Irish nationalism: "If all this were done, it should not be very difficult . . . to bring about a tone of thought which would make it disgraceful for an educated Irishman—especially of the old Celtic race, MacDermotts, O'Conors, O'Sullivans, MacCarthys, O'Neills—to be ignorant of his own language—would make it at least as disgraceful as for an educated Jew to be quite ignorant of Hebrew." National comparisons of Irish and Jewish cases went back to the first Gaelic history of Ireland by the lay priest Geoffrey Keating in the early seventeenth century. "No People except the Jews, whose Writings were divinely inspired, have more genuine or earlier Accounts of the Concerns of their Ancestors than the Chronicles and ancient Records that give Being to the present History," he wrote there.[24] Hyde's later and impassioned plea for replacing a colonial language like English would echo throughout similar nationalist maneuvers, whether to favor Gaelic in Ireland, Hebrew in Palestine, or African languages on that continent. In the event, Zionism proved even more successful in reestablishing Hebrew as the primary national language of an entire country than Irish nationalism did with Gaelic.

Two years after Hyde's speech came the anti-Semitic Dreyfuss Affair in France, which resulted in the trial and wrongful conviction of a Jewish captain in the French army on charges of treason. The resultant outcry led to a national and international scandal, sparked by Zola's famous indictment "J'accuse." It also resulted in the embrace of Zionism by a young Austro-Hungarian journalist covering the trial, Theodore Herzl. Indeed, according to historian Walter Laqueur, the term "Zionism" first appeared in the same year as Hyde's "De-Anglicising" speech, 1892, and according to the *Oxford English Dictionary* only in English in 1896.[25] Influenced like George Eliot by

Harriet Beecher Stowe's *Uncle Tom's Cabin* (and later by *Daniel Deronda*), Herzl had been urged by his friend Alphonse Daudet (ironically, an anti-Semite) to write a novel rather than a political tract: "A novel can reach farther. Think of *Uncle Tom's Cabin*." Herzl thought, too, of the Irish example, resolving in his diary from 1895 that "I shall be the Parnell of the Jews."[26] In the event, Herzl produced both a novel and a tract, first the founding pamphlet of Zionism, *Der Judenstaat* (The Jewish State), in 1896 and then the novel *AltNeuland* (OldNew Land) in 1902. *The Jewish State* moved from a nationalist insistence that "We are a people—one people" through a long practical section on organization and logistics to an idealistic but naive conclusion that "the Jews, once settled in their own state, would probably have no more enemies."[27]

But Jews did have enemies, then and now, and Herzl's eloquent *The Jewish State* finds its dark double in the hate-filled *Protocols of the Elders of Zion,* forged in 1903 by the czar's secret police and circulated widely by anti-Semitic hatemongers ever since, even though unmasked long ago as a fabrication. The forgery provided the basis of the czarist claim that Jews were Bolsheviks, a charge gleefully adopted by the Nazis. It circulated widely in both Ku Klux Klan and Nation of Islam circles in the United States and circulates even more pervasively in Arab countries today, which obsessively rebroadcast the forty-one-part Egyptian television series "Horse without a Horseman" based on it and shown repeatedly since its debut in 2002. Those tempted to sympathize uncritically with organizations like Hamas today might go on the Internet and read Article 32 of the Hamas charter: "The Zionist plan is limitless. After Palestine, the Zionists aspire to expand from the Nile to the Euphrates. When they will have digested the region they overtook, they will aspire to further expansion, and so on. Their plan is embodied in the *Protocols of the Elders of Zion*."[28]

Such sentiments fall far from what Herzl hoped for when he wrote *The Jewish State* and even farther from the vision of intergroup cooperation that he envisaged in his novel *AltNeuland* a few years later. There the scientist Professor Steineck calls for ameliorating the lot of the other group besides Irish and Jews in this study:

There is still one problem of racial misfortune unsolved. The depths of that problem, in all their horror, only a Jew can fathom. I mean the

Negro problem. Don't laugh, Mr. Kingscourt. Think of the hair-raising
horrors of the slave trade. Human beings, because their skins are black,
are stolen, carried off, and sold. Their descendants grow up in alien
surroundings despised and hated because their skin is differently pig-
mented. I am not ashamed to say, though I be thought ridiculous, now
that I have lived to see the restoration of the Jews, I should like to pave
the way for the restoration of the Negroes.[29]

The notion of a special sympathy between Blacks and Jews because of their
respective suffering was commonplace a century ago and articulated by intellectual leaders and the popular press of both groups.

The same affinity with the Exodus story begins before that, of course, in
the moving rhythms of African-American spirituals sung in the slave South.
Part of an ongoing vernacular and oral tradition, these songs first made
their way into print at the start of the nineteenth century in a collection by a
Black church leader. They focused often on the travails of the children of
Israel in Egypt, particularly the story of Moses and the Exodus. In that typology, Egypt often figured as the slave South, heaven as the free Northern
States, the ancient Jews as modern African Americans, and any liberationist
leader as a Moses. One of the most prominent was Harriet Tubman, an es-
caped slave who over time led more than 300 of her people to freedom in the
North. Her first biographer, Sarah H. Bradford, subtitled her biography
"The Moses of Her People" and explained that "I only give her here the
name by which she was familiarly known, both at [sic] the North and the
South." Song after song like "Wade in the Water" paralleled the suffering of
the two peoples. Here is a verse from perhaps the best known of all, "Go
Down, Moses," which Tubman's biographer took care to quote:

Oh go down, Moses,
Way down in Egypt's land,
Tell old Pharaoh,
Let my people go.

The enormous pathos of such songs eased the pain of bondage and promoted hopes of freedom in a typical maneuver by oppressed peoples of
words that might mean one thing to their alien overlords (here, acquiescent

piety) but quite another to themselves (here, a call for freedom and escape). They also indelibly inscribed parallels between Black and Jewish experience that endured well beyond the nineteenth century. Ralph Ellison remarked in a 1976 interview that "'Go Down, Moses' is an absorption of certain Jewish religious traditions and that's my possession; no one can take that away from me."[30]

Those parallels carried over into print traditions as well. They pervade the Harlem Renaissance, for example, whose landmark anthology of 1925, *The New Negro*, proclaimed that "Harlem has the same role to play for the New Negro as Dublin has had for the New Ireland." James Weldon Johnson observed in the same year that "it is not possible to estimate the sustaining influence that the story of the trials and tribulations of the Jews as related in the Old Testament exerted upon the Negro."[31] And toward the end of the same movement, Zora Neale Hurston based her novel *Moses, Man of the Mountain* (1939) on a triple analogy among ancient Hebrews in bondage in Egypt, African Americans in the slave South, and Jews trapped in Nazi Germany.

I turn here to a now almost forgotten member of the Harlem Renaissance, Theodore Henry Shackelford, who died young. The grandson of escaped slaves who followed the Underground Railroad through the Northern free states all the way into Canada, Shackelford was born in 1888 in Windsor and produced two books of poetry before his untimely death in 1923. His second collection, *My Country and Other Poems*, included the poem "The Big Bell in Zion," which became his best-known work when James Weldon Johnson selected it for his landmark anthology *The Book of American Negro Poetry* (1922). In his preface to the original edition Johnson argued that "What the colored poet in the United States needs to do is something like what Synge did for the Irish; he needs to find a form that will express the racial spirit by symbols from within rather than by symbols from without." Two stanzas of "Big Bell in Zion" apply the biblical story of the Exodus from Egypt even more explicitly to contemporary politics than had the old spirituals and draw a parallel between the land of Canaan and the free state of Ohio, just as Stowe and many others did:

> My bruthah jus' sent word to me,
> > Ding. Dong. Ding.

That he'd done set his own self free.
  Ding. Dong. Ding.

Ole massa said he could not go,
  Ding. Dong. Ding.
But he's done reached Ohio sho'.
  Ding. Dong. Ding.[32]

Affiliation between Black and Jewish liberations did not stop with ancient Israel and nineteenth-century African Americans, nor with songs of freedom and biblical tropes. They extended as well into practical politics and political philosophy, particularly the interweaving of African nationalism and Zionism as twin causes. That conception informs the work of Edward Blyden (1832–1912), whom the *Oxford Companion to African American Literature* describes as "the most important African thinker of the nineteenth century." Born in Saint Thomas in the Caribbean, Blyden made his way first to America and eventually to Liberia and Sierra Leone, where he led a successful career as journalist, writer, and politician, serving eventually as Liberian secretary of state and then ambassador to the Court of St. James, among other distinguished posts. The Exodus analogy was central to this thought. He wrote, "The Negro leader of the exodus, who will succeed, will be a Negro of Negroes, like Moses was a Hebrew of the Hebrews—even if brought up in Pharaoh's palace he will be found."[33] Though sketched by rare scholars like Hollis Lynch and Paul Gilroy, the importance of Jews and Zionism to Blyden goes unmentioned in major anthologies and reference books, such as the *Oxford Companion*. Blyden himself, however, had no doubts of a lifelong affinity, and in his pamphlet *The Jewish Question*, written at the end of the century, he extolled "that marvelous movement called Zionism."[34] Blyden dedicated that work to his Jewish friend Louis Solomon, a Liverpool merchant, expressing the hope that "you and your friends may have the record of the views held by an African of the work and destiny of a people with whom his own race is closely allied, both by Divine declaration and by a history almost identical of sorrow and oppression; and that, if possible, members of the two suffering races—Africans and Jews—who read these pages, may have a somewhat clearer understanding and a deeper sympathy with each other." That alignment of Jews and Blacks for political purposes would echo throughout the writings of later Black thinkers, such as W. E. B. Du Bois, Marcus Garvey, and a host of others.

In *The Jewish Question* Blyden recalled that he was "born in the midst of Jews" on Saint Thomas and that the awe and reverence that he felt at listening to synagogue services followed him all his life. He testified, too, to the support for his endeavors from Jewish acquaintances, both on Saint Thomas and throughout his career, and of his efforts to study Hebrew to read the Old Testament and Talmud in the original. Besides pressing the parallels between Black and Jewish dispersal and suffering, Blyden throughout urged not merely a political but also a spiritual view of Zionism as contributing to human welfare. He closed with a ringing endorsement of brotherhood that Frederick Douglass would have understood as he gazed at that Irish cabin and that Blyden himself borrowed from Rabbi S. Singer of London:

> We are all apt to think evil of others of whom we are ignorant. The more ignorance, the more hatred among people of different races and creeds. A man once told a very curious thing that happened to him. I was going over the hills one foggy morning, and at a distance as far as my eye could reach I saw coming towards me a strange object, which I thought was a monster; when we came nearer to each other I saw it was a man, and when we got close up to each other, lo! And behold, it was my own brother! (p. 24)

That concept of brotherhood, of course, underlies the analogies that this chapter has been exploring. The great Black, Jewish, and Irish thinkers of the past extended it beyond their own group to all groups, and if we follow their diminished modern epigones in restricting the term only to our own groups, we contradict their teachings and diminish ourselves as well as our world. In that way we would mirror the dehumanizing views of others shown by their oppressors.

The 1881 cartoon "Time's Waxworks" by the caricaturist Sir John Tenniel in the British humor magazine *Punch* (Figure 10) shows how dehumanizing those views were. In it Father Time shows Mr. Punch a "chamber of horrors" featuring a Zulu warrior from the 1880 revolt in South Africa and a Irish Fenian dynamiter from the Land War of 1879–1882, with Chinese figures in the background suggesting the two Opium Wars earlier in the century. Both

TIME'S WAXWORKS.

(1881 *JUST ADDED TO THE COLLECTION.*)

Mr. P. " HA ! YOU 'LL HAVE TO PUT HIM INTO THE CHAMBER OF HORRORS ! "

Figure 10. "Time's Waxworks," *Punch,* 31 December 1881. (Courtesy, University of Michigan Library.)

the Zulu and the Fenian carry weapons of violence, wear outlandish costumes, and have dark skins. Most important of all in terms of racial theory, both display simian or apelike features that assign them to a lower rank on the evolutionary scale than their imperial conquerors. The *Punch* cartoon thus dehumanizes the rebels as animalistic, prone to violence, and dangerous—"horrors" indeed. Their fellow Zulus and Irish might take a very different view, seeing the rebels as nationalist heroes instead. The imperial power thus associates the rebels negatively with each other, while the opposing forces would see them positively. They could draw both solace and inspiration from each other. The *New Negro* volume of 1925 provides one of countless examples, with its insistence that "Harlem is the home of the Negro's 'Zionism'" and that "Harlem has the same role to play for the New Negro as Dublin has had for the New Ireland" (pp. 7, 12). I should like to extend that notion of championing one's own group but still believing in interracial and interethnic brotherhood through three final examples from the first quarter of the twentieth century—the writing of the Zionist leader Israel Zangwill, the Black political thinkers W. E. B. Du Bois and Marcus Garvey, and finally a crucial scene in James Joyce's novel *Ulysses.*

Liberationist Links: Zangwill, Du Bois, Garvey, and Joyce

Now largely forgotten, Zangwill was once an important Zionist leader. He was also the author of a now little-performed or read play whose title survives in a phrase that pops up in nearly all interracial and intergroup discussion, *The Melting Pot,* and that figures centrally in the next chapter. It is popular today to denounce the play (often without reading it) as favoring suppression of individual groups by a dominant culture. But Zangwill intended just the opposite, arguing in an afterword that "The process of American amalgamation is not assimilation or simple surrender to the dominant type, as is popularly supposed, but an all-round give-and-take by which the final type may be enriched or impoverished."[35] He carefully wrote into the play the transformation of initial hostility between the Irish maid Kathleen and the elderly Jewish Frau Quixano into fervent mutual loyalty. He also made sure to associate the anti-Semitic bigots with anti-Black sentiments as well and to denounce the practice of lynching. In the afterword, he presented himself as a Zionist leader and paralleled the Jewish immigrants as "the toughest of all the white elements that have been poured into the crucible" to amalgamate with African Americans, for whom he predicted that "even the Negrophobia is not likely to remain eternally at its present barbarous pitch." Zangwill's views fit well with those of Herzl, who as we saw also associated Zionism with both Irish and Black causes.

They also fit well with perhaps the greatest African-American intellectual of the early twentieth century, Du Bois, who became aware of the Jewish problem in 1893 while studying in Germany and who saw Zionist and African aspiration as cut from the same cloth. "The African movement means to us what the Zionist movement must mean to the Jews, the centralization of race effort and the recognition of a racial fount," he wrote in his editorial "Not 'Separatism'" for the NAACP journal *Crisis.*[36] Such affinities carried practical as well as theoretical freight. The first Pan-African conference was

held in London in 1900, only three years after the first Zionist Congress in
Basel, and Zionism helped inspire Du Bois's Pan-African Congresses between 1919 and 1927. Throughout his life Du Bois learned of Zionism from
his many close Jewish friends, including Joel Spingarn of the NAACP and
Madame Calman-Levy of the French-Jewish community. At a board meeting of the NAACP he even distributed copies of a pamphlet by Paul Otlet,
popularly called "the father of the League of Nations" because of his writings on the subject, which stressed that "The initiators of the Pan-African
movement believe that there is a strong analogy between the situation of
blacks and that of the Jews." Du Bois made a similar point in the essay that
he contributed to *The New Negro* in 1925, "The Negro Mind Reaches Out,"
where he movingly endorsed analogies between "two international groups—
the Jews and the Modern Negroes" (p. 411). He intertwined Black and Jewish causes over many decades, including (for example) his linkage of Black
and Jewish nationalisms in the essay "Africa, Colonialism, and Zionism"
of 1919, his bold condemnation of Hitler's policies in "The Present Plight of
the German Jew" of 1936, his support for creation of the state of Israel
in "The Case for the Jews" of 1948, and his meditation on the Holocaust in
"The Negro and the Warsaw Ghetto" of 1952.

The Pan-African leader who most emphasized the triangle of Black, Jewish, and Irish causes was Marcus Garvey. Born in Jamaica in 1887, Garvey
became the most famous Black nationalist of his time, especially after setting up his Universal Negro Improvement Association (UNIA) and moving
its headquarters to Harlem. Though increasingly given to anti-Semitic out-
bursts about Jews and economics, he regularly praised both Zionism and
Irish Nationalism as political movements and upheld them as ideals for
Black liberation movements as well. Garvey vibrated deeply to the tropes of
Exodus and Moses; to this day, one of the best biographies of him is called
Black Moses, and his followers regularly made that comparison. A Garvey
supporter in South Africa in 1919 observed that "Africans have the same
confidence in Marcus Garvey which the Israelites had in Moses." "The Universal Negro Improvement Association is no joke," Garvey wrote that same
year. "It is as serious a movement as the movement of the Irish today to have
a free Ireland, as the determination of the Jew to recover Palestine."[37] Garvey would echo those sentiments repeatedly, even obsessively. And when
UNIA held its first convention in Madison Square Garden in 1920, Garvey

began his rousing remarks by reading first a telegram of congratulations from the Zionist leader Louis Michael that said "As a Jew, a Zionist, and a Socialist I join heartily and unflinchingly in your historical movement for the reclamation of Africa" (2:499). Garvey then went on to read a telegram he himself had sent congratulating the Irish revolutionary leader Eamon de Valera on the success of the Irish revolution. Irish nationalism fascinated Garvey perhaps even more than Zionism did. For instance, he named his UNIA headquarters in Harlem "Liberty Hall" because the Irish nationalist and socialist James Connolly had previously given his headquarters in Dublin that name. After Garvey designed the black, red, and green Pan-African flag still often seen at Black Power or Black nationalist rallies, he repeatedly indicated that the green stood for Ireland, which he saw as the first British colony to gain independence in the twentieth century and as a model for African aspirations.

Zionist leaders paid homage to the Irish, too. For example, while fighting the British in Palestine, Yitzhak Shamir, later prime minister of Israel, adopted the code name "Michael" in tribute to the Irish guerilla leader Michael Collins. "It was to the heroes of the Irish revolution that I was to pay tribute years afterwards by choosing 'Michael' as my underground alias," he wrote in his autobiography.[38] And, of course, Chaim Herzog, the son of the Chief Rabbi of Ireland, himself fought for Israeli independence and eventually served as the sixth president of the State of Israel. Practically though improbably, Vladimir (Ze'ev) Jabotinsky, the founder of militant Revisionist Zionism and its armed force, Irgun, travelled to Ireland in 1938. He solicited support for a Jewish state from then-President Eamon de Valera and learned Irish guerilla tactics from Robert Briscoe, the highest-ranking Irish Jew in the nationalist movement.

Born into a nationalist household so militant that he had a brother named Wolfe Tone after the organizer of the United Irishmen uprising of 1798, Briscoe had headed gun-running operations from Germany for the Irish Republican Army. In later life he became a member of the Dail (the Irish parliament) and eventually the first Jewish lord mayor of Dublin (the only other one was his son Ben). When he travelled to Boston in that capacity, Mayor John Hynes of Boston introduced him with the endorsement, "We have here with us two fine fellows—an Irishman and a Jew. I give him to you now, Lord Mayor Robert Briscoe." That displayed far more wit than the dreadful doggerel beginning "'Bob' Briscoe, a fighting Irish Jew / Stalwart son of Erin—Brave and True" that celebrated Briscoe as both Irish and Zionist nationalist.[39] Briscoe struck up a friendship with Jabotinsky and later served as board member and fund-raiser for the Revisionists. But his greatest practical help was to teach Jabotinsky proven guerilla tactics. "Jabotinsky came to Ireland to learn all he could of the methods we had used in training our young men and boys for the Revolution against England in order to form a physical force movement in Palestine on exactly the same lines as Fianna Eireann and the I. R. A.," he wrote in his autobiography. "I then began to work closely with Jabotinsky in organizing Irgun on the lines of the I. R. A." Briscoe saw the fruits of that collaboration on a later trip with de Valera to Israel after independence, which deepened their sense of "the remarkable likeness between Israel and Ireland" in both history and struggle for independence.

The confluence of Irish, Jewish, and Black nationalisms reaches one high-water mark in James Joyce's novel *Ulysses,* with its continual inscriptions of Zionism, Irish nationalism, and minority liberation of all kinds, right from that first chapter with Stephen and Buck Mulligan in the Martello tower through to the end of Molly's soliloquy. They cluster most thickly in Chapter 12, "Cyclops," where the problematic Irish Jew Leopold Bloom encounters in a pub the even more problematic narrow nationalist known in the novel as the Citizen and based on the historical Michael Cusack, founder of the Gaelic Athletic Association. As the scene builds to its violent confrontation, our familiar triangle emerges. I have argued in a recent book called *Material Modernism: The Politics of the Page* that Joyce expanded the parallels and allusions to Irish, Jewish, and Black causes as he continually revised this scene and others in the process of composition. One epitome of that comes in the late invocation of the song now beginning "If the man in the moon was a jew, jew, jew" with its archaeology of links between Irish, Jewish, and Black liberation that we noted in the last chapter.[40] The antagonisms that Joyce seeks to counter rise to a crescendo earlier in the scene, when the Citizen challenges Bloom's claims to be an Irishman rather than a "half and half" by asking insultingly, "What is your nation if I may ask?" (p. 272). Bloom responds with the note of simple humanity that Seamus Heaney in his wonderful poem "Traditions" cited in reference to current troubles in Northern Ireland: "Ireland, says Bloom. I was born here. Ireland." But the Citizen and his cronies refuse Bloom's claims and provoke him to identify with Jewry:

And I belong to a race too, says Bloom, that is hated and persecuted. Also now. This very instant. . . . Robbed, says he. Plundered. Persecuted. Taking what belongs to us by right. At this very moment, says he, putting up his fist, sold by auction in Morocco like slaves or cattle.

   —Are you talking about the new Jerusalem? Says the citizen.

   —I'm talking about injustice says Bloom. (p. 273)

Bloom's outburst reminds us that the Zionism that pervades the novel was a response to Jewish mistreatment not only in Europe (as is often said nowadays) but also to mistreatment in the Arab lands where Jews had existed for over two millennia. Joyce was well aware of that at the time of writing the novel, for newspapers had recently described the custom in Morocco of the Muslim majority subjecting the Jewish population to "compulsory service" for servile tasks, an obligation that could be bought or sold in the marketplace along with slaves and cattle. Indeed, the Jewish population figures for Morocco and other Arab countries before and after establishment of the State of Israel indicate the nationalist ingathering of these diasporic and often mistreated populations. Here are a few of them, first for the year of the establishment of the Israeli state and then for the year 2001:[41]

	1948	2001
Morocco	285,000	5,700
Libya	38,000	0
Algeria	140,000	< 100
Iraq	135,000	< 100
Yemen	55,000	< 200
Egypt	75,000	< 100

Yet that account of persecution is not Bloom's final position, nor should it be ours. Bloom goes on to give his final verdict and his final value:

   —But it's no use, says he. Force, hatred, history, all that. That's not life for men and women, insult and hatred. And everybody knows that it's the very opposite of that that is really life.

   —What? Says Alf.

   —Love, says Bloom. I mean the opposite of hatred. (p. 273)

If pressed, I hope that we will all take our stand with Bloom. I suggest throughout this book that our constructions of the past are inevitably misconstructions. Our current misconstructions have seized on the elements of Bloom's force, hatred, and persecution that certainly pervade history. But we have scanted Bloom's opposites of hatred among groups—love, alliance, and compassion—that also appear there. The history of interrelations among Irish nationalism, Zionism, and Pan-Africanism shows us the humane and broad vision that the late nineteenth-century and early twentieth-century inventors of those movements displayed at their best. It would be well for us to recover and practice them at our best, too.

3

Melting Pots

"What Then Is the American, This New Man?"

When Joyce's Leopold Bloom insists that his country is Ireland ("I was born here"), he overtly pledges his nationalism but covertly implies the other side of the nationalist coin—assimilation. For if Bloom can claim an Irish identity, then it must mean that as the son of an immigrant he can assimilate to Irish society enough to join it. In truth Bloom is more Irish than Jewish, though like the Citizen not everyone in the novel sees him that way. And Bloom remains Irish with a difference, as so many recent arrivals do in their new countries, on whatever side of the Atlantic or Pacific they land. They adjust not by transforming themselves into some ideal but imaginary "pure" ethnic or racial identity, which we have seen does not exist anyway, but by nudging both themselves and their societies toward a new hybridity. That was certainly the understanding of Israel Zangwill, the English Jew whose 1908 play *The Melting Pot* popularized a key term in ethnic discourse ever since. Besides making the point clear in the play itself, he spelled out the notion of mutual interaction—of change on both sides—in his 1914 afterword: "The process of American amalgamation is not assimilation or simple surrender to the dominant type, as is popularly supposed, but an all-round give-and-take by which the final type may be enriched or impoverished."[1] Zangwill signaled the stress of such eventual mutual accommodation through his fondness for words like *seething, boiling,* and *crucible* (he originally titled his play *The Crucible*) and insistence that it would take place in the future rather than the present. Wrongly attacked in his own day from the racist right for advocating "mongrelization" of the races and by the progressive left for substituting homogeneity for pluralism, Zangwill stoutly held to his understanding of the melting pot as an ongoing *process* rather than product. In that way, too, he, like Bloom, could reconcile nationalism with acculturation.

So, too, could a poet from whom Zangwill quoted in that same afterword, the Jewish American Emma Lazarus, with her keen double vision of the fate of modern Jews. She could sing as profoundly of immigration and assimilation as she does of expulsion and exile. That happens, for example, in the poem she chose as opening lyric for *Songs of a Semite* (1882), "The New Year: Rosh-Hashanah, 5643." The title and subtitle themselves gesture toward the predicament of the immigrant torn between two cultures, with the former in English ("The New Year") but the latter ("Rosh-Hashanah") a transliteration from the Hebrew into English. By giving the date 5643 according to Jewish reckoning rather than the corresponding 1882 c.e. of the Christian or Common Era, Lazarus again invokes a clash of cultures. The poem itself offers alternate solutions to exile, whether toward a Jewish state in then Turkish Palestine or toward a pluralistic one in the United States:

> In two divided streams the exiles part,
>   One rolling homeward to its ancient source,
> One rushing sunward with fresh will, new heart.
>   By each the truth is spread, the law unfurled . . . [2]

Sympathetic though she was to the stream of proto-Zionist efforts in Palestine ("One rolling homeward to its ancient source"), she focused more on the other current, the huge wave of Jewish immigration to America just getting under way in 1882 ("One rushing sunward with fresh will, new heart").

Lazarus treated those and other immigrants more directly in her famous sonnet "The New Colossus," subsequently inscribed on a plaque on the Statue of Liberty in New York harbor:

> Not like the brazen giant of Greek fame,
> With conquering limbs astride from land to land;
> Here at our sea-washed, sunset gates shall stand
> A mighty woman with a torch, whose flame
> Is the imprisoned lightning, and her name
> Mother of Exiles. From her beacon-hand

Glows world-wide welcome; her mild eyes command
The air-bridged harbor that twin cities frame.
"Keep, ancient lands, your storied pomp!" cries she
With silent lips. "Give me your tired, your poor,
Your huddled masses yearning to breathe free,
The wretched refuse of your teeming shore.
Send these, the homeless, tempest-tost to me,
I lift my lamp beside the golden door!"[3]

The sonnet deploys a traditional Petrarchan rhyme scheme *(abbaabba cdcdcd)* to subvert the usual contents both of that form and of the social formations that it had earlier supported, particularly those of gender and subject matter. For the Petrarchan sonnet was originally a form invented by men to idealize women, starting with Petrarch and his Laura, and presented the male poet as agent and speaker, with the female beloved as object of love and inspiration. In contrast, Lazarus (who herself once translated Petrarch) speaks here as a female rather than male poet, and her female figure of Liberty herself also speaks. Furthermore, she does so in a political rather than amorous realm, with her words pertaining directly to a major political event of the years starting with the Russian pogroms of 1881 and the May Laws of 1882, and not ending until the closing of mass immigration to the United States in the early 1920s—the wave of immigration from Eastern and Southern Europe, with Jews and Italians conspicuously joining earlier and ongoing large arrivals of Irish.

Lazarus wrote the poem as part of a fund-raising campaign for the massive pedestal of the Statue of Liberty, the French having contributed the statue itself. She read it aloud at the gala opening of the Art Loan Exhibition in Aid of the Bartholdi Pedestal Fund for the Statue of Liberty in 1883; the dedication itself took place in 1886, just after the wave of mass immigration started. Remarkably, the poem actually revised the statue's original meaning, shifting it from a French to an American context. Originally conceived by the group of moderate republican intellectuals centered around Edouard-René Lefebvre de Laboulaye, the statue first bore the title "Liberty Enlightening the World." Their intention was to erect a major statue in America that would reflect America's absorption of French ideals of liberty and facilitate the reinjection of those republican ideals into the France of the Second

Empire. That tactic formed part of their eventually successful campaign to establish the Third Republic, which lasted up until the Nazi conquest. The sculptor Frédéric Auguste Bartholdi himself conceptualized the statue in those terms, with Liberty intended to reflect back to the Old World the participation of the New in a worldwide political movement. In contrast, Lazarus's poem reinterpreted Liberty as a specifically American goddess (the "Mother of Exiles") welcoming refugees from the oppressive Old World to the emancipated new one, especially those from the bottom of the social order—"tired," "poor," "huddled masses." In that way Lazarus's inversion of historical politics matches her inversion of gender ones. As the poet James Russell Lowell enthusiastically wrote to her, "your sonnet gives its subject a [new] raison d'etre."[4]

Despite the fervor of Lowell and others, the poem sank into obscurity for fifteen years after that. It appeared in only one newspaper (the *New York World*) and not in any collection of Lazarus's poetry during the brief remainder of her life, though she did inscribe it first in her own notebook collection of her verse. The period of obscurity ended in 1903, when Lazarus's friend Georgina Schuyler succeeded in having the sonnet inscribed on a bronze tablet placed inside the pedestal of the statue. With its inscription on the tablet, the poem becomes not simply a sonnet about a monument but rather part of the monument itself. The block capitals used throughout the inscription heighten this monumental status, just as the devoted inscription evokes the maker of both the statue and the poem: "THIS TABLET, WITH HER SONNET TO THE BARTHOLDI STATUE OF LIBERTY ENGRAVED UPON IT, IS PLACED UPON THESE WALLS IN LOVING MEMORY OF EMMA LAZARUS BORN IN NEW YORK CITY JULY 22ND 1849 DIED NOVEMBER 19TH 1887." The tablet is physically affixed to the statue, just as the poem's revisionary meaning has been for generations of Americans.[5]

That meaning rests on a solid foundation. During the period of this study, the United States not only absorbed more immigrants than any other nation but it absorbed more than all of the other nations combined.[6] Immigration reached a peak in the decade surrounding *The Melting Pot* and reached an all-time high of 1,285,349 the year before the play opened in 1908. Further, immigration increased in every decade from 1820 through the outbreak of World War I. Prominent among these waves were Jews and Irish. The Irish were the largest group during the Famine years and their aftermath and still figured in the top half dozen in the decade leading up to the war. Jews (often called "Hebrews" in official documents) constituted the second largest group to Italians in absolute numbers and the largest as a proportion of their world-wide population. The Immigration Commission's own *Dictionary of Races and Peoples* estimated the number of Hebrew immigrants for the twelve years ending with 1910 as over a million and the Irish as half a million. The influx caused alarm, and a series of congressional acts used first crime, then literacy, and then mental health as restrictions before hitting on national origins in laws culminating in the Immigration Act of 1924. That finally slashed the high and rising numbers from Eastern and Southern Europe, though not those of the Great Migration of African Americans from the South to Northern cities that began around the beginning of the war and would eventually total over 4 million people.

While Zangwill's play popularized the term "melting pot," its term's evolution goes back at least to the French visitor and sometime settler J. Hector St. Jean de Crevecoeur, who spent almost three decades in North America as soldier, farmer, and eventually French consul. In a passage from Letter III of his celebrated *Letters from an American Farmer* (1782), Crevecoeur posed the question "What then is the American, this new man?" His answer, while restricted to European ancestry and omitting the word "pot," captured the spirit of Zangwill's later phrase in emphasizing "that strange mixture of blood, which you will find in no other country": "I could point out to you a family whose grandfather was an Englishman, whose wife was Dutch, whose son married a French woman, and whose present four sons have now four wives of different nations. *He* is an American, who, leaving behind him all his ancient prejudices and manners, receives new ones from the new mode of life he has embraced."[7] The mixture of nationalities anticipates that of Zangwill's play, while Crevecoeur's insistence that "Here individuals of all nations are melted into a new race of men, whose labors and posterity will one day cause great changes in the world," prefigures both the central metaphor in *The Melting Pot* and its central theme of future effect.

Melting Pots and Crucibles: A New Hybridity

In the next century Ralph Waldo Emerson prominently picked up Crevecoeur's insight. Then as now, high levels of immigration prompted defensive reactions from those who felt threatened by the new arrivals. One such group alarmed particularly by high levels of Irish immigration in the 1840s and 1850s was the Native American Party, popularly called the Know-Nothings. Emerson in turn opposed them. An entry in his journal for 1845 began in a manner Leopold Bloom would have understood by invoking a wide love against a narrow nationalism. It ended by conjuring the image of a "smelting pot" that featured Irish and Africans among others:

> I hate the narrowness of the Native American Party. It is the dog in the manger. It is precisely opposite to all the dictates of love and magnanimity.... Man is the most composite of all creatures.... Well, as in the old burning of the Temple at Corinth, by the melting and intermixture of silver and gold and other metals a new compound more precious than any, called the Corinthian brass, was formed; so in this continent,—asylum of all nations,—the energy of Irish, Germans, Swedes, Poles, and Cossacks, and all the European tribes,—of the Africans, and of the Polynesians,—will construct a new race, a new religion, a new state, a new literature, which will be as vigorous as the new Europe which came out of the smelting-pot of the Dark Ages.[8]

Emerson's vision extends backward in time to classical antiquity just as it extends outward in space to Africa and Polynesia before imagining a future for nineteenth-century America. The ideas of mixture, of a new compound created from the old elements, and of a new culture able to rival old overseas ones reappear continually in this tradition. The historian Frederick Jackson Turner included them in his influential 1893 paper "The Significance of the Frontier in American History," which located the ongoing amalgamation not in the constricted cities of the East Coast but in the ever-moving western frontier. "The frontier promoted the formation of a composite nationality for the American people.... In the crucible of the frontier the immigrants were Americanized, liberated, and fused into a mixed race, English in neither nationality nor characteristics," he wrote. "The process has gone on from the early days to our own."[9] Going back to the Puritan colonial poet Edward Taylor, the image of America as crucible stretches forward to Zangwill's time and to ours. Zangwill even thought of using it as title for the play, which evolved from the manuscript "The Mills of God" to "The Crucible" of the typescript and finally to "The Melting Pot," entered by hand on the typed version submitted to the Lord Chamberlain's Office.

Melodramatic rather than naturalistic, the plot of *The Melting Pot* treats three generations of the Quixanos, an immigrant Jewish family from the Pale of Settlement in Russia. It includes the Yiddish-speaking grandmother Frau Quixano, the music teacher and musician Mendel, and the grandson and violinist David. David is a "pogrom orphan" whose parents and sister perished in the terrible Kishineff (or Kishinev) pogrom of 1903, widely reported in the international press. The Russian word "pogrom" itself means a violent mass attack; in modern times a widespread series of them, beginning in 1881 after the assassination of Czar Alexander II, triggered the mass Jewish immigration of the following decades. After an opening scene between the Irish housemaid Kathleen O'Reilly and elderly Frau Quixano that inaugurates a subplot running throughout the play, the main plot dramatizes David's growing love for the upper-class, Russian-Christian settlement house worker Vera. Vera's father, Baron Revendal, travelling with his new wife, belongs to the Russian nobility and turns out to have commanded the troops at the Kishineff massacre, so that his face has haunted David ever since. As the star-crossed lovers of this plot reminiscent of *Romeo and Juliet* move toward an eventually happy rather than tragic conclusion, David works on his American Symphony, which the rich and bigoted Europhile Quincy Davenport derides but his orchestra conductor, the German immigrant master musician Herr Pappelmeister, encourages. All comes together in the final act, set on a Sabbath that is also the Fourth of July, at which Pappelmeister's orchestra triumphantly performs David's symphony at the settlement house. The panorama described in the final stage direction highlights the Statue of Liberty, about which David talks in the play, and Zangwill quotes five lines from Lazarus's sonnet in the afterword.

Zangwill's staging of the crucible image grows more comprehensive as the play develops. At the beginning it pertains particularly to "all the races of Europe," a more ambitious fusion at the time than it sounds now, partly because the melting pot succeeded so well with what were then viewed as separate European stocks but now simply as "White." In its *Dictionary of Races and Peoples* of 1911, for example, the Immigration Bureau said that it "recognized 45 races or peoples among the immigrants coming to the United States, and of these 36 are indigenous to Europe."[10] In Act I, when David

claims inspiration for his American Symphony in "the seething of the Crucible," Vera responds: "The Crucible? I don't understand!" David launches
into an impassioned explanation:

> Not understand that America is God's Crucible, the great Melting-Pot
> where all the races of Europe are melting and re-forming! Here you
> stand, good folk, think I, when I see them at Ellis Island, here you stand
> in your fifty groups, with your fifty languages and histories, and your
> fifty blood hatreds and rivalries. But you won't be long like that, broth-
> ers, for these are the fires of God you've come to—these are the fires of
> God. A fig for your feuds and vendettas! Germans and Frenchmen,
> Irishmen and Englishmen, Jews and Russians—into the Crucible with
> you all! God is making the American. (p. 33)

Numbering Jews and Irish in the six groups that he cites from among the
fifty, David stresses their melting and re-forming to create a new whole in
which all are changed into brothers freed from their blood hatreds. Yet even
at his most rhapsodic he posits the result as a future change rather than a
present reality. "The real American has not yet arrived," he explains. "He is
only in the Crucible, I tell you—he will be the fusion of all races, perhaps the
coming superman" (p. 34).

The violence signaled by the word "seething" erupts in Act II when David
confronts the rich and bigoted Quincy Davenport, significantly the only
native-born American in the play. Denouncing Davenport's luxurious party
adorning the grounds of his estate for flaunting Venetian canals complete
with gondolas even as women and children starved to death in New York,
David erupts, "Not for you and such as you have I sat here writing and dream-
ing; not for you who are killing my America!" Further enraged by Quincy's
retort, "*Your* America, forsooth, you Jew-immigrant," David labels himself a
Jew who knows that "your Pilgrim Fathers came straight out of his Old Testament" and adds, "There shall come a fire round the Crucible that will melt
you and your breed like wax in a blowpipe" (pp. 86–88). The exchange dramatizes Zangwill's repeated insistence that the melting pot does not mean
that new immigrants lose their identity in existing structures but rather that
they modify and even replace those structures, with here Quincy's own Anglophile class being remade as much as any newer immigrant group. Zangwill

underlined that point in his afterword, stating again what the play had already made clear: "The process of American amalgamation is not assimilation or simple surrender to the dominant type, as is popularly supposed, but an all-round give-and-take by which the final type may be enriched" (p. 203).

By the end of Act IV, that amalgamation has expanded to include "all race-differences and vendettas" (p. 179) rather than just European ones. Reunited with Vera, David breaks into his great closing speech that includes Africans and Asians unmentioned in the earlier sketching of the crucible in Act I: "There she lies, the great Melting Pot—listen! Can't you hear the roaring and the bubbling? There gapes her mouth—the harbour where a thousand mammoth feeders come from the ends of the world to pour in their human freight. Ah, what a stirring and a seething! Celt and Latin, Slav and Teuton, Greek and Syrian,—black and yellow." At that point Vera interrupts to add the categories perhaps most relevant to their own romantic union, "Jew and Gentile" (p. 184). Vera's words echo the same New Testament passage from Galatians 3.28 that Bloom invokes in *Ulysses* for his own vision of harmony in the New Jerusalem: "There is neither Jew nor Greek, there is neither slave nor free person, there is not male and female." Zangwill includes all three categories of nation, slavery, and gender in his vision. The last words of the play iterate one more time that this will take place in the future, with David insisting "Here shall they all unite to build the Republic of Man and the Kingdom of God" and invoking not the God of our fathers but "the God of our *children*."

The growing love between Vera, the daughter of the monster who executed the Kishineff massacre, and David, the only survivor of it from his immediate family, offers a paradigm for the action of the melting pot. Act by act they progressively exemplify Zangwill's belief expressed in the afterword "that in the crucible of love, or even co-citizenship, the most violent antitheses of the past may be fused into a higher unity" (p. 203). Vera begins by confronting her own anti-Semitism. Visiting the Quixano household to see whether David will play the violin at the settlement house, she recoils in outrage when Kathleen calls her a Jewess—"I, a Jewess! How dare you?"— and when Mendel enters, the stage direction shows her "struggling with her anti-Jewish prejudice" (pp. 11, 14). Yet later in the same scene she remembers that the biblical namesake of David created and sung psalms. In Act II she defends David against Davenport's indignation by saying, "I was thinking only of his genius, not his race," and in the act's closing love scene exclaims "Oh, David. And to think that I was brought up to despise your race" (pp. 72, 92). By the third act she proclaims her intention to marry David to her father the baron, who retorts, "I—love—a Jew? Impossible." But what is impossible for the parents is open to the children, and toward the close of the scene Vera invokes biblical precedent in telling David, "I say in the words of Ruth, thy people shall be my people and thy God my God!" (pp. 125, 154). After their estrangement and reconciliation in the final act, Vera adds "Jew and Gentile" to David's list of groups stirring and seething in the melting pot. Similarly, David must overcome both his abhorrence at the Kishineff pogrom and his exclusive devotion to his art in order for his love for Vera to reciprocate hers for him. Their relationship adapts but transforms into fictional narrative Zangwill's own experience of loving and marrying in 1903 a Christian woman, the English writer and feminist Edith Ayrton, with whom he would have three children. Such interfaith or mixed marriages then seemed as much interracial as interreligious, as the terms "race" and "racial" in the play make clear.

Other characters in *The Melting Pot* mirror in the subplots Vera and David's changes in the main one. The play opens with a short monologue of the elderly music teacher Mendel, whose pupil Johnny has left without taking his practice music with him. Mendel's display of affectionate yet prejudiced abuse ("Brainless, earless, thumb-fingered Gentile!") prepares us for the varied stream of more serious bigotry later in the play, including Mendel's own. Initially opposed to David's attraction to Vera, Mendel later asks "what true understanding can there be between a Russian Jew and a Russian Christian?" yet also admits, "I never thought a Russian Christian could be so human" (pp. 40–41). By the end of the play, he admits to the stricken David, "I'd rather see you marry her than go about like this" (p. 165). Even the genial German musician Pappelmeister has put his scruples aside to conduct Davenport's orchestra, but as the play progresses his admiration for David leads him to reveal his true feelings, start his own orchestra, and perform David's symphony at the settlement house. Only Quincy Davenport, the only native-born American in the play, and the snobbish Baroness Revendal remain mired in their prejudices, with even the abhorrent baron melodramatically offering his pistol to David and asking to be shot.

The subplot most pertinent to *The Colors of Zion* stages the growing understanding between the two major groups represented by the Irish maid

Kathleen and the Jewish grandmother Frau Quixano. With relations often tense between Jewish immigrants and the slightly earlier but overlapping Irish ones, the overcoming of such conflicts appeared in a host of popular dramas, like the long-running *Abie's Irish Rose,* and songs such as "If It Wasn't for the Irish and the Jews." In the play we first see the two women bickering over Frau Quixano's demands to observe kosher rules for cooking and crockery. "And who *can* work wid an ould woman nagglin' and grizzlin' and faultin' me?" asks Kathleen in stage Irish. "Mate-plates, butther-plates, *kosher, trepha,* sure I've smashed up folks' crockery and they makin' less fuss ouver it" (p. 5). By the last act Kathleen will fault others for not keeping Jewish rules, but here her exasperation boils over. Yet she becomes more than a stage Irish stereotype. Kathleen perceptively notes the three levels of Jewish observance in the house—represented by Frau Quixano, Mendel, and David—and she resists the simianization of the Irish at the time in exclaiming "I'm not a monkey," even if she does follow it up with a stage Irish question about her Orthodox antagonist, "Why doesn't she talk English like a Christian?" (p. 7). Yet already by the second act Kathleen joins boisterously in the Purim celebration and chides Mendel for forgetting it, even as she refers to "our" Passover (pp. 58–59). By the end of the act she even responds to Quincy's question about why they wear false noses as Purim costumes, "Bekaz we're Hebrews!" (p. 72). By the last act she loyally trudges up flights of stairs with Frau Quixano rather than ride an elevator on the Sabbath. When Frau Quixano wanders off, Kathleen's last lines of the play mix Irish and Jewish elements in her own linguistic melting pot: "*Wu geht Ihr,* bedad?"; "Houly Moses, *komm' zurick!*"; and finally, "Begorra, we Jews never know our way" (p. 170). Elsewhere in the play, influences from multiple languages jostle together, as they did in the larger society then and do now as well. The melting pot functions on a linguistic level, too. As Zangwill noted in his afterword, "this play alone presents scraps in German, French, Russian, Yiddish, Irish, Hebrew, and Italian" (p. 203).

However much the play focuses on the melting of what were then viewed as European races and peoples, it does include in its vision of amalgamation both Asians and Blacks, as the final image of the crucible made explicit. With their numbers limited by the Chinese Exclusion Act of 1882 and other measures, Asians remained far less numerous than African Americans, to whom Zangwill referred repeatedly in ways that often link them to other groups, especially Jews and Irish. Repulsed by the mixing in American public

transportation such as streetcars, the baron objects, "But surely no gentleman would sit in the public car, squeezed between working-men and shop-
girls, not to say Jews and Blacks" (p. 106). His anti-Semitism and anti-Black
racism reinforce each other. The baron thus segues from the pogrom massacres and lynching of Jews to those in America of Blacks, in the process
becoming the only character in the play to use the n-word. "Don't you lynch
and roast your niggers?" he inquires rhetorically (p. 111). The homegrown
bigot Davenport one-ups him with the response "Not officially." Zangwill
worried about American race relations at length in his afterword, particularly in the aftermath of slavery, which had been abolished only forty years
before his play. He named "negrophobia" as "that black problem, which is
America's nemesis for her ancient slave-raiding" (p. 204). Throughout he
argued against the racialist pseudoscience of his day even while occasionally
reflecting it and insisted that social prejudice divided Black and White at
least as much as racial antipathy. He thus maintained that "accusations
against the black are largely panic-born myths" and that "neither colour has
succeeded in monopolising all the virtues and graces in its specific evolution from the common ancestral ape" (pp. 205–206). For Zangwill the slan-
ders against African Americans mirrored those against Jews in marshalling
racial pseudoscience, animal imagery, and distortions of character to render
both groups inferior to mainstream society. Yet the majority groups cast up
numerous champions of the oppressed ones. Aware like many others of the
work of George Eliot and Harriet Beecher Stowe, Zangwill approvingly
quoted a distinguished Christian clergyman who called *The Melting Pot*
"calculated to do for the Jewish race what 'Uncle Tom's Cabin' did for the
coloured man" (p. 208).

Mainstream society differed about which group formed the biggest challenge to the melting pot, but Jews, Blacks, and Irish usually emerged as the
leading candidates. Zangwill himself nominated two candidates in his afterword to the play. "The Jewish immigrant is, moreover, the toughest of all
the white elements that have been poured into the American crucible," he
posited, partly because of its exposure to alien majorities for over 2,000
years. Yet he clearly saw the "barbarous pitch" (p. 204) of anti-Black feeling
as an even bigger obstacle, to which he carefully inserted the references that
we noted in the play. Others might nominate the Irish. Less than twenty
years before *The Melting Pot*, the influential New York humor magazine

Puck published a cartoon called "The Mortar of Assimilation—And the One Element That Won't Mix" (Figure 11). In it a figure representing America uses the spoon "Equal Rights" to stir a cup labeled "Citizenship" and filled with various ethnic types, including a Black toward the left and a Jew toward the right. The rebel is a simian Irishman wielding a knife in one hand and a green flag marked "Clan na Gael" in the other and sporting a sash that says "Blaine Irishman." Besides its reflection of anti-Irish stereotypes, the cartoon carries a particular political meaning. The inscription on the sash refers to Senator James G. Blaine, the Republican candidate for president in 1884 defeated by Grover Cleveland. Blaine himself, along with many others, attributed his defeat in part to his failure to repudiate characterization of Democrats with the slogan "Rum, Romanism, and Rebellion" (referring to liquor interests, Catholics, and Southern states) popularized by a Protestant clergyman supporting Blaine and sharing a platform with him. The cartoon appeared in full color and occupied the entire back page of *Puck*. The editorial page of the same issue featured an extended answer to the question "What is an American?" and impugned the Irish on charges of dual loyalty, a libel that would be directed at Jews and Blacks on other occasions. Ironically, the same page included a cartoon called "The Melonium Has Come" that made stereotyped fun of African Americans for fondness for watermelon and punned on the word "millennium." Though given to racial stereotyping of all kinds, including Blacks and Jews, *Puck* displayed particular rancor toward Irish people ranging from immigrants to politicians running Tammany Hall.

Though distinguishing among various groups, Zangwill became ever more keenly aware that the groups themselves were mixtures of other groups in an endlessly receding sequence. When he first met the most important Zionist theorist, Theodor Herzl, in 1895, Zangwill had disappointed Herzl by his then relatively narrow construction of Jewish identity. "His point of view is a racial one—which I cannot accept if I so as much look at him and at myself. . . . We are an historical unit, a nation with anthropological diversities. . . . No nation has uniformity of race," recorded Herzl in his diary. Two years later the diary celebrated "wonderful things" about Kurdish, Persian, Indian Jews, and even "Jewish Negroes who come from India. They are the descendants of slaves."[11] Zangwill increasingly adopted Herzl's position on diversity within each race, including the Jewish one. In his well-received

THE MORTAR OF ASSIMILATION — AND THE ONE ELEMENT THAT WON'T MIX.

Figure 11. "The Mortar of Assimilation," *Puck*, 26 June 1889. (Courtesy, University of Michigan Library.)

speech at the 1911 Race Congress in London, he surveyed the history and current condition of the Jews before noting their variety and kinship with other races:

> Not only is every race akin to every other, but every people is a hotch-potch of races. The Jews, though mainly a white people, are not even devoid of a coloured fringe, black, brown or yellow. There are the Beni-Israel of India, the Falashas of Abyssinia, the disappearing Chinese colony of Kai-Fung-Foo, the Judaeos of Loango, the black Jews of Cochin, the negro Jews of Fernando Po, Jamaica, Surinam, etc., the Daggatuns and other warlike nomads of the North African deserts. . . . If the Jews are in no metaphorical sense brothers of all these people, then all these peoples are brothers of one another. . . . [The Jew] is the pioneer by which the true race theory has been experimentally demonstrated . . . even the colour is not an unbridgeable and elemental distinction.[12]

Unlike many race theorists and group advocates of the time, then, Zangwill came to see the mixed nature of all groups as a sign of their common brotherhood. Hence he could glory in the colored members of a predominantly White race. He applied that sentiment to his own country as well as to Jews or to the United States. Citing the British explorer and colonial administrator Sir Harry Johnston, Zangwill observed in his afterword that "there is hardly an ethnic element that has not entered into the Englishman, including even the missing link," along with a Negroid type, Gaels, Aryans, Germans, Norse, and others (pp. 213–214). Like the Jews and all other peoples, the English were a mixed race.

The Melting Pot was a smash hit at its debut in Washington, D.C., on 5 October 1908, not least due to the presence of President Theodore Roosevelt and his wife, Secretary of State Elihu Root, and other luminaries. Roosevelt's response was immediate, positive, and public. Mrs. Zangwill rejoiced in a letter to a friend that "there were cries for Zangwill after every act. The President was most enthusiastic. When Israel appeared before the curtain at the end, the President shouted across the theatre: 'That's a great play Mr. Zangwill.'"[13] Endorsement by the president of the United States helped make the drama famous. Roosevelt remained firm in his support. When

Zangwill wrote for permission to dedicate the book version to him, the president agreed and added that "I do not know when I have seen a play that stirred me as much."[14] Roosevelt even persuaded Zangwill to revise a line in the play legitimizing divorce so that it applied not to all Americans but only to "unemployed millionaires like Mr. Davenport" (p. 124). Three years later the work still echoed in Roosevelt's head. "That particular play I shall always count among the very strong and real influences upon my thought and my life," he wrote in an unpublished letter. "It has been in my mind continually, and on my lips very often, during the last three years." The admiration was mutual, with Zangwill repeatedly praising Roosevelt's openness to ethnic groups in general and to Jews in particular. No wonder that he inscribed the dedication to the play to Roosevelt "in respectful recognition of his strenuous struggle against the forces that threaten to shipwreck the great republic" (p. v). The publisher, Macmillan, reprinted the book yearly until the United States entered World War I in 1917.

The Melting Pot Debates

The play provoked widespread public reaction, with productions all across the country and longer runs in Chicago, New York, and eventually London. Its posing of hot-button issues ranging from Russian massacres to assimilation and racial mixing led to a wide spectrum of responses. Chicago reviewers and audiences generally loved *The Melting Pot,* which came with glowing testimonials by such leaders as the social work pioneer Jane Addams and the famous trial lawyer Clarence Darrow. Burns Mantle of the *Chicago Daily Tribune,* for example, praised the play as "something of a master work," while *Unity* called it "a mighty prophecy." One of the few detractors, Amy Leslie, writing in the *Chicago Daily News,* noted the juxtaposition of Irish and Jewish characters in the opening scene but invoked all three of our groups in objecting to the overall theme: "Jews do not want to be melted up, however, and Americans are not anxious to be melted up with them or the Irish or the Dutch or the Hottentots."[15] New York newspapers took a more mixed view of the controversial work and sometimes vied with each other in invective about both theme and technique. The *Times,* for example, blasted the play in a review headlined "New Zangwill Play Cheap and Tawdry"; the *Evening Sun* called it "an awful Zangwill stew" that "isn't a play at all"; and the *New*

York Press pronounced it "not a drama but a lecture in four acts." When the play reached London in 1914, most reviewers liked it better than that. True, English reviewers of the play and book, like conservative G. K. Chesterton and his younger brother Cecil, evinced an ugly anti-Semitism in their remarks. Influential *Times* reviewer A. B. Walkley's attack on the drama as "romantic claptrap" involving "rhapsodising over music and crucibles and statues of Liberty" inspired a response from Zangwill himself in his afterword (p. 199). But the *English Review* approved *The Melting Pot* as showing "a rare honesty," and the *Athenaeum* accurately stressed the future orientation of the "racial" play and welcomed it to the London stage. There as in America, though, Jewish journals showed some ambivalence, on the one hand reveling in Zangwill's huge public success but on the other worrying about whether his view of assimilation posed a threat to Jewish survival.[16]

With more time to reflect than reviewers, prominent intellectual voices both progressive and reactionary produced critiques that sometimes missed Zangwill's insistence on mutual modification and realization only in the future. Philosopher Horace Kallen, a German-born Jew who took a PhD from Harvard and became lifelong friends with the Black philosopher Alain Locke whom he met there, did that in his two-part essay "Democracy versus the Melting-Pot" in the *Nation* in 1915, in a long quarrel with Edward Alsworth Ross's nativist book *The Old World and the New*. A founding Pluralist, Kallen traced the separate arrival of immigrants from various groups, including Irish and Jews along with "nine million negroes" mostly in the South. He rejected the notion of unison or one-way assimilation in favor of a symphony with separate instruments playing in harmony, an early image that would later lead to talk of salad bowls and the like. He did not notice that the symphony was the other major image to the crucible in Zangwill's play, which of course featured David Quixano's American Symphony. Kallen closed with his own musical image: "As in an orchestra, every type of instrument has its specific timbre and tonality . . . so in society each ethnic group is the natural instrument." Kallen's essay influenced another prominent progressive, the New Jersey-born WASP and public intellectual Randolph Bourne, who in his celebrated essay "Trans-National America" proclaimed "the failure of the 'melting-pot.'" Bourne equated "Americanizing" with "Anglo-Saxonizing," which Zangwill had resisted, and argued for America as a "federation" of national groups that would lead to cosmopolitanism and multiple allegiances. "It is apparently our lot rather to be a federation of cultures," he concluded, and in that way America would become not a nationality but a transnationality. Bourne expanded his point with particular references to Jews (though again he also mentioned Irish in his lesser-known essay "The Jew and Trans-National America" later that same year). There again he misunderstood Zangwill as arguing for a melting pot that would assimilate all Europeans into the prevailing Anglo-Saxon type and argued again for a "co-operation of cultures" instead. He acknowledged the impact of Kallen's *Nation* article on him and in passages that would have warmed the cockles of Leopold Bloom's heart argued that the same person could be a Jew, an American, and a Zionist sympathizer.[17]

Conservatives proved as adept at misconstruing Zangwill as progressives did. One of the most colorful, the industrialist Henry Ford, regarded himself as "more a manufacturer of men than of automobiles."[18] He instructed the sociological department at his sprawling Detroit factory to set up a Ford English School in 1914, which graduated 16,000 workers before disbanding in 1921. Ford blatantly aimed to assimilate the workers to what cultural historian Lawrence W. Levine calls "Anglo-conformity." A contemporary spokesman for Ford Motor explained, "We prefer that classes be mixed as to race and country, for our one great aim is to impress these men that they are, or should be, Americans, and that former racial, national, and linguistic differences are to be forgotten." The school held a unique graduation ceremony featuring a huge melting pot, presided over by the teachers and by the school's principal, Clinton C. DeWitt, dressed up as Uncle Sam. Clad in their native garb, the immigrant workers climbed a ladder at one side of the large pot and descended into it. They then emerged one at a time on the other side dressed in derby hats with coats, pants, vests, and ties, replete with a tiny American flag in one hand and a Ford Motor Company badge on their lapels. Far from Zangwill's ideal of an all-around give and take, the Ford workers learned to cast off all traces of their native culture to assimilate to already existing Anglo-American norms.

Fear that the immigrants would fail to assimilate fully drove the other side of conservative reaction, exemplified by sociology professor Henry Pratt Fairchild, who also served as president of the American Eugenics Society. Like Kallen and Bourne, Fairchild noted the lack of full American unity during World War I, especially on the part of German Americans and others. Also like Kallen and Bourne, he detected a plurality of groups rather than a unity. But unlike them, he drew opposite conclusions—to defend the Anglo-centric character of the United States, to promote racial improvement through eugenics, and above all to choke off the flow of immigrants from Southern and Eastern Europe as well as from Asia. Hence he supported the Chinese Exclusion Act along with the "Gentleman's Agreement" that restricted Japanese immigration, and he lobbied hard for the series of acts that by 1924 finally cut off the bulk of European immigrants that he deemed undesirable. He combated "this stupendous injection of foreign elements" explicitly in his 1926 book, *The Melting-Pot Mistake.*[19] Tracing the crucible image condescendingly to "Israel Zangwill's little drama," he saw its historical importance as "staving off the restriction of immigration" for as long as it did (pp. 9, 11). But he maintained that "the Melting-Pot did not melt" and that "with its great immigration movement the United States tried to do something and failed" (p. 12). Fairchild saw that failure as rooted in a refusal to appreciate accurately the roles of race and nationality in establishing group unity, with the primary basis as racial, as Lothrop Stoddard and others had argued. Beginning in 1882, a new and diverse immigration replaced the earlier and heavily British waves to create what Fairchild saw as "increasingly a racial problem" and inevitably "the additional problem of race mixture," which he termed "mongrelization" (pp. 112, 125). In terms of Zangwill's play, Fairchild spoke for the Quincy Davenports of the world in rejecting mass immigration and characterizing it as corrupting America. "Unrestricted immigration . . . was slowly, insidiously, irresistibly eating away the very heart of the United States," he intoned at the end. "What was being melted in the great Melting Pot, losing all form and symmetry, all beauty and character, all nobility and usefulness, was the American nationality itself" (p. 261). Those forces of reaction finally triumphed in the immigration quota acts, with tragic consequences for the 1930s and the Holocaust, before being swept away by the wave of reaction against racialist thinking after World War II.

European and American Pogroms

One thing that both sides of the melting pot debates often lost sight of was the formative role of foreign oppression in stimulating immigration in the first place, and especially of the Russian pogroms like that at Kishineff. A prominent Irish exception was the nationalist leader Michael Davitt (1846–1906), who successively belonged to the Irish Republican Army, served a prison term, cofounded the Land League, and served both as member of Parliament and as political journalist before dying less than two years before the premiere of *The Melting Pot*. At the beginning of Joyce's *Portrait of the Artist as a Young Man*, Dante (Mrs. Riordan) has two brushes, one for Davitt and the other for Parnell (whom she later condemns at the time of the Parnellite split). In 1903 the Hearst newspapers commissioned Davitt to travel to Russia to report on the Kishineff pogrom of April for the *New York American* and *Evening Journal*, whose wide circulation included many Russian Jewish immigrants. Davitt collected his published articles and other material into his book *Within the Pale: The True Story of Anti-Semitic Persecutions in Russia*, published at the end of that same year. The murder of a Christian boy in a nearby town shortly before Easter and Passover led to invocation of the centuries-old blood libel that Jews required the blood of Christian children to make ceremonial matzohs (later investigation identified the true murderer as one of the boy's own relatives). Kishineff itself was at the time the capital of Bessarabia and according to Davitt included 50,000 Moldavians, 50,000 Jews, 8,000 Russians, and a miscellany of smaller populations. Unrestrained and sometimes even aided by police and troops, mobs rampaged through the Jewish quarter on April 6–7, killing 49 Jews, severely wounding 92, and injuring another 500 while looting and burning over 700 houses.

Travelling to Kishineff itself as an investigative reporter, Davitt staunchly defended the Jews against the perpetrators of the pogrom. The parallels to another religiously oppressed people, the Irish of the nineteenth century, impressed Davitt, and he even quoted New York Cardinal Manning's phrase about the "penal laws" that afflicted the Jews of Russia as they had the Catholics of Ireland. An ardent Irish nationalist, Davitt sympathized with Jewish nationalism, too. He began his preface by announcing "the twofold aim of this book,—to arouse public feeling against a murder-making legend, and to put forward a plea for the objects of the Zionist movement,—and to tell the story of the Russian Jew, apropos of recent massacres."[20] For Davitt the blood libel was "an atrocious fabrication" leading to the "cowardly racial warfare" of anti-Semitism. In tones as applicable to the very first blood libel in 1144, which led later to the murder of nearly all the Jews of Norwich, as to propaganda in the Middle East and elsewhere today, he stated bluntly that "the peculiar atrocity of most of the crimes perpetrated against the Jews of the city at Easter were directly attributable to the horrible influence of the ritual-murder propaganda upon untutored minds possessed of an ignorant and fanatical conception of religion" (p. x). He also came away "a convinced believer in the remedy of Zionism," which he saw as "a noble racial effort" (pp. 86, 244). Davitt returned from Kishineff, revised his articles into a book, and even organized a fund for surviving victims of the pogrom. His courage in revealing the truth about what had happened and his material efforts to support the survivors won him widespread praise from the Jewish community, which to commemorate his death held a rally in New York large enough to be reported in the *New York Times.*[21]

Davitt did not have to travel to Russia to discover anti-Semitism. Though over the centuries Ireland showed itself more tolerant of Jews than most European countries, the trickle of the vast tide of immigration from Russia that found its way to Irish shores led to increasing tension culminating in the worst outbreak in modern Irish history, the Limerick "pogrom" of 1904. The Jewish population remained small: the decennial census shows that the Jewish population of Ireland numbered only 285 in 1871, rose to 1,111 by 1891, and to 5,148 in 1911.[22] But even that was enough to cause trouble, with nationalists like Arthur Griffith and Redemptorist priests like Father John Creagh stirring anti-Jewish feeling for their own ends. In contrast, Davitt stoutly defended the tiny Jewish minority. For instance, in 1893 he vigorously opposed a call at a Labour Federation meeting that "the Jews ought to be kept out of Ireland." "The Jews have never to my knowledge done any injury to Ireland," he wrote in a letter to the same *Freeman's Journal* for which the fictional Leopold Bloom sold advertising. "Like our own race, they have endured a persecution the record of which will forever remain a reproach to the 'Christian' nations of Europe."[23] When Father Creagh's fiery sermons in Limerick led first to violence in 1904 and then to a two-year boycott of Jewish merchants, Davitt—with memories of the Russian pogroms fresh in his mind—spoke up again. The level of violence was lower in Limerick, of course, but Creagh had rung the familiar tones of classic anti-Semitism in branding Jews as leeches, economic bloodsuckers, killers of Christ, and by insinuation ritual murderers. Davitt protested as both Irishman and

Catholic against "the spirit of barbarous malignity being introduced into Ireland." So, too, did the leader of the Irish Parliamentary Party, John Redmond, who declared, "I have no sympathy whatever with the attacks upon the Hebrew Community in Limerick or elsewhere." Unlike in Russia, no major politician in Ireland endorsed Creagh's anti-Semitic rants and the level of violence remained much lower, though Limerick Jews themselves thought of it as a pogrom and the community declined in size.

Davitt's articles and book resonated particularly with American condemners of the pogroms, who linked the mob violence and legal discrimination against Jews in Russia to that against African Americans in the United States. Zangwill himself helped lead the way, labeling the 1906 race riots in Atlanta as a "Black pogrom" and worrying about "trusting the Russian Jew among the Southern savages."[24] He found a famous ally in the same president of the United States, Theodore Roosevelt, to whom he would dedicate *The Melting Pot*. In a letter quoted by Davitt among the testimonial appendices to *Within the Pale*, Roosevelt hoped that the Russian government "takes the same view of those outrages that our own government takes of the riots and lynchings which sometimes occur in our country" and endorsed "the historic American position of treating each man on his merits as a man, without the least reference to his creed, his race, or his birthplace" (pp. 266–267). Jewish writers expressed similar views, both in English and in Yiddish. Reacting to the East St. Louis race riot of 1917 that killed at least forty African Americans, the *American Israelite* editorialized that "Apparently the civilized world cannot do without pogroms . . . our own country has demonstrated its ability to substitute Russia as it was under the . . . Czar and his bureaucracy, by the pogrom which took place in East St. Louis last week."[25] The Yiddish press spoke up even more militantly and frequently. The largest circulating Yiddish paper, the *Forward* of New York, bluntly announced, "Kishinev and St. Louis—the same soil, the same people. . . . The same brutality, the same wildness, the same human beasts." A year earlier the *Forward* pointed out that "the situation of the Negroes in America is very comparable to the situation of the Jews . . . in Russia. The Negro diaspora, the special laws, the decrees, the pogroms, and also the Negro complaints, the Negro hopes are very similar to those which we Jews . . . lived through." The same paper had condemned in 1900 what it termed "bloody pogroms against the negroes" and three years later painted the Evansville, Indiana, riots as "negro pogroms." Similar perceptions led the *Yidisher Kurier* in Chicago to conclude in 1912 that "the Jew is treated as a Negro and the Negro as a Jew."

Perhaps surprising to our ears now, the African-American press and leaders reciprocated the identification. W. E. B. Du Bois and Booker T. Washington argued over many things, but they agreed about the parallels between the treatment of Jews in Eastern Europe and Blacks in the American South. In the September 1917 issue of *The Crisis,* which featured Du Bois's blistering exposé of the East St. Louis riot, he branded it a "pogrom" in his introductory editorial. Correspondingly, in his 1912 memoir of a trip through Europe, *The Man Farthest Down,* Washington catalogued the Jim Crow–like restrictions against Jews in the Pale of Settlement. For Russian Jews as for Southern Blacks he saw education as the key: the story of the Jews showed "what education can do and has done for a people who, in the face of prejudice and persecution, have patiently struggled up to a position of power and preeminence in the life and civilization in which all races are now beginning to share."[26] In founding the Tuskegee Institute, he hoped to contribute to a similar uplift through education for African Americans, starting especially with manual arts. The Black press at the time took a regular interest in the treatment of Russian Jews and its parallel with that of Blacks. The *Cleveland Gazette* opined that Russian Jews were "treated worse than our people in the South have ever been," and the same paper joined others to encourage rallies against the treatment of both Russian Jews and Southern Blacks, arguing that this "can do no harm and might do both the Jews in Russia and the southern Afro-American 'a world of good.' By all means let us encourage both protests." African-American papers like the Baltimore *Afro-American* leapt to defend Jews against the charge of blood libel that had helped spark the Kishinev and other pogroms, as did the Washington, D.C., *Colored American.* "The persecution of the Jews, the prejudice directed against them, are sad commentaries on Christianity . . . by representatives of Christianity," declared the Baltimore paper. Faced with the parallels and shared knowledge of suffering, the Black press recognized a deep source of amity even while at other times it criticized Jews along with others. "Surely there must be a strain of sympathy in the heart of every Negro for the Jewish people," declared the St. Louis *Argus.* James Weldon Johnson spoke for many when he explained why to readers of the New York *Age:* "It is the American Negro

who can best appreciate the reason for the joy [of American Jews] because
we are the only other people who have a deep understanding of what the
Jews in Russia have suffered."[27]

James Weldon Johnson and the Color Line

Johnson himself published in 1912 the first African-American novel to be
masked and marketed as an autobiography, just three years after *The Melting Pot*. His *Autobiography of an Ex-Colored Man* tells the story of a light-
skinned African American who crosses back and forth over the color line.
Growing up in Connecticut, he thinks he is White until a schoolteacher asks
the White students to stand and, when he rises, instructs him to wait for the
colored group. Musically gifted, he moves south to study at Atlanta University, but when a newfound Black friend steals his money he continues south-
ward to Jacksonville, Florida (Johnson's own home town), and works at a
cigar factory. Moving again, this time to New York City, he gambles and
plays ragtime piano in a colored club until a rich White gentleman (who is
never named) discovers him and asks him to play for his friends. Eventually
the anonymous millionaire takes him to Europe, where he attends cultural
events and plays ragtime for Europeans. Upon returning home to create a
blend of rag and classical music for the benefit of his race, he witnesses a
lynching that frightens and shames him into crossing the color line one more
time, ending up back in New York as a rich real-estate developer whom
people see as White. Besides presenting the title character, the novel fulfills
Johnson's aim in the preface to create "a composite and proportionate presentation of the entire race." In the course of doing so he deconstructs the
stereotyped view of Blacks as all alike into three different classes, each with
a complement of colorful characters.

The very title of Johnson's novel calls the stability of racial categories into
question. If one can become an "ex-colored" man, then racial terms like
"colored" lose their inevitability in categorizing and separating people and
peoples. We see that in concrete terms as the same title character passes
back and forth over the color line, sometimes taken for and taking himself
as White, sometimes as African American. In that way, the novel joins a
host of others by Blacks and Whites reflecting anxiety and doubt over the
color line, including William Wells Brown's *Clotel, or the President's Daugh-*

ter (1853), Mark Twain's *Pudd'nhead Wilson* (1894), Charles W. Chesnutt's *The House behind the Cedars* (1900), Nella Larsen's *Passing* (1929), and George S. Schuyler's satiric *Black No More* (1931). The destabilizing notion of passing can lead to identifications with other groups. Johnson does not invoke the Irish here, though in his groundbreaking anthology *The Book of American Negro Poetry* he did proclaim that "What the colored poet in the United States needs to do is something like what Synge did for the Irish; he needs to find a form that will express the racial spirit."[28] But the *Autobiography of an Ex-Colored Man* does persistently provide Jewish analogies. As a boy the hero reads feverishly and excitedly of "the trials and tribulations of the Hebrew children"; on the way back from Europe he converses with the Negro physician about "the race problem, not only of the United States, but as it affected native Africans and Jews"; when passing as White in the Southern smoking car he notes with admiration "the diplomacy of the Jew" in walking a middle course; and he marvels how "Go Down, Moses" "stirs the heart like a trumpet call" (pp. 16, 111, 116, 131). The identifications reflect a cultural ability to cross lines between groups that mirrors his physical ability to do so racially.

The ex-colored man increasingly aims to move toward a cultural and racial melting pot through music, particularly a fusion of classical music with ragtime. While still in Jacksonville he ranks ragtime among the four great African-American achievements in the arts, along with the Uncle Remus stories, the Fisk Jubilee songs, and the cakewalk. By the time he lives in New York, he recognizes that ragtime, while created largely by Blacks, "possesses at least one strong element of greatness: it appeals universally; not only the American, but the English, the French, and even the German people find delight in it" (p. 73). With that recognition, he goes on to become a great player of ragtime, not so much as separate African-American music but as culturally able to cross boundaries and mix with other traditions. "It was I who first made ragtime transcriptions of familiar classic selections," he boasts. "I used to play Mendelssohn's 'Wedding March'" (p. 84). Significantly, the club in which he plays that hybrid form attracts both White and Black admirers. The next stage of evolution toward musical mixing or melting comes when he leaves New York for an extended stay in Europe with his millionaire patron, who gives a party in Berlin for musicians, writers, and artists. Asked to play the "new American music," the hero is astonished when a bush-headed German rushes over and takes a ragtime theme through various musical forms. "I sat amazed. I had been turning classic music into ragtime, a comparatively easy task; and this man had taken ragtime and made it classic," he thinks. "The thought came across me like a flash—It can be done, why can't I do it? From that moment my mind was made up. I clearly saw the way of carrying out the ambition I had formed when a boy" (pp. 103–104). The fusion of American Negro ragtime with European classical music would create a musical melting pot that redounds to the credit of the narrator's race. Returning to the United States with that intent, he witnesses a lynching and narrowly escapes the mob himself, an experience that causes him to pass for White for the remainder of the novel. Yet the abdication of his dream for worldly success does not bring him happiness. In the last sentence of the novel, he invokes a biblical Jewish analogy one more time in reflecting, "I cannot repress the thought that, after all, I have chosen the lesser part, that I have sold my birthright for a mess of pottage" (p. 154). It is important to recognize that the birthright he sells contains not simply racial identification but also his hybrid dream of joining ragtime to classical music. Like that other dreamer of musical hybridity, David Quixano in *The Melting Pot*, the narrator yearns to create an American music, but unlike David he forsakes that ideal for worldly success.

That was not true of James Weldon Johnson himself, who in the course of a varied career gained admittance to the Florida bar; wrote over 200 popular songs with his brother, John Rosamond Johnson; served as a U.S. consul, first in Venezuela and then in Nicaragua during the administration of Theodore Roosevelt (for whom he had campaigned); wrote and edited distinguished volumes of prose and poetry; became the first African-American general secretary of the NAACP; acted as a prime force in the Harlem Renaissance; and ended up a professor of creative literature and writing at Fisk University. Like Israel Zangwill, he saw no contradiction between activities on behalf of his race and those on behalf of mankind. For example, he and his brother made his 1900 poem "Lift Every Voice and Sing," originally written to commemorate Abraham Lincoln, into a song that the NAACP later nominated as the "Negro National Anthem." During the same period, in 1902 he with his brother and their frequent collaborator Bob Cole wrote the hit song "Under the Bamboo Tree," which sold the then immense total of over 400,000 copies and helped make the Irish-themed Broadway musical

Sally in Our Alley a success. The story of a royal maid of a "dusky shade" who meets "a Zulu from Matabooloo," Johnson's lyric included the lines "One live as two, two live as one / Under the bamboo tree."[29] In a manner that would have delighted the ex-colored man, those lines and others resurface in T. S. Eliot's high cultural "Fragment of an Agon" nearly three decades later. There Eliot reworks the poem into a minstrel-like rendition complete with the Tambo and Bones of the old (and often demeaning) minstrel shows; revealingly, Eliot assigns the Tambo role to the Jewish-sounding "Swarts." Like the mixture of ragtime and classical music in *Autobiography of an Ex-Colored Man*, the mixture of popular and high culture in Eliot's poem represents in cultural terms the mixing that the melting pot advocated in racial and religious ones. The next chapter investigates those popular cultures and the institutions that made them possible. In his own autobiography, *Along This Way*, Johnson speculated on "the blending of the Negro into the American race of the future." While in some ways attracted to a separatist vision, he doubted its feasibility. "It seems probable that, instead of developing them independently to the utmost, the Negro will fuse his qualities with those of the other groups in the making of the ultimate American people, and that he will add a tint to America's complexion and put a perceptible permanent wave in America's hair" (*Writings*, p. 596).

4

Popular and Institutional Cultures

The Fluidity of Cultures

Melting pots bubble especially visibly in the realm of popular cultures and the institutional frameworks that support them and other social formations. That was as true 100 years ago as it is today in the age of Barack Obama, with its high-profile multiethnic figures like the singer Mariah Carey, the golfer Tiger Woods, and the television anchor Soledad O'Brien. Contemporary African-American theorist Cornel West hears mixture even in the realm of jazz. Arguing that "from the very beginning we must call into question any notions of pure traditions or pristine heritages," West instead labels them "hybrid," as indeed they are. "By hybrid, of course, we mean cross-cultural fertilization," he writes. "Every culture that we know is a result of the weaving of antecedent cultures." The claim fits both the cultures themselves and their components. Taking a chief example from the United States, West, as we saw earlier, points out that "there is no jazz without European instruments."[1] West picks a deliberatively provocative example of a cultural form rightly identified with African Americans. Yet even there, not just in the physical instruments but in the music itself and the musicians that played it, other ethnicities and races contributed to an overall give and take that continues to this day not only in America but in international jazz around the world. Popular culture is incorrigibly hybrid. The first part of this chapter explores that hybridity first in jazz and then in the popular song of Tin Pan Alley, using Louis Armstrong and George Gershwin as primary examples in jazz and Tin Pan Alley composers like Irving Berlin in popular song. It then probes the phenomenally successful play *Abie's Irish Rose* and its imitators as chief examples for drama and film and concludes with a look at high cultural fascination with popular hybridity in the poetic rendering of our three groups by T. S. Eliot and Ezra Pound. The second part examines institutional cultures that support multicultural dissemination, especially book publishers, as transition to the schools and activist organizations treated in the next chapter.

Critics and artists both now and at the turn of the last century share West's point of view. Opposing the identity politics of the later twentieth century, the theorist Edward Said writes of transgressive elements in music and literature, instanced by composer Richard Wagner's attacks on Jewish influences and Aschenbach's resistance to Asiatic ones in novelist Thomas Mann's *Death in Venice.* He argues that "to focus more narrowly upon what is purely European, or German, or French, or Jewish, or Indian, Black, Muslim, etc., is then to accept the very principle of a separate essentialization— the separation of the Jewish essence from the German, or the black from the white, etc.—and along with that to purify the types and to turn them into universals . . . [by which a] dominant culture eliminated the impurities and hybrids that actually make up all cultures." For Said, such essentializing aligns politically with totalitarian and imperialist enterprise, whereas recognition of hybridity resists both. The historian Gary Gerstle in his recent *American Crucible: Race and Nation in the Twentieth Century* finds a concrete example of such crossing in swing musicians of the 1930s. They "fought to attain in their bands and in the broader society as well what they had achieved in their music—racial mixing, hybridity, and respect," writes Gerstle. "Benny Goodman began participating in interracial recording sessions in 1933 and formally integrated his band in 1936. Artie Shaw's orchestra toured with the black singer Billie Holliday [*sic*] for eight months in 1938, and Charlie Barnet's orchestra did the same with another black singer, Lena Horne, in 1941."[2]

Sentiments like those of West, Said, and Gerstle closely echo those of a central figure in the Harlem Renaissance, the philosopher and critic Alain Locke. In his 1930 essay "The Contribution of Race to Culture," Locke urged students to "do away with the idea of proprietorship and vested interest— and face the natural fact of the limitless interchangeableness of culture goods." He instead held cultures to be "composite." With one eye on the rise of Nazi and other European nationalisms he declared notions of cultural ownership "vicious in the face of the natural reciprocity and our own huge indebtedness."[3] Recognizing cultural hybridity would protect against national chauvinisms and a bimodal split between "us" and "them." Jazz musicians expressed themselves with less eloquent words (except to some songs) but with similar intent.

Jazz: The Negro Art?

Arguably the most important figure in the history of jazz, Louis Armstrong insisted many times on musical ability rather than race as the key factor in performance. "These people who make the restrictions, they don't know nothing about music. It's no crime for cats of any color to get together and blow," he once said in a characteristic remark. "Race-conscious jazz musicians? Nobody could be who really knew their horns and loved the music." The pianist Duke Ellington, whom some consider the greatest jazz composer, shared Armstrong's view and tied it more tightly to the melting pot. He told an interviewer at the end of World War II:

> Twenty years ago when jazz was finding an audience, it may have had more of a Negro character. The Negro element is still important. But jazz has become a part of America. There are as many white musicians playing as Negro. . . . We are all working along more or less the same lines. We learn from each other. Jazz is American now. *American* is the big word.[4]

Mindful of such contributors as Bix Beiderbecke, Jack Teagarden, Bennie Goodman, Artie Shaw, George Gershwin, and many others, Ellington embraced the hybrid "American" label rather than retreating to the alleged purity of a Negro art. Like Zangwill, he saw such mixing as an ongoing process, with jazz as a prime example of Zangwill's "all around give-and-take" just as more classical music had been in Zangwill's play itself, where David Quixano longs to write his American Symphony.

While present-day commentators speak of a Black-White dichotomy or mixing, depending on their perspective, those of an earlier time saw clearly which groups among those we now label "white" contributed most to the development of jazz. Foremost among them were Jews, as three of the five names (Goodman, Shaw, and Gershwin) in the list above suggest. Claiming that many Europeans could play or sing jazz tunes correctly but lacked the spirit behind them, the musician, writer, and political activist James Weldon Johnson exempted Americans, and one group among them in particular. "Among white Americans those who have mastered these rhythms most completely are Jewish-Americans," he wrote in the preface to his *Book of American Negro Spirituals* (1925). "Indeed, Jewish musicians and composers are they who have carried them to their highest development in written form."[5] Characteristically, Johnson did not see Jewish jazzmen as appropriating much less stealing Black music because like most of the leading African Americans of his time he, like Locke, thought that culture had no color and was hybrid to begin with, though he remained proud of Black contributions when he could find them, as in Negro spirituals themselves. As we have seen in his autobiography, *Along This Way*, Johnson sketched a dream in which if a genie told him he couldn't be Black, then he'd choose to be Jewish.

The greatest jazzman of them all, Louis Armstrong would have understood Johnson's choice. Satchmo wore a Star of David around his neck almost his entire life. The Jewish jazz photographer Herb Snitzer captured a memorable image of Armstrong sporting it during a road trip in the summer of 1960 as part of a spread for *Metronome* magazine (Figure 12). As Snitzer explained about the star later, "It was a gift from the Karnovsky family in New Orleans when Pops was just a child. They cared for him, fed and clothed him. He wore the Star his entire life. He was the least prejudiced musician I ever knew."[6] Snitzer took multiple versions of the photo: the one that *Metronome* put on its cover shows Armstrong introspectively gazing downward in a moment of private meditation, whereas the one from Snitzer's later book depicts him holding a cigarette and looking directly at the observer. Both show his white-striped shirt unbuttoned, with the star clearly visible hanging from the chain round his neck. Armstrong knew the photos would be published and reach a wide public, particularly in the jazz world to which *Metronome* belonged. Far from concealing his Jewish empathy, he displayed it proudly.

Armstrong's sympathies had always been wide and extended far beyond Blacks and Jews. In an interview with Richard Meryman for *Life* magazine in 1966, Armstrong talked about how buying a cheap Victrola record player as a young teen extended the range of influences on his music beyond what

Figure 12. Louis Armstrong with Star of David necklace, 1960. (Photo © Herb Snitzer.)

he could hear from Black and White bands in his native New Orleans, which included above all his mentor Joe "King" Oliver along with Kid Ory and others. But in the *Life* interview he reeled off a list of White artists that reached from Dixieland jazz to operatic singers: "Big event for me then was buying a wind-up victrola. Most of my records were the Original Dixieland Jazz Band—Larry Shields and his bunch. They were the first to record the music I played. I had Caruso records too, and Henry Burr, Galli-Curci, Tettrazini—they were all my favorites. Then there was the Irish tenor, McCormack—beautiful phrasing."[7]

The Original Dixieland Jazz Band had scant claim to the fidelity of its own name, for of course Black bands preceded them. But they were the first to make records of New Orleans jazz, and Armstrong happily learned from them. The others on the list show that genre limited Armstrong's influences no more than race or nationality did. The Italian singer Enrico Caruso became one of the greatest tenors in history, while Amelita Galli-Curci and Luisa Tetrazzini (for whom the dish turkey tetrazzini is named) were leading operatic sopranos of their day. The other two names belonged to singers of Celtic background: the Canadian Henry Burr (born Henry McClaskey) starred as a singer of popular songs, while the even more famous Irish tenor John McCormack started as a singer of church music and opera, later giving recitals that ranged from art songs to popular Irish ballads and taking American citizenship. Armstrong's influences, then, represent a melting pot of their own.

Armstrong repeatedly called attention to the Jewish elements, though, and in ways that went beyond wearing the Star of David around his neck and allowing photographs of him wearing it. That devotion perhaps surfaced most explicitly in his short memoir "Louis Armstrong + the Jewish Family in New Orleans, La., the Year of 1907," a manuscript in his hand written during treatment at Beth Israel Hospital in spring of 1969 (in appreciation of the health care he received, Armstrong through his foundation would later fund the "Louis Armstrong Department of Music Therapy" there). Although Armstrong scanted early Jewish influence in his other published memoirs, he stressed them in this one, which has special claims on us as the latest of the lot and as one that he did not publish and so did not have to trim to suit imagined audiences. The memoir begins with perception of a shared burden. "The neighborhood was consisted of Negroes, Jewish people and lots of Chinese," recalled Satchmo, who like most people of the time referred to Jews as a separate race. "But the Jewish people in those early days were having problems of their own—Along with hard times from the other *white* folks *nationalities* who felt that they were better than the *Jewish* race."[8] He went on to record his "long time admiration for the Jewish people" along with the belief that his own Negro people "were having a little *better* break than the *Jewish* people" (p. 8) and like Booker T. Washington and W. E. B. Du Bois, among others, urged that Negroes imitate Jewish behavior for success. Armstrong even dedicated the memoir to his Jewish manager Joe Glaser ("The best Friend That I've ever had"; p. 6), and extolled in it the warmth and support shown to him by the Karnofsky family as a boy. The Karnofskys did far more than employ him on their delivery wagon in the red light district of Storyville. They offered him meals, warmth, and encouragement, and according to this memoir (the story differs in other accounts) staked him to the five dollars necessary to buy a cornet he saw in a pawn shop window. "The Karnofsky Family kept reminding me that I had Talent. . . . They could see that I had music in my Soul. . . . It was the Jewish family who instilled in me Singing from the heart" (pp. 15–18). Armstrong responded not only to the Karnofskys' emotional and material support but also to their penchant for the lullaby that these Russian-Jewish immigrants and their older children would sing with Satchmo to put the younger children to sleep. The "Russian Lullaby" haunted Armstrong both in the memoir and in his life, and he quotes a passage in the memoir itself, beginning "Every Night you'll hear me Croon / A Russian Lullaby / Just a little plaintive tune / When Baby Starts to Cry." That plaintive tune, of course, did not originate in Russia but was a famous hit song by Irving Berlin, who himself came to the United States as a Russian-Jewish immigrant at age five.

Armstrong recorded several hits by Irving Berlin that went on to become top-selling records. A notable example was Berlin's first breakthrough hit, "Alexander's Ragtime Band" (1911), which itself drew on African-American elements, including Scott Joplin's popular rags. In turn, famous Black singers, like Bessie Smith in 1927 and Armstrong himself in 1937, cut versions that climbed high on the charts, and as late as 1959 Ray Charles's big-band version did the same. Ella Fitzgerald and Armstrong sang numerous hit duets of Berlin's songs, many of them gathered in the double CD set *Ella Fitzgerald Sings the Irving Berlin Songbook,* including famous numbers like "Cheek to

Cheek," "Isn't This a Lovely Day," and "I've Got My Love to Keep Me Warm." Neither Berlin on one hand, nor Smith, Armstrong, Fitzgerald, and Charles, on the other saw themselves as "appropriating," let alone stealing, work by someone from a different ethnic group; to all, such musical interchange formed part of the give and take among top-notch artists. Armstrong sang and recorded several explicitly Jewish-themed songs, including his hit "Shadrach," based on the biblical story of Shadrach, Meshach, and Abednego from the Book of Daniel and set by the White Louisiana composer Robert MacGimsey. One of Armstrong's boldest cross-cultural ventures came during his famous Hot Five and Hot Seven recordings of 1926–1927 that loom so large in the history of jazz. Sandwiched between "You Made Me Love You" and "Willie the Weeper" was "Irish Black Bottom," a Hibernization by Percy Venables and Louis of the original New Orleans "Black Bottom." Along the way Armstrong ad libs "I was born in Ireland" before breaking into characteristic raucous laughter. The song ends with the line "Cause Ireland's gone Black bottom crazy now." With such multiracial and multinational examples, no wonder that trombonist Trummy Young recalled Armstrong's response nearly thirty years later to a group of Arab musicians with whom the All Stars played in Lebanon before going on to Israel. When some Lebanese journalists challenged Satchmo about planning to play in the Jewish state, too, Armstrong responded, "Let me tell you something, man. That horn. You see that horn? That horn ain't prejudiced. A note's a note in any language."[9]

Louis Armstrong was not the only Black musician who wore a Star of David around his neck. So, too, did Willie "The Lion" Smith, the great stride pianist born four years before Satchmo. In his memoir *Music on My Mind* he described his ancestry as French, Spanish, Negro, and Mohawk Indian, and called himself "an American pianist" in the subtitle.[10] His mother worked for a Jewish family who let him take Hebrew lessons along with their own children. After discovering that he had a Jewish ancestor, Smith converted, had a Bar Mitzvah, and even served as a cantor in the synagogue on 122nd Street and Lenox Avenue, where he collaborated with Cantor Goldman on several Yiddish compositions, including "Wus Geven Is Geven" (What's Gone Is Gone), written as a memorial to his mother (pp. 12, 246). Again, no one accused Willie the Lion of appropriating a Jewish language or Jewish songs, just as no one judged Paul Robeson that way when he sang the "Chasidic

Chant" in large concert halls. Those desperate to maintain the view of exploitation rather than hybridity might claim that Willie the Lion converted to help his career, but no evidence supports that view. On the contrary, Smith himself records a doubter saying to him, "Lion, you stepped up to the plate with one strike against you—and now you take a second one right down the middle." He concluded, "They can't seem to realize I have a Jewish soul" (p. 12). Indeed, Smith composed his comic song "What's My Name?" after being asked that question during a conversation in Hebrew with a rabbi during a transatlantic flight to Paris. He ascribed his own nickname to being called "the Lion of Judah," later shortened to the Lion, because of his Jewish identification. The notion of a musical melting pot did not faze Smith, who paused in his memoir to record the pianist Eubie Blake avowing the influence of the Hungarian classical composer Franz Lehár. As we have seen, Blake became friends with Al Jolson and attended his funeral.

If African-American jazzmen like Armstrong and Smith identified with Jews, many White musicians, especially Jewish ones, identified with Blacks. The one who plunged most deeply into African-American identity was Mezz Mezzrow, born Milton Mesirow, another Jewish clarinetist and saxophone player who became even better known for his colorful personality, drug dealing, and stint as Louis Armstrong's manager. His autobiography, *Really the Blues,* records a journey that reverses the hero of James Weldon Johnson's *Autobiography of an Ex-Colored Man.* Where Johnson's protagonist hops back and forth across the color line but ultimately passes for White, Mezzrow does the same before ultimately choosing to become what he calls "a voluntary Negro."

An early incident recounted in *Really the Blues* helped catalyze Mezzrow's racial crossing. Riding the rails with other Jewish youths from Chicago, Mezz and his pals went for a meal in Cape Girardeau on the Mississippi River in southeastern Missouri only to be told by the owner, "Where the hell did you come from? We don't serve niggers in here."[11] The encounter shaped Mezzrow's life. "We were Jews, but in Cape Girardeau they had told us we were Negroes," he recalled. "Now, all of a sudden, I realized that I agreed with him. . . . By the time I reached home, I knew that I was going to spend all my time from then on sticking close to Negroes." In Mezzrow's case that meant not only becoming a jazz musician but also marrying a Black woman, moving to Harlem, and even insisting to prison guards that he be housed with Black inmates rather than White ones. He became a passable though not great saxophonist and clarinetist who also supplied his fellow musicians with marijuana and sometimes other drugs. He served briefly as Louis Armstrong's manager and hit his high point in recording sessions involving such great African-American jazzmen as pianist Teddy Wilson and Sidney Bechet, a much better clarinetist and saxophonist than himself. Mezz also operated one of the first high-profile racially mixed bands and proudly recorded in his autobiography the full-page headline in *Billboard* magazine reading "Mixed Band Bows on Broadway" and subtitled "Mezzrow Takes Sepia & Ofay Swingsters out in the Open." The article itself highlighted the racial mixing of "15 musical swing stars culled from both the Caucasian and Negroid races. . . . Since music recognizes no language save its own . . . there is no color line in the playing of swing music and followers are representative of every race" (p. 289). For Mezz, as for Satchmo, Willie the Lion, Jean Toomer, Paul Robeson, and so many others, Jews and Blacks together claimed a special place in that crossing. Encouraged by the Irish warden Big John McDonnell to organize a Jewish choir in prison, Mezzrow says that he found out "once more how music of different oppressed peoples blends together. Jewish or Hebrew religious music. . . . When I add Negro inflections to it they fit so perfect, it thrills me" (p. 316).

Even more influential than Mezzrow was the clarinetist and band leader Artie Shaw, born Arthur Jacob Arshawski in 1910, whose greatest hit was "Begin the Beguine." First hearing Louis Armstrong and his Hot Five on race records in 1927 marked a turning point in his career and caused him to make a pilgrimage to Chicago to meet Satchmo and later to spend time playing with Willie the Lion in Harlem, where he retreated during one of his many difficult periods and deepened his identification with Black culture. Besides hanging out in Harlem with Willie the Lion, Shaw toured with singer Billie Holiday for eight months in 1938, the first major White bandleader to feature an African-American songstress. The *Chicago Defender,* an African-American newspaper, sponsored a Christmas charity concert featuring Shaw as "King of the Clarinet Players" and Holiday as "America's First Lady of Song." *Billboard* enthusiastically reported that "all attendance records were broken and Artie with his sepia songstress Billie Holiday had to work an extra half hour after pleading with the throng to go home. The crowd couldn't get enough of Shaw's jiving." As with Black reaction to Al Jolson in

The Jazz Singer, actual African-American reactions to racial crossing at the time differ sharply from our contemporary back-projections. The Jewish-Black combination of Shaw and Holiday ran into considerable racial hostility during the Southern part of the band's tour, with Holiday often excluded from restaurants and hotels.[12] Sometimes the band countered in humorous ways, as in painting a dot on Billie's forehead and telling a desk clerk that she was an Indian aristocrat rather than a Black. At other times the racism hurt, but Shaw and Holiday kept on. Wild charges abounded after the two separated and persisted until Shaw's death in 2004. He pointed out to interviewer Stuart Nicholson in 1993 that those who accused him of firing Holiday because she was Black forgot that "When I hired her she was black too!" Despite some acrimony at their parting, Holiday loyally defended Shaw's racial attitudes. "There aren't many people who fought harder than Artie against the vicious people in the music business or the crummy side of second-class citizenship which eats at the guts of so many musicians," she recalled. "He didn't win. But he didn't lose either. It wasn't long after I left him that he told them to shove it like I had."

The Shaw-Holiday collaboration typified a range of racial crossings in the service of musical art. Besides Holiday and Smith, for example, Shaw played memorably with Roy Eldridge, engaging in what critic David Yaffe has termed a "call and response" interaction on the model of other African-American patterns.[13] But Shaw was by no means the only one. Encouraged by the legendary producer John Hammond, the Jewish clarinetist Benny Goodman, for example, broke through racial barriers in the 1930s by entering a recording studio with an integrated band that included Lionel Hampton on vibes, Teddy Wilson on piano, Charlie Christian on guitar, and Billie Holiday doing vocals. Goodman played with some of those same musicians in first his trio and then his quartet later in the 1930s, when he also led the first major integrated band in live performances. The chemistry was instantaneous. As Goodman described playing with Wilson in 1935, "Teddy and I began to play as though we were thinking with the same brain." In similar fashion, saxophonist Stan Getz would later describe pianist Kenny Barron as "the other half of my heart," a phrase echoing Charlie Parker's famous remark about Dizzy Gillespie. Getz's original name was Gayetzky, just as Goodman's was Gutman, and, as we have seen, Shaw's was Arshawsky and Mezzrow's was Mesirow. The name changes do far more than sound more mellifluous;

they transform Eastern European Jewish nomenclature into an Anglo-Saxon register. In that way they become a kind of reverse Jew-face, inversely analogous to blackface, in which Jews cross racial lines into mainstream American far more obviously and successfully than blackface minstrelsy allowed them to do. Even the Al Jolson character in *The Jazz Singer* changed from Jakie Rabinowitz into Jack Robin, a transformation far more effective for that purpose than its companion strategy of blacking up. Conversely, Black jazz and blues singers like Willie the Lion Smith, Duke Ellington, and Ethel Waters all performed Hebrew and Yiddish songs. "I always loved to sing it," explained Waters about her fondness for "Eli, Eli" (My God, My God). "It tells the tragic history of the Jews as much as one song can, and that history of their age-old grief and despair is so similar to that of my own people that I felt I was telling the story of my own race too."[14] Far from re-senting Waters's performance of the song as appropriation or exploitation, Jewish audiences thronged the theaters to hear it, as did those of other ethnicities.

Such hybridities inform both the work and reception of George Gershwin, which epitomizes melting pots of both race and culture as well as within cultures. Like so many Jews in the music world, Gershwin anglicized his name, from the Jacob Gershowitz given him by his Russian immigrant parents to its more assimilated form. Born in Brooklyn, he grew up in New York and reflected its melting pot in both his life and work. Biographically, Gershwin encountered African Americans and their music early, absorbed important elements from that culture into his own creations, and spent considerable time with Black artists of various kinds. His work itself performed a vertical integration of cultural levels sometimes kept distinct, such as classical music, jazz, and popular songs, to the vast approval of audiences even if occasional sniping by critics. Gershwin himself called his sensationally successful *Rhapsody in Blue* a "musical kaleidoscope of America—of our vast melting pot." He wrote in 1926 that the American soul "includes the wail, the whine, and the exultant note of the old 'mammy' songs of the South. It is black and white. It is all colors and all souls unified in the great melting pot of the world."[15] No wonder that, for example, *Opportunity*, the magazine of the National Urban League, cited the *Rhapsody* approvingly in a 1925 editorial on jazz as showing "recognition of common passions, instincts,—human qualities" between Blacks and others (the same piece also cited Al

Jolson's songs). No wonder, too, that what the great scholar of American popular song Charles Hamm sees as "distinctive in [Gershwin's] career was his affinity for the music of blacks" and cites the African-American bandleaders James Reese Europe and Will Voldery along with ragtime pianists James P. Johnson and Luckey Roberts among Gershwin's early influences.

Gershwin's first big break in popular song came when Al Jolson performed his tune "Swanee," but *Rhapsody in Blue* a few years later established his reputation across genres and audiences as well as ethnic groups. The well-known bandleader Paul Whiteman especially commissioned the piece for his famous "Experiment in Modern Music" concert held on the symbolically important date of Lincoln's birthday in 1924 and dedicated to introducing jazz to more mainstream listeners. *Rhapsody in Blue,* which Gershwin originally planned to call *American Rhapsody,* stole the show. Scored for jazz band and piano with the composer himself as featured soloist, it opened with a memorable and wailing clarinet passage followed by three main sections and a coda. The audience included leaders of both the classical and jazz worlds: composers Serge Rachmaninoff and John Philip Sousa; conductors Walter Damrosch and Leopold Stokowski; violinists Mischa Elman, Jascha Heifetz, and Fritz Kreisler; singers Amelita Galli-Curci and the Irish tenor John McCormack (both of whose recordings had enwrapt the young Louis Armstrong); along with stride pianist Willie the Lion Smith and the great bluesman W. C. Handy. Louis Armstrong himself transferred an easily recognizable passage to his performance of "Ain't Misbehavin'" for the *Hot Chocolates* hit show of 1929, and J. Rosamond Johnson praised *Rhapsody* as the "greatest one-hundred-percent expression of Negro American idioms and characteristics" he had heard. "George, you've done it— you're the Abraham Lincoln of Negro music," he told the composer (Melnick, pp. 57, 47–48). Critics generally approved, too, and F. Scott Fitzgerald worked a brief allusion into his novel *The Great Gatsby* and a longer one into that book's earlier version, *Trimalchio.*

The give and take between Gershwin's work and the world of jazz, especially African-American jazz, continued even more prominently with his famous song "I Got Rhythm." The musical *Girl Crazy* (1930) showcased the number in a breakthrough performance by Ethel Merman that established her career, particularly when she held a high note on the word "more" for sixteen bars. Not the high notes, though, but rather the chord changes in the song sparked ongoing interethnic exchange by artists that included Dizzie Gillespie, Charlie Parker, and Thelonious Monk. As cultural scholar David Yaffe has recently observed, those changes became

> a basis for Duke Ellington's "Cottontail," Charlie Christian's "Seven Come Eleven," Charlie Parker's "Salt Peanuts," Thelonious Monk's "Rhythm-a-Ning," and much more. Gershwin's 1-6-2-5 chord structure served as a guiding theme for the birth of bebop, and even if he was a Jew who was overt in his indebtedness to black music, the exchange worked both ways. Dizzy Gillespie's Minton's sessions would often start with playing the chords to "I've Got Rhythm"—known as "Rhythm" changes. . . . To this day, calling for "Rhythm" changes is a universally understood directive on the bandstand, it is a common language of bop, and while Gershwin came up with his chord sequence borrowing from the swing and stride he heard from black musicians in Harlem, the beboppers returned the favor.[16]

Other jazz classics by African Americans that work off the song's basic structure include Sidney Bechet's "Shag," Count Basie's "Blow Top," Coleman Hawkins's "Chant of the Groove," and other tunes by Parker, like "Shaw 'Nuff" and "Anthropology" (Pollock, p. 480). The history of "I've Got Rhythm" and its influences shows clearly the hybrid nature of artistic and cultural interaction, even in such a form as identified with African-American achievement as jazz. Such give and take is normative rather than exceptional. When Derek Walcott reworks Homer's *Odyssey* in *Omeros* or Zora Neale Hurston transfers the biblical Exodus story to Black dialect in *Moses, Man of the Mountain,* no one thinks that they appropriate or steal "white" art, anymore than Monk or Gillespie or Parker thought that Gershwin had done so with "black" stride piano; indeed words like "appropriate" and "white" have little if any meaning in this context. The art may arise from specific socioeconomic circumstances and formations, but once it does so it exists beyond them. As Satchmo said, anyone who thinks otherwise does not know their horns and does not love the music.

Such questions surface again with Gershwin's most extensive work, the folk opera *Porgy and Bess* (1935), derived from the White Du Bose Heyward's novel *Porgy,* set among African Americans of Gullah background living on the Carolina coast in Catfish Row. The work itself crosses over many lines, not only in race but also in genre; it is at once an opera and an elevated Broadway show, infused with elements from classical opera, jazz, and hit musicals. After Crown kills Robbins in a crap game and flees, he leaves his girlfriend Bess to suffer the advances of Sportin' Life, a drug dealer from New York. Bess finds protection in the arms of the handicapped Porgy, whom she leaves for Crown and then returns to. After a storm drowning Clara and her husband Jake, Crown returns for Bess but Porgy kills him instead. Once the police haul Porgy off to jail, Bess flees to New York with Sportin' Life, and after Porgy's release he sets off for New York to find her once again. The show contains some of Gershwin's most memorable music, including "It Ain't Necessarily So," "Summertime," and "I Got Plenty o' Nothin'." Gershwin himself traveled to Folly Beach in 1934 to experience Gullah culture firsthand and returned to New York able to tutor Northern singers in Gullah ways. The opera drew on Heyward and his wife Dorothy's stage adaptation of the novel, a Theatre Guild hit of the 1920s that featured a mostly Black cast of sixty-six, including twenty-two principals. James Weldon Johnson judged *Porgy and Bess* the work where "the Negro performer removed all doubts as to his ability to do acting that requires thoughtful interpretation and intelligent skill. . . . Here was a large company giving a first-rate, even performance."[17] Johnson's comment alerts us to the largely positive African-American response to the play, which carried over to the opera.

Because after its initial success *Porgy and Bess* in recent years has attracted the usual charges of appropriation and larceny on the one hand and stereotyping and racism on the other, I want to highlight the responses of African-American subjects, artists, and critics of the time, nearly all of whom enthusiastically praised the work. We may start with an elderly Gullah Negro who listened to Gershwin throw himself into the call and response at an island church and then exclaimed, "By God, you can sure beat out them rhythms, boy. I'm over seventy years old and I ain't never seen no po' little white man take off and fly like you. You could be my own son" (p. 578). The old man's enthusiasm matched that of the African-American performers in the original cast. With Paul Robeson away in Europe for most of 1934–1935, Gershwin settled instead on Todd Duncan, who had performed in New York productions like *Cavalleria Rusticana,* taught at Howard University, and initially scorned the idea of playing the original Porgy as something smacking of Tin Pan Alley and beneath him. Gershwin persisted, however, and Duncan rejoiced that he did. "I literally wept for what this Jew was able to express for the Negro," he told the composer Ned Rorem and particularly cited his final song "I'm on My Way" as moving him to tears (p. 595). The youngest principal, Anne Brown (Bess), stoutly defended the opera to her own father, who accused it of recycling clichés of Black people as dope peddlers and prostitutes. "I thought that DuBose Heyward and Gershwin had simply taken a part of life in Catfish Row, South Carolina, and rendered it superbly." Brown herself went on to direct productions *of Porgy and Bess* in Norway and France, where she told audiences that "Gershwin's opera was concerned with humanity" (p. 597). Similarly, Eva Jessye, who directed the choir, said that Gershwin "had written in things that sounded just right, like our people" and that the opera expressed "our inheritance, our own lives."

After the work's premiere the praise continued. The composer of the music for "Lift Every Voice and Sing," J. Rosamond Johnson, whose brother James Weldon Johnson had written the lyrics for that unofficial "Negro Anthem," had created the role of "Lawyer Frazier" in *Porgy and Bess.* He hailed Gershwin as "the Abraham Lincoln of Negro music." To him if the work was not "one hundred per cent Negroid," as *Rhapsody in Blue* had been, it was still "at least eighty percent" so, with the rest a blend of American Indian, cowboy, and mountain music. He considered it "a monument to the cultural aims of Negro art" and praised "this young man's musical exposition and development of folklore, emanating from street cries, blues and plantation songs of the Negro." The opera ran for 124 performances during the depths of the Depression and attracted largely favorable reviews. Those that were not, like that in the *New York Times,* expressed doubts about the music or technique, but most praised the production as the best American opera to date and admired its sincerity and freshness. Arthur Pollock in the *Brooklyn Daily Eagle* reported that "This is the sort of thing that Pulitzer Prizes are not good enough for." The Black press praised the play, too. Pianist-composer Carl Diton lauded the "well-sounding score" and closed his review for the *New York Amsterdam News* with "the sincerest hope that George Gershwin's 'Porgy and Bess' may never die!" (pp. 587–598, 604, 607). Those who did critique aspects of the opera usually focused on the music as twangy or stiff but, like

Hall Johnson in *Opportunity,* stoutly declared Gershwin "as free to write about Negroes in his own way as any other composer to write about anything else." *Porgy and Bess* was Gershwin's last major work; within two years he died from a brain tumor. But the melody lingered on in covers by myriad artists Black and White, including a who's who of African-American musicians: Louis Armstrong, Art Tatum, John Coltrane, Billie Holiday, Sam Cooke, Ella Fitzgerald, Miles Davis, and Natalie Cole, among many others. It was love, not theft.

The affinity of not only Blacks and Jews but also of Irish came through in the 1952 production of *Porgy and Bess* by the Irish-American director Robert Breen. Sent to tour the United States and then Europe for the State Department, that revival starred William Warfield as Porgy, Leontyne Price as Bess, and Cab Calloway as Sportin' Life, among other luminaries. In rehearsal Breen told the cast of his own Irish background and exhorted them to recover the vitality of African-American folk culture. "If I were cast in any Irish folk play, I would come up with all the richness of the Irish countryside, all the local color . . . and I would revel in it." The cast caught his enthusiasm. "I was always amazed that he was not put among the great stage directors of all time," remarked Martha Flowers, who later played Bess. "No one had ever done *Porgy and Bess* that way before, with the subtleties, the touches that were so natural and beautiful." Most Black papers liked the production, though some did not. Paul Warfield spoke for the majority when he defended it as "a celebration of our culture, and not an exploitation of it. The work didn't snigger at African-Americans. It ennobled the characters it depicted . . . a story of triumph, not degradation. . . . The folk opera transcended purely racial orientation and achieved that universality that characterized other world masterpieces rooted in German or Italian or other ethnic themes" (Pollack, pp. 614–617). Gershwin himself sometimes composed under Irish inspiration, as did other composers of Tin Pan Alley. In the early 1920s, for example, he wrote "Irish Waltz," described as "Three-Quarter Blues for Piano," a title that nicely displays the Black and Irish affinities of this Jewish composer. His first biographer, Isaac Goldberg, picked up on them in 1930. "The Negro blue note, of course, has its peculiarities of origin and of use," he wrote. "Yet, when the folk music of Ireland and of Jewish Poland . . . betray a similar departure from our diatonic norm, there seems to be room for further co-ordination."[18] Goldberg held the then familiar but now bizarre-sounding theory of such similarities deriving from "a common Oriental ancestry in both Negro and Jew," a view that he expressed at greater length in his book *Tin Pan Alley* the previous year.

Tin Pan Alley and Multicultural Crossover

Popular music typified by Tin Pan Alley and musical theater thought of itself and was thought of by others as even more of a melting pot than jazz, though the borders often blurred. Gershwin himself planned to write a work called *The Melting Pot*, though he completed only "Three Preludes" for it, and as we have seen thought of *Rhapsody in Blue* that way. An anecdote from *The Jerome Kern Song Book* captures the multicultural spirit as Oscar Hammerstein recalls considering doing a musical adaptation of a book by the Irish writer Donn Byrne:

> Jerome Kern and I were one time contemplating writing a musical version of Donn Byrne's *Messer Marco Polo*. Discussing the general problems of adaptation, I confronted Jerry with what I considered to be a serious question about the score. I said, "Here is a story laid in China about an Italian and told by an Irishman. What kind of music are you going to write?" Jerry answered, "It'll be good Jewish music."[19]

Kern's remark highlights the mixing and crossing of cultural barriers common in both Tin Pan Alley and Broadway in those years. Sometimes they reflected racial and ethnic stereotypes, too, though for better or worse people worried less about that back then than they do now and did see ethnic types as materials for melting pots. Irving Berlin told an interviewer for a front-page article in the *American Israelite* in 1922 that his music was more syncopation than jazz. "It's a distinctive form of music, a typically 'melting pot' form I call it, for it's derived from the music of so many countries, of many centuries." He aimed at an appeal across groups. The interviewer cited the popular military grouse against buglers, "Oh, How I Hate to Get up in the Morning," from the show *Yip, Yip, Yaphank* as "a striking example of Irving Berlin's genius in appealing to the crowd by striking a universal chord of sympathy." The Jewish duo Rodgers and Hart even wrote that sentiment into their song "Bugle Blow" from the show *Betsy* (1926), which also displayed a medley of "national dances." "We've a race that's het'rogeneous / With folks from all the earth," the song declared, and "All were diff'rent when they came, / But jazz has made them all the same!"[20]

Some observers demurred, usually those opposed to racial mixing and affiliated with Anglo-Saxon America. Henry Ford's *Dearborn Independent,* for example, denounced jazz as "Yiddish moron music" in two articles of 1921. Associating Jewish music with Black sexuality, these screeds claimed that African-American music with its "monkey talk, jungle squeals" required Jewish "cleverness to camouflage the moral filth" and went on to remind readers that Jews had invented camouflage uniforms during World War I. Similarly, a letter writer to the *New York Times* argued "against the statement so frequently made that jazz is typically American music." Instead, he branded jazz "the Hebrew interpretation of African and Eastern rhythms . . . the African jungle or the bazaars of the East" and asked "Is there anything at all suggestive of the great open spaces of America or of the fine spirit that dominates our country?"[21] At a higher level of musical awareness, composer and critic Virgil Thomson smarted at the overshadowing of his own *Four Saints in Three Acts* (with libretto by Gertrude Stein) by *Porgy and Bess.* He brought Blacks, Jews, and Irish together in a negative way by assigning Gershwin to Tin Pan Alley and declaring that school "straight from the melting pot. At best it is a piquant but highly unsavory stirring-up together of Israel, Africa, and the Gaelic Isles." Thomson dismissed Gershwin's expressive substance or architectonics though granted him talent and charm. He found little drama in *Porgy and Bess* and damned the melodies with faint praise as "prettily Negroid."[22]

Among the stars of Tin Pan Alley, none shone brighter than Irving Berlin. Another son of a cantor, like Gershwin and other Russian-Jewish composers and lyricists, he changed his name as part of his crossover from ethnic to national popularity. Starting life as Israel Isidore Baline, he used a misprint in one of his first pieces of sheet music to adopt the name he made famous as composer of "God Bless America," "White Christmas," and "Easter Parade," among other unlikely titles for a Jewish immigrant. Inspired by sources including the broad multiethnic musical comedy of Edward Harrigan and Tony Hart in *The Mulligan Guards* and its successors from 1878 onward, Tin Pan Alley turned out an array of ethnic-based songs. The *Mulligan Guards* series had included characters like the Irish saloon owner Dan Mulligan, in whose establishment the multiethnic guards gather; the African-American washerwoman Rebecca Allup (played in a gender bender by Hart himself); and representatives of most New York minorities of the time. In the next generation, Tin Pan Alley composers followed suit. For example, Irving Berlin's early work included his first song, "Marie of Sunny Italy," "Sadie Salome (Go Home)," "Oh How That German Could Love," and "Molly-O! Oh, Molly," among many others. His breakthrough came in 1911 with the smash hit "Alexander's Ragtime Band," later recorded by Bessie Smith, Louis Armstrong, and other Black artists. As much a march as a true rag, the song inspired the legend that Berlin had paid an African American to write it (a similar malicious rumor swirled about Gershwin having a little colored boy to help him). Stung by the false charge, Berlin responded by asking "if a negro could write 'Alexander,' why couldn't I?" Such ethnic crossings were common in those days, as in many other periods. The Gentiles Joseph McLeon, Harry Piano, and Raymond Walker wrote the "Yiddisha Rag" of 1909, and Berlin responded with "Yiddle, on Your Fiddle, Play Some Ragtime." Ethel Waters and Louis Armstrong did famous renditions of Berlin's "Blue Skies," and Thelonious Monk varied it for his "In Walked Bud," a tribute to Harlem bebop pianist Bud Powell. Among many other Black singers, Waters and Armstrong performed two of the most vibrant versions of Harold Arlen's "I've Got a Right to Sing the Blues," and Waters once called Arlen "the Negro-ist white man" she had ever known.[23]

Tin Pan Alley and its ethnic crossovers extended to the Irish as well. Best-known among composers (as well as singers, dancers, and lyricists) was Irish-American George M. Cohan, whose many hits included the patriotic songs "Over There!" and "It's a Grand Old Flag" along with "Give My Regards to Broadway" and "I'm a Yankee Doodle Dandy." His sixteen-year alliance with the Jewish Sam Harris generated numerous hit shows that pioneered the integration of songs, choreography, and dialogue in popular musical comedies. Other famous Irish-Jewish teams included the popular act (first in vaudeville during the 1910s and then on Broadway in the 1920s) Gallagher and Shean, which featured the Irish-American Edward Gallagher and the Jewish Al Shean, an uncle of the Marx brothers, whose original name was Schoenberg. Their well-known theme song, "Mister Gallagher and Mister Shean," ended each stanza with the exchange "Absolutely, Mister Gallagher?" followed by "Positively, Mister Shean!" The longevity of their alliance paled though beside that of Jewish George Burns and Irish Gracie Allen, who became successively stars of vaudeville in the 1920s, radio in the 1930s, and eventually television and film. Much of their humor featured the interplay of Burns as straightforward Jew and Allen as slightly ditzy denizen of a large Irish Catholic family, which led to exchanges like George's query, "Did the nurse ever drop you on your head when you were a baby?" to which Gracie responded, "Oh, no, we couldn't afford a nurse; my mother had to do it."[24] Such collaborations continue right up to the present, of course, as in Mel Brooks and Thomas Meehan's work on *Young Frankenstein*.

Irish-Jewish alliances grew so pervasive in popular culture during the early twentieth century that they inspired songs like Billy Murray's "If It Wasn't for the Irish and the Jews" of 1912. Historian of the Irish song in America William Williams notes that Tin Pan Alley churned out numerous comic songs displaying odd racial or ethnic combinations and that 44 percent of the Irish songs of the 1900s fell into that category and 39 percent for the 1910s.[25] While some of them featured Native Americans, Germans, or Hawaiians, the largest number paired Irish and Jews. Those included "It's Tough When Izzy Rosenstein Loves Genevieve Malone" (1910), "My Yiddisha Colleen" (1911), "Yidisha Luck and Irisha Love" (1911), "Moysha Machree" (1916), "There's a Little Bit of Irish in Sadie Cohen" (1916), and "Kosher Kitty Kelly" (1926) from the play of the same name. "If It Wasn't for the Irish and the Jews" cast an even wider net than such romantic pairings. Appropriately, an Irishman and a Jew collaborated in writing it. Billy Jerome came from upstate New York, and in a reversal of Jews changing their surnames to more Christian-sounding ones, he dropped his last name of Flannery in favor of his more Jewish-sounding middle name, Jerome. Jean Schwartz, meanwhile, had emigrated to the United States with his Hungarian Jewish family while still a boy. The pair did hundreds of songs together, including ethnic hits of the time like "Chinatown, My Chinatown" and the still-popular "My Irish Molly O," with lines like "Molly—my Irish Molly—My sweet acushla dear."

"If It Wasn't for the Irish and Jews" took off partly because it was recorded by one of the top singers in the United States at the time, Billy Murray, the son of Irish immigrants. The song portrayed a traveler glad to return to America after a European jaunt who extols Jewish-Irish cooperation in business, politics, and entertainment. Toward the end he sings:

Talk about a combination,
Hear my words and make a note,
On St. Patrick's Day Rosinsky,
Pins a shamrock on his coat,
There's a sympathetic feeling,
Between the Blooms and McAdoos,
Why Tammany would surely fall,
There'd really be no hall at all,
If it wasn't for the Irish and the Jews.

The lines about the Democratic machine stronghold Tammany Hall are not altogether fantasy; no less an authority than Tammany's sub-boss George Washington Plunkett (who coined the phrase "honest graft") praised the politician Johnny Ahearn for earning support from both ethnicities in a district that was half Irish and half Jewish. The two groups collaborated even more tightly in the entertainment industry, which the song invokes through its reference to the theater impresario David Belasco, born in San Francisco to Sephardic Jewish parents and known as "the king of Broadway":

I once heard Dave Belasco say,
You couldn't stage a play today,
If it wasn't for the Irish and the Jews.

Jerome and Schwartz's lines refer primarily to collaborations in writing, acting, and producing and perhaps secondarily to stereotyped routines from both vaudeville and the more legitimate stage. But that was about to change.

Broadway and Film: The Vogue for Irish-Jewish Romances

The 1920s saw a vogue for Irish-Jewish romances first on the stage and then on film. The improbable catalyst was *Abie's Irish Rose*, a play that barely made it to Broadway at all after its successful run in California, before opening in May 1922 and becoming first a smash hit and then the longest-running Broadway play up to that time, lasting for five years and 2,327 performances. Besides theatrical revivals, it lived on through a novelization and two film versions (in 1928 starring Buddy Rogers and Nancy Carroll and in 1946 starring Richard Norris and Joanne Dru) as well as an NBC radio show during World War II. Its author, the Georgian-born playwright Anne Nichols, had to mortgage her house and secure funding from the Jewish gangster Arnold Rothstein (who helped fix the 1919 World Series and inspired creation of the character Meyer Wolfshiem in *The Great Gatsby*) to bring it to New York. Producers doubted that a romance between a Jew like Abie and an Irish Catholic woman like Rose would appeal to audiences. Herself a Southern Baptist, though with some Irish ancestry, Nichols repeatedly claimed that "a spirit of tolerance" animated the work.[26] The 1920s badly needed that tolerance as a series of congressional acts closed down the more open immigration that had brought so many new ethnics to the United States.

In portraying Catholics and Jews, *Abie's Irish Rose* featured two groups excluded from bastions of WASP privilege in America. The farcical plot treats Abraham Levy and Rosemary Murphy, who met in France during World War I and subsequently married in a ceremony performed by a Methodist minister. The first of the three acts presents Abie's Jewish family, to whom he introduces Rose as Rose Mary Murpheski to appease their insistence that he marry a Jewish girl. The opening lines by the neighbor Mrs. Cohen gives an idea of the broad dialect that pervades the play: "Isaac call the doctor, I know ven I god a differend pain. Ven my indigestive tablets don't voik, I know how I veel!" Occasional Irishisms create a similar effect when Rose's father, Patrick Murphy, enters with Father Whelan in the second act. Despite initial hostilities between the two groups, Mr. Cohen's own opening action prefigures an eventual harmony. The Jewish Cohen relishes "Maggy and Jiggs," the Irish couple featured in the longtime comic strip "Bringing up Father," penned by the Irish-American cartoonist George McManus. Pretending that they are not married and that Rose is Jewish, the young couple agrees to be married by a rabbi to placate Abie's parents. But her father, Patrick Murphy, fresh off a train from California, erupts into the ceremony accompanied by Father Whalen, whom Murphy expects to conduct a Catholic wedding. A publicity photo from the original 1922 production (Figure 13) illustrates the range of ethnic types. It shows from left to right Rosie, Abie, Father Whalen, Solomon Levy, Patrick Murphy, and Rabbi Samuels. Improbably, the rabbi and the priest bond through their common experiences comforting troops during the war. Eventually Father Whalen conducts a third wedding ceremony for Rose and Abie, but the fathers remain estranged.

Figure 13. Marriage scene from *Abie's Irish Rose*, 1922. (Billy Rose Theater Division, The New York Public Library for the Performing Arts, Astor, Lenox and Tilden Foundations.)

Reconciliation comes in the third act, set in Abie and Rose's apartment on Christmas eve a year later. In this comic takeoff on the Romeo and Juliet theme, the marriage and parenthood of the younger generation replaces the tragedy and death of Shakespeare's lovers. Again, the religious figures take the lead, as the rabbi, priest, and two fathers all drop by to view the boy and girl twin babies of the young couple. Father Whalen remarks, "Now if the Jews and the Irish would only stop fighting, and get together, they'd own a corner of the world!"[27] Following common usage of the time, Nichols refers to both Irish and Jews as "races" when Patrick and Solomon begin their bantering rapprochement, as Patrick exclaims "That's the trouble with your race; they won't give in," and Solomon replies "Give in, is it? That's the trouble with the Irish! Dod's the reason it took you so long to get free!" Ireland had only recently achieved independence at the time, as we saw in Chapter 2, and the dialogue reproduces in comic mode the association of Irish and Jewish patriotism. "Well, at least we've always had a country—that's more than you can say!" teases Patrick. Solomon replies, "Ve god a country, too! Jerusalem is free! Ve god it back!" The play diverges markedly from racist attacks on intermarriage by lauding it instead and featuring the "biracial" twin babies as agents of reconciliation. The twins carry that even in their names, with little Rebecca named for Abie's deceased mother and little Patrick for Rose's father. The dialogue progresses until Solomon wonders, "Maybe we could apologize and esk them to fergive us," and Patrick admits that "I can feel ashamed of myself." The exchanges and play end with the older Patrick exclaiming, "Merry Christmas, Sol!" and Solomon responding, "Goot Yonteff, Patrick!"

The vogue of *Abie's Irish Rose* spawned a host of imitators during the 1920s. First and most popular was the Broadway comedy *The Cohens and the Kellys* (1926), in which the daughter, Nannie, of Jewish dry-goods merchant Jacob Cohen secretly marries the son of Irish cop Patrick Kelly. The marriage of the children leads to reconciliation of the fathers, who become business partners. The plot resembled that of Anne Nichols's play so closely that she sued in federal court for plagiarism and copyright infringement. In *Nichols v. Universal Pictures,* Judge Learned Hand wrote for the court that broad concepts and stock figures cannot be copyrighted and that their use does not constitute infringement. Buoyed by that decision, Universal continued its series of films, during which the Cohens and the Kellys successively visited Paris, Atlantic City, Scotland, and Africa. The bizarre plot of the now rare *Cohens and the Kellys in Africa* (1930) sketched a journey to that continent by the unlikely business partners, this time searching for ivory to make piano keys for their factory. Along the way they visit unexplored territory and are captured by cannibals who turn out to have a Jewish chief from New York, whom the explorers beat in a game of miniature golf. The film's campy ending featured both explorers and African tribe in a spirited jazz song, at the end of which a giant gorilla exclaims "Mammy!" as he strikes the one-knee pose that Al Jolson had made famous in *The Jazz Singer*.

Other works besides the *Cohens and Kellys* series mined the vein first popularized by *Abie's Irish Rose,* often starting out as a play and then being adapted to film. Brian de Costa's *Kosher Kitty Kelly* became in turn a play, film, and popular song as it sketched the interactions of the Irish Kellys and

Jewish Feinbaums in exploring what *Film Daily* called "the racial question." Owen Davis's play *The Shamrock and the Rose* retained both the sympathetic priest and reconciliation through the birth of a mixed child from *Abie's Irish Rose*. *Clancy's Kosher Wedding* featured a romantic triangle among Leah Cohen, Tom Clancy, and the Jewish boxer Izzy Murphy, whose name itself combines both groups. In all, over seventeen films from the 1920s exploited the Irish-Jewish romantic theme.[28] The earlier one-act comic sketch *The American Idea* by Lillian P. Heydemann, writing as Lily Carthew, had anticipated the various cross-ethnic romances by announcing the offstage marriage of Abe and Esther Goldman's daughter Rachel (who has renamed herself Mignon and sings songs by Irving Berlin) to a mysterious John Kelly. But Heydemann draws back from the overt mixing of the later works by revealing at the end that the bridegroom is really a Jew who has changed his name from Yankele Operchinsky to the Irish-sounding John Kelly. As Mignon explains in the last line, "Yes, father, that's the American idea." Presentation of racial mixing involving African Americans would have to wait until after World War II, but for all their stock types these works pioneered a way in overcoming the racial prejudice of their own day.

Like divisions between groups, efforts to classify culture by level ultimately succumb to the fluidity of cultures. "The squirming facts exceed the squamous mind," observed Wallace Stevens, contrasting the fluidity of reality with the mind's stiffness like that of scaly plates.[29] As the largely mistaken notion of modernism as an elite enterprise hostile to popular culture fades, the interpenetration of "high" and "low" emerges more clearly. Culture usually works that way, of course, as elements of Chaucer or Shakespeare show. So, too, does the Gershwin song "Mischa, Jascha, Toscha, Sascha," written the same year (1922) that saw publication of Eliot's *The Waste Land* and Joyce's *Ulysses*. The title of this novelty ditty refers to four Russian-born Jewish violinists of the day who emigrated to the United States and became American citizens—Mischa Elman, Jascha Heifetz, Toscha Seidel, and Sascha Jacobsen. Part of the work's wit lies in constructing a popular song around four masters of the classical violin. Ira Gershwin's lyrics to George's music make explicit both the element of mixing and the contribution of Jews to that hybridity:

> We're not high-brows, we're not low-brows
> . . . we're Hebrows from the start.[30]

The song acts out its own statement, as the highbrow Hebrews mix high and low in constructing their own identity as "Hebrows," just as George Gershwin himself did in his own career at the time or as Leonard Bernstein would do later. The barriers between cultures, as between races, melting pots, or even nationalisms, turn out more porous than we sometimes think.

Eliot and Pound: Mixing High and Low Culture along with Blacks, Jews, and Irish

I turn briefly to the work of two poets often mischaracterized as "elite" but who in fact were captivated by elements of popular culture and refashioned it in their own work—T. S. Eliot and Ezra Pound. I intend here not to engage with the large recent literature on that subject or on their relation to individual groups but rather to call attention to their tendency to associate Blacks, Jews, and Irish together. In doing that they particularly utilized folk and musical elements, especially jazz. In his famous essay "Change the Joke and Slip the Yoke," Ralph Ellison argued that "the Negro American writer is also an heir of the human experience which is literature." He explained that "I use folklore in my work not because I am Negro, but because writers like Eliot and Joyce made me conscious of the literary value of my folk inheritance."[31] So, too, did Eliot and Pound use folk materials, even going so far as to pick names from the then-popular Uncle Remus tales in their correspondence with each other. Eliot signed his letters "Possum" and occasionally "Tar Baby," while Pound used the trickster "Br'er Rabbit" signature and persona. First published in 1881, Joel Chandler Harris's famous renderings of Southern African-American dialect enjoyed an enormous vogue worldwide among both Blacks and Whites. Besides in the United States, they circulated particularly in the then British Isles, where in Ireland the newspaper *Freeman's Journal* organized an Uncle Remus Club, Joyce invoked them in *Finnegans Wake*, and the late Victorian poet Rose Kavanagh (for whom Yeats wrote an obituary) used "Uncle Remus" as a pen name. Jazz would shortly have a similar vogue and similar cultural crossing, though not everybody would approve. Putting jazz and modernist poetry together, a columnist for the *New York Times* in 1924 huffed, "Jazz is to real music exactly what most of the 'new poetry,' so called, is to real poetry. Both are without the structure and form essential to music and poetry alike, and both are the products, not of innovators, but of incompetents."[32]

Jazz particularly pervades that masterpiece of modernism, T. S. Eliot's *The Waste Land,* both in specific allusions and in overall structure and rhythm. In his equally well-known essay "Hidden Name and Complex Fate," Ellison confessed that the poem "seized my mind" because of that fusion. "Somehow its rhythms were even closer to those of jazz than were those of the Negro poets, and even though I could not understand then, its range of allusion was as mixed and varied as that of Louis Armstrong" (p. 160). Besides its rhythms, the poem reframed specific jazz and popular song works, such as "The Shakespearian Rag" at lines 128–130, in the middle of the "Game of Chess" section. That popular song by Gene Buck and Herman Ruby with music by David Stamper from the 1912 Ziegfeld Follies provided the phrases "That Shakespearian rag, Most intelligent, very elegant" commandeered by Eliot. They not only allude to a past song but also describe Eliot's own poem, particularly its bringing together of what we wrongly dichotomize as high culture (Shakespeare once himself part of the popular culture of his day) and popular jazz or ragtime. The confluence of Black, Irish, and Jewish elements with high culture loomed even larger in the original opening section of *The Waste Land,* which Eliot deleted at Pound's instigation and which featured a Boston Irish pub crawl in which one character sings lines from George M. Cohan's "Harrigan": "I'm proud of all the Irish blood that's in me, / There's not a man can say a word agin me."[33] The same section also invokes lines from two more popular songs, Thomas Allen's 1904 coon song "The Watermelon Vine" (also known as "Lindy Lou") and Mae Sloan's 1901 vaudeville minstrel "My Evaline," before citing with slight alteration lines from "The Cubanola Glide" by the Irish-Jewish songwriting team of Vincent Bryan (words) and Harry von Tilzer (music): "Tease, squeeze, lovin' and wooin' / Oh, babe, what are you doin'?" Along with the minstrel songs and Irish names, Eliot carefully included a reference to the Jewish "little Ben Levin the tailor." It would be hard to imagine an opening more indebted to popular culture.

Eliot similarly drew on popular culture and associated Blacks, Jews, and Irish with it in his Sweeney poems, both those incorporated into his *Poems* (1920) volume from the earlier *Ara Vus Prec* and the slightly later *Sweeney Agonistes* fragments of a syncopated drama. In Chapter 1 we noted Eliot's adoption of typical imagery of vermin, apes, and the like for our three groups in the earlier Sweeney poems, and Chapter 3 sketched his adaptation of James Weldon Johnson's "Under the Bamboo Tree" from the later drama. Here I focus on *Sweeney Agonistes,* which Eliot once considered sub-titling "Fragments of a Comic Minstrelsy." David Chinitz has suggested the nineteenth-century Irish-American minstrel and banjo virtuoso Joel Walker Sweeney as an additional source for Eliot's title figure, along with the Irish king Sweeney and the Irish pub keeper mentioned by Eliot himself (Chinitz, p. 105). The stage direction "Swarts as Tambo. Snow as Bones" from the "Fragment of an Agon" section aptly invokes that heritage, since Tambo and Bones were important characters in the minstrel shows; assigning the Tambo role to the Jewish-sounding Swarts in a sort of reverse blackface continues the Jewish association as well. In Eliot's musical drama they sing Johnson's "Under the Bamboo Tree." Eliot invoked jazz as well, in 1924 confiding to Arnold Bennett his desire to write a "jazz play" (North, p. 224). As with *The Waste Land,* the syncopated rhythms of *Sweeney Agonistes* reflect the popular musical heritage driving Eliot's adaptations. The work aptly fulfills Eliot's remark to his friend Mary Hutchinson in 1920 that "it is a jazz-banjorine that I should bring, not a lute" (Chinitz, p. 21). A banjorine was a short-necked banjo popular with banjo orchestras and bands from the 1880s through the 1930s.

Popular culture fascinated Ezra Pound, too, especially in his lifelong obsession with dialect. Pound wove Blacks, Jews, and Irish into the text of *The Cantos* as it evolved over decades, whether in denouncing usury, invoking anthropologist Leo Frobenius's work on the African city of Wagadu, or sketching important Irishmen like W. B. Yeats, James Joyce, and Arthur Griffith. He even imported their respective dialects into the very language of his epic. Canto LXXIV, the first of the *Pisan Cantos* that Pound wrote in the prison camp there toward the end of World War II, offers ready examples. Pound not only incorporates Joyce into his list of deceased "lordly men" but renders him singing with an Irish accent, "Blarrney castle me darlin'/you're nothing now but a StOWne."[34] Similarly, when Pound invokes the goodwill of the African-American prison guard Mr. Edwards in the same canto, he records the guard's use of Black dialect. "Doan you tell no one/I made you that table," cautions Edwards. And in Canto LXXIV as elsewhere, Pound refers to Jews as "yidds," a derogatory term deriving from the Yiddish word for "Jew," a Yid. These and other intonations echo throughout the 800 pages of Pound's epic, creating a linguistic potpourri matching the cultural melting pot of the poem.

The dialects surface in other works as well, including some of Pound's translations. As though the cross-cultural challenge of rendering Japanese Noh dramas or Chinese Confucian odes were not enough, Pound does so by supplementing standard English with ethnic dialects. The effect can be startling, as in *The Confucian Odes*. There Pound renders a whole poem invoking a yellow bird entirely in a version of African-American dialect that owes much to the Uncle Remus tales: "Yalla' bird, you stay outa dem oaks," he writes.[35] Pound used Irish dialect even more expansively while working on his translations of Japanese Noh plays. He was serving as Yeats's secretary at the time and hit on the idea of experimenting with Irish syntax and diction to render speech. That resulted in curious passages, as in the dialogue between the ghosts of the two lovers in *Nishikigi*. There the hero tells his lady, "Times out of mind am I here setting up this bright branch," and says to the priest, "They are names in love's list surely." Such sentences could drop seamlessly into the plays of John Synge or Lady Gregory, in which Pound was well versed. Pound himself recorded of *Nishikigi* that "Mr. Yeats tells me that he has found a similar legend in Arran" (p. 226). Less attractive was Pound's adaptation of Jewish speech. He combined that with the popular association of African Americans and Jews in jazz in his little-known "Yiddischer Charleston Band," which appeared in his disciple Louis Zukofsky's *An Objectivist Anthology* (1932), a collection dedicated to Pound himself. Performed in Black communities from the turn of the century onward, the Charleston jazz dance became popular in the 1920s after the song "The Charleston" by James P. Johnson appeared in the African-American musical *Runnin' Wild* in 1923, a successor to the breakthrough *Shuffle Along* of 1921. Pound's poem combined his distaste for Christianity with his dislike of Jews into a sexualized account of Jesus and Mary Magdalene that referred to Eliot's King Bolo along the way. The end of the stanza on Calvin Coolidge illustrates the use of dialect: "Vuddunt giff notding but his name vass lent / For deh yidtischer Charleston pband."[36] In one way the lines clearly offend; in another they extend Pound's efforts to break standard patterns of meter and diction in his search to make them new. Either way they display the mixing of groups and levels characteristic not only of melting pots and popular cultures but of modernism in general.

Cultural Institutions: The Music and Publishing Industries

That mixing reveals itself further in the institutions that brought such cultural products into physical existence. Jazz, popular song, theater, film, and literature all required networks to produce and distribute them (as they still do today). Music, for example, needed a range that included live performance, publication of sheet music (even more popular a century ago than now), recording, and distribution. Plays and film both required original stagings followed by either regional licensing and road companies or cinematic reels (or, now, digital files) for national dispersal in theaters across the country. And books required editing, designing, printing, and distribution to bookstores. In that vein I want to look briefly at a smash musical hit of 1903, "Bedelia," before devoting the remainder of this chapter to the book publishing industry as another instance of cultural distribution. Both the song and the industry exemplify the way in which both the production and distribution of culture displays an intergroup hybridity that matches the mixing represented in the works themselves.

The same Irish-Jewish team of William Jerome and Jean Schwartz who wrote "If It Wasn't for the Irish and the Jews" scored a major success in 1903 with their song "Bedelia." In those days tunes gained national distribution and popularity not through radio or recordings, both of which had been invented only recently, but primarily by sheet music. The cover of the sheet music for "Bedelia" repays careful study (Figure 14). It labels that tune a "novelty song" (like other ethnic tunes), though it was a popular hit that sold over a million copies. The subtitle combines two of our groups in calling it "The Irish Coon Song Serenade." The terminology so offensive to our ears should not mislead us into hasty blanket condemnation. "Coon songs" won enormous popularity for thirty years beginning in the 1880s. Scholar Russell Sanjek explains in his authoritative *American Popular Music and Its Business* that "any song in black dialect was labeled a 'coon song,' as was any involving black persons."[37] The spectrum ran from the frankly offensive to neutral and even positive. Many African-American composers of the day wrote such tunes, including Ernest Hogan, Sam Lucas, Bob Cole, and Bert Williams. Even Hogan's famous "All Coons Look Alike to Me" turns out more complicated than its title might suggest, for Hogan put that title line not into the mouth of a bigoted White person but of a Black woman jilting

Figure 14. Cover of "Bedelia" sheet music, by William Jerome and Jean Schwartz, 1903.

her lover in favor of another African-American man. The lyrics to "Bedelia" in fact have nothing to do with Blacks but rather depict a purely Irish love story in which the male proclaims, "I'll be your Chauncey Olcott if you'll be my Molly O" (Olcott was a famous Irish-American entertainer of the day). The subtitle then may try simply to cash in on a current musical craze, but it does associate Irish and Blacks, just as the two authors William Jerome and Jean Schwartz combine Irish and Jewish in their own backgrounds. Further, the publisher was Shapiro, Remick, and Company, which had so recently succeeded Shapiro, Bernstein, and Company that an ad for the earlier Tin Pan Alley firm graces the entire inside cover. Led by M. Witmark and Company, such new Jewish firms increasingly dominated the distribution of popular music, particularly that involving different ethnic groups. The Shapiro, Bernstein ad alone included among other ethnic titles the Irish "Shule, Shule, Shule Aroon" and "Mister Dooley"; the Asian "My Little Japaneesee" and "On a Chinese Honeymoon"; and the Black "When Sousa Comes to Coontown" and "My Pretty Zulu Lou."[38]

The rise of new book publishers matched that of new music ones both in the creation of new networks and in promoting work by different ethnic groups. Before 1900 American publishing centered on the Northeast, with family firms like Houghton Mifflin and Little, Brown in Boston holding sway. After 1890 and especially with the outbreak of World War I, the publishing industry's center of gravity shifted from Boston to New York. Even so, old-line WASP houses continued to dominate and to publish primarily White, Anglo-Saxon authors. Literature by emerging groups including Blacks, Jews, and Irish, like that of Anglo-Saxon but avant-garde modernists or recent Europeans, had to seek out newer, more marginal firms to reach a market at all. That marginality often evades commentators today, because so many once upstart new houses have turned into bastions of today's publishing world—Alfred A. Knopf, Viking, and Simon and Schuster among them. The management of most such houses matched their innovative nature: they were staffed largely by Jews who had bumped up against glass ceilings in the traditional houses. Publishing historian Charles A. Madison observes that at the time "gentlemen publishers . . . would not employ a Jew and made little or no effort to seek out Jewish writers."[39] Alfred Harcourt of Harcourt, Brace—one of the few Gentile publishers to promote ethnic literature, especially African American—captured the situation well in a retrospective look from a 1937 lecture. Citing the "flood of European immigrants" to the United States beginning in the late nineteenth century, Harcourt observed acutely that "While Boston publishers were bringing out sets of Longfellow and Emerson in new bindings, new publishers sprang up in New York, notably Huebsch, Knopf, and Liveright, who began to publish translations of contemporary foreign authors and books by young American authors who had broken away from the Victorian point of view."[40] If they were not Irish, Black, or Jewish, those "young American authors" usually belonged to the avant-garde. Understanding their publishing context creates new angles to see the literature of different groups as sharing in the larger modernist enterprise and, conversely, displays modernism as a more varied venture than earlier views often suggest.

B. W. Huebsch, the son of a rabbi, could legitimately claim to be first of the new publishers, beginning in the first decade of the twentieth century rather than the second or third as did the others. His small firm published an extraordinary number of valuable books, including work by European authors like Maxim Gorki's *The Spy,* Eduard Bernstein's *Evolutionary Socialism,* Gerhardt Hauptmann's *The Weavers,* August Rodin's *Venus,* and further afield Mahatma Gandhi's *Young India.* Part of the Irish-inflected group that met at Petitpas's restaurant in New York and featured John Butler Yeats (the poet's father) and Mary and Padraic Colum, Huebsch scored his greatest coup in becoming James Joyce's American publisher for his early works. That included the first American edition of the *Dubliners* stories as well as the first edition anywhere of *Portrait of the Artist as a Young Man,* both in 1916. He also published modernists like Sherwood Anderson and D. H. Lawrence. No wonder that his contemporary Christopher Morley puckishly observed in the *Saturday Review* that "It used to be waggishly said that any Irish, Hindu, or German artist could find a home in Mr. Huebsch's list when no other publisher would take a chance on him." Huebsch saw such international cross-fertilization in very positive terms. Correlating a rise in European books with American imprints like his own to the wave of new immigration, he praised the "interchange of literatures and of the cultures they represent" in a way that anticipates conclusions of hybridity theorists of our own day, like Cornel West and Anthony Appiah. "The land that depends solely on indigenous writing has no standing in the larger world of culture; the great books all come from lands that have ever drawn on foreign sources," he wrote. "Every language owes a debt to every other."[41] For Huebsch, payment of the debt to hybridity involved featuring rather than concealing his own Jewishness. Huebsch adopted as his press mark the seven-branched Jewish candelabra known like the nine-branched one of Hanukkah as a menorah and described in Exodus 31; it is featured on the frieze adorning the Arch of Titus in Rome that commemorates destruction of the Jewish kingdom and temple in Jerusalem in 70 A.D. In a gesture that surely would have pleased the philo-Semitic Joyce, Huebsch used it on the title pages of works like Joyce's own *Exiles* when he published it in 1918 (Figure 15).

Huebsch did not publish much work by African-American authors through his own firm, but that changed when he joined the newly founded Viking Press in 1925 as vice president, bringing his backlist with him. Unlike Huebsch but like most of their contemporaries, Viking's founders Harold Guinzburg and George Oppenheimer enjoyed college educations, Guinzberg at Harvard and Oppenheimer at Williams. In their very first year, Viking brought out James Weldon and Rosamond Johnson's *The Book of American Negro Spirituals* with splashy fanfare and followed it up the next year with *The Second Book of Negro Spirituals,* followed in turn by James Weldon's *God's Trombones* and autobiographical *Along This Way.* Viking published other high-profile African-American books as well, including Richard Wright's *Twelve Million Black Voices* in the 1930s and W. E. B. Du Bois's *The World and Africa* in the 1940s. Viking's Irish authors included James Joyce (whom Huebsch brought with him upon joining) and Sean O'Faolain; their Jewish ones featured Muriel Rukeyser, Dorothy Parker, and Lillian Hellman; and their other modernists numbered Lawrence and Anderson from Huebsch's list along with John Steinbeck and the muckraking Upton Sinclair. Foreign additions included Franz Werfel and Stefan Zweig.

The pattern of publishing African-American, Irish, and Jewish authors along with translations of foreign ones started by Huebsch at his own press and then Viking continued in the influential house of Alfred A. Knopf, operated by Knopf together with his wife, Blanche, from 1915 onward. Knopf began chiefly with foreign authors, including the Russians Gogol and Turgenev. He also published the Irish Liam O'Flaherty's novel of betrayal during "The Troubles," *The Informer,* along with modernist volumes like T. S. Eliot's *Poems* and *The Sacred Wood* (both 1920), Ezra Pound's *Lustra* and

EXILES

A PLAY IN THREE ACTS

BY

JAMES JOYCE

NEW YORK

B. W. HUEBSCH

MCMXVIII

Figure 15. Title page of James Joyce's *Exiles*, published by B. W. Huebsch, 1918. (Courtesy, University of Michigan Library.)

Pavannes and Divisions, all the major poetry of Wallace Stevens from *Harmonium* in 1923 onward, and several D. H. Lawrence books after Huebsch migrated to Viking. Knopf's Jewish titles included the first two plays of Lillian Hellman and Siegfried Sassoon's *Prehistoric Burials.* Those works all create interesting contexts for reading the major African-American books that Knopf promoted, including both of Nella Larsen's novels, *Quicksand* and *Passing,* and particularly Langston Hughes's poetry from *The Weary Blues* in 1926 onward and important prose volumes like his autobiographical *The Big Sea.* The Knopfs did not shy away from controversy: they issued both Walter White's *The Fire and the Flint* about the Atlanta riots, which other houses had rejected because of subject, and Carl Van Vechten's *Nigger Heaven,* touchy because of its title and its White authorship. Publishers like the Knopfs did not operate in isolation, of course, but as part of a network of connections and acquaintances that sometimes blossomed into friendships. In his memoir *The Big Sea,* Langston Hughes has left a vivid portrait of attending a triple birthday party given by Van Vechten for himself, James Weldon Johnson, and Alfred A. Knopf Jr.:

> For several pleasant years, he gave an annual birthday party for James Weldon Johnson, Young Alfred A. Knopf, Jr. and himself, for their birthdays fell on the same day. At the last of these parties, the year before Mr. Johnson died, on the Van Vechten table there were three cakes, one red, one white, and one blue—the colors of our flag. They honored a Gentile, a Negro, and a Jew—friends and fellow-Americans. But the differences of race did not occur to me until days later, when I thought back about the three colors and the three men.
>
> Carl Van Vechten is like that party. He never talks grandiloquently about democracy or Americanism. Nor makes a fetish of those qualities. But he lives them with sincerity—and humor.
>
> Perhaps that is why *his* parties were reported in the Harlem press.[42]

Hughes might have said the same thing about his own publisher Alfred Knopf's list, which displayed similar democratic qualities allied to an aristocracy of merit wherever it surfaced. Knopf's Borzoi book imprint materialized that credo in the books themselves, providing the same high-quality craftsmanship to every book regardless of the race, creed, or color of its author. They set a new standard for the industry.

The strength of such networks extended even to the one Gentile house that published numerous Black titles, Harcourt, Brace, through its Jewish vice president Joel Spingarn, first Knopf's favorite professor at Columbia and later his friend. While teaching comparative literature at Columbia for twelve years before his dismissal in 1911, Spingarn also instructed Alfred Harcourt and Donald Brace. Harcourt and Brace both worked at Henry Holt & Co. until the restrictive policies there propelled them to resign and found their own firm, taking with them such upcoming authors of Harcourt's as Sinclair Lewis. They promptly recruited their former teacher Spingarn first as literary advisor and then as vice president and partner. By that time Spingarn had thrown himself into biracial social activism and become first cofounder and then chairman of the board of the NAACP, where he allied himself closely with W. E. B. Du Bois. He put his comparative literature background to use at Harcourt, Brace by directing their European Library series and drew on his civil rights experience by recruiting African-American writers. Under his guidance Harcourt, Brace promptly published Du Bois's prose *Dark Shadows* in 1920; Claude MacKay's first book of poems in the United States, *Harlem Shadows* (1922); and James Weldon Johnson's *Book of American Negro Poetry*, along with work by Arna Bontemps, Sterling Brown, and other African Americans. They also published Carl Sandburg's *The Chicago Race Riots, July 1919*, Louis Untermeyer's influential anthology *Modern American Poetry*, and Sinclair Lewis's *Main Street*, while the European Library featured work by the Frenchman Remy de Gourmont, the Italian Benedetto Croce, and the German Heinrich Mann. The book that made the firm's early reputation and finances, John Maynard Keynes's *Economic Consequences of the Peace*, opened important links to the Bloomsbury modernists in England, including E. M. Forster and Virginia Woolf, along with their sometime fellow traveler T. S. Eliot.

In 1917 the Harvard-educated Boni brothers came together with the flashy self-made product of the Jazz Age, Horace Liveright, to create Boni and Liveright, another upstart Jewish firm that would publish work by various ethnic groups along with modernist Anglophone and European writers of any ethnicity. For their first dozen titles they created the still extant and influential Modern Library series, featuring cheap reprints by Friedrich Nietzsche, Oscar Wilde, Fyodor Dostoevsky, and others at sixty cents a volume. They soon moved into more contemporary work as well, publishing the first books by the Black writers Jean Toomer (who disliked being termed a "Negro"), the West Indian Eric Walrond, and the novelist Jessie Fauset. Irish authors included Liam O'Flaherty, George Bernard Shaw, and W. B. Yeats, along with the Irish American Eugene O'Neill. Their Jewish writers numbered Dorothy Parker, Waldo Frank, Ben Hecht, and Mike Gold, reflecting a general left-liberal tilt. The firm even boasted perhaps the most distinguished assistant in New York publishing with the young Lillian Hellman. Other major modernist work included Hart Crane's *White Buildings* and *The Bridge;* William Faulkner's first two novels, *Soldier's Pay* and *Mosquitoes;* Ernest Hemingway's *In Our Time;* and several works by Ezra Pound and Theodore Dreiser. Liveright also secured Pound's services as translator by agreeing to one of the most unusual clauses in publishing history: "Mr. Liveright agrees not to demand Mr. Pound's signature on the translation of any work that Mr. Pound considers a disgrace to humanity or too imbecile to be borne." The Jewish character of the firm apparently did not trouble the increasingly anti-Semitic Pound, but it did bother William Faulkner, who apparently associated Jews with Blacks and was happy to switch to Harcourt, Brace after two books with Boni and Liveright. "I'm going to be published by white folks now," he told his great-aunt Alabama. "Harcourt Brace & Co. bought me from Liveright. Much nicer there."[43] The partnership of the Bonis and Liveright proved unstable: the brothers had operated a Greenwich Village bookshop that sponsored the avant-garde journal *The Glebe,* from whose sheets they issued the breakthrough verse anthology *Des Imagistes* in 1914, while the brash Liveright cut his teeth on Wall Street. By the mid-1920s the Bonis had left to found their own firm, A. and C. Boni, which published the signature anthology of the Harlem Renaissance, Alain Locke's *New Negro,* among other works. Another influential refugee from the firm was Bennett Cerf, who served as vice president for two years before leaving in 1925 to found Random House, buying the Modern Library series to take with him.

Four books published by Boni and Liveright and influential in different ways exemplify its ethnic range and create a new context for viewing cultural works often kept apart from one another (Figure 16). Earliest came *Irish Fairy and Folk Tales,* edited by W. B. Yeats and one of the first titles in the Modern Library series, as a close look at the publisher's device on the title page indicates. Originally published in London at the start of the Celtic Twilight movement, the volume helped to inject ideas of folkloric and

IRISH FAIRY and FOLK TALES

Edited By W · B · YEATS

BONI AND LIVERIGHT, INC.

PUBLISHERS   NEW YORK

OUR AMERICA

BY

WALDO FRANK

BONI AND LIVERIGHT
PUBLISHERS   NEW YORK

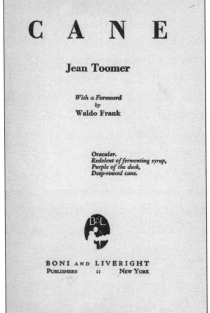

C A N E

Jean Toomer

With a Foreword
by
Waldo Frank

Oracular.
Redolent of fermenting syrup,
Purple of the dusk,
Deep-rooted cane.

BONI AND LIVERIGHT
PUBLISHERS   ::   NEW YORK

THE WASTE LAND

BY

T. S. ELIOT

" NAM Sibyllam quidem Cumis ego ipse oculis meis
vidi in ampulla pendere, et cum illi pueri dicerent:
Σίβυλλα τί θέλεις; respondebat illa: ἀποθανεῖν θέλω.'

NEW YORK
BONI AND LIVERIGHT

Figure 16. Title pages of four Boni and Liveright Editions, 1917–1923. (Yeats, Frank, and Eliot: Courtesy, University of Michigan Library; Toomer: General Research and Reference Division, Schomburg Center for Research in Black Culture, The New York Public Library, Astor, Lenox and Tilden Foundations.)

mythic structure and content into the Irish Renaissance and modernism in general. Its numerous subdivisions included separate groupings on fairies, ghosts, paradises, giants, and others. And its content offered access to a spiritual power in contrast to modern materialism. The Irish tales also carried a nationalist and ethnic edge, recovering or perhaps creating a neglected tradition, as books of stories by various ethnic groups or by women do in our own time. It was followed by the Jewish author and critic Waldo Frank's *Our America* (1919), which passionately argued for creation of a new historical and spiritual consciousness "in revolt against the academies and institutions which would whittle America down to a few stale realities current fifty years ago when our land in all but the political surface of its life was yet a colony of Britain."[44] Inclined more toward pluralist conceptions like those of Horace Kallen, Frank saw a welter of new cultures contributing to an American renaissance that ranged from indigenous Native Americans to immigrant Jews. He devoted an entire chapter to the latter group, arguing that they had fallen into the waste land of contemporary American materialism but showed signs of rising up again artistically and spiritually, and most of another chapter to Mexicans and Native Americans. Polyglot New York fascinated Frank, particularly its mix of European ethnic groups, including Jews and Celts.

Frank also admired the rise of an African-American culture in New York and took the manuscript of the first major novel of the Harlem Renaissance, Jean Toomer's *Cane,* to his own publisher, Horace Liveright. He not only persuaded Liveright to issue a contract but also telegraphed the news to Toomer and then championed the book in a foreword for the first edition. There he praised "the book's chaos of verse, tale, drama, its rhythmic rolling shift from lyricism to narrative" in a way that implicitly aligned it with other modernist work. *Cane,* too, deployed jumps between discrete units, mixed forms, a potpourri of elevated and everyday language, and a sense of mythic presences behind everyday occurrences. Those works throw an unexpected cross-light on the fourth example, that famous modernist poem *The Waste Land* (1922) by T. S. Eliot, who was previously published in America by Alfred Knopf and later by Harcourt, Brace. Its presence in the Boni and Liveright list recontextualizes it in terms of African-American, Jewish, and Irish modernist work and reveals its affinities with all three groupings. And Liveright's worry that the poem was too short for a separate book led to Eliot's composition of the famously erudite prose notes. Often seen as a pure product of WASP high culture, *The Waste Land* in the context of book history instead discloses its sometimes lost connections to other ethnic literatures and to popular cultures in general. Indeed, its very title page proclaims its debt to modern Jewish publishing even as Eliot himself deprecated that group. The poem's (and the manuscript's) invocations of Black and Irish culture match its material presence among Black and Irish works on the Boni and Liveright lists. Its polyglot nature and place of publication reinforce each other. In that way, the material form of *The Waste Land* reenacts its content. To see that, as with so much else in this chapter and book, we need to turn from current readings that often misread these works and look again at original contexts and their implications.

5

The Gathering Storm:
The 1930s and World War II

New Restrictions and New Righteousness

The glass ceilings experienced by Jews in American publishing during the 1910s and 1920s mark a shift from the old restrictions to a new wave of them in education, culture, and politics that would intensify as the twenties turned to the thirties and culminated in first the rise of Nazi Germany and then World War II. In the thirties the growing "blood-dimmed tide" of violence detected by W. B. Yeats as early as 1920 in his poem "The Second Coming" swelled and would result in the horrors of the war and the Holocaust. Together those would legitimate revulsion against earlier prejudices and make possible their eventual mitigation in the postwar period, but that lay in the future. During the period between the wars and during World War II, barriers of race and religion grew stronger, and under the pressure of Ireland's neutrality and its effect on many Irish Americans, the cooperation between the Irish and our other two groups diminished but did not die out. But the connections between Blacks and Jews if anything grew stronger, whether in confronting obstacles to higher education, nurturing groups like the NAACP, opposing the horrors of lynching, or publicizing parallels between the treatment of Jews in Nazi Germany and of African Americans in the Jim Crow South. These historical developments inform literary works as varied as Karl Shapiro's poem "University," renditions of the anti-lynching song "Strange Fruit" by Billie Holiday and others, the major Nazi exhibition *Entartete Kunst* (Degenerate Art), Zora Neale Hurston's novel *Moses, Man of the Mountain,* and Arthur Miller's play *Incident at Vichy.* They culminate in the concept of the "Righteous Gentile" codified in the legislation establishing the Israeli Holocaust museum Yad Vashem, which labels it a duty to recognize those non-Jews who helped Jews escape extermination by the Nazis. Only by refusing to demonize all Gentiles (from Latin *gens,* meaning nation or tribe) or people outside the group, however wronged, can we disrupt the ongoing perpetuation of grievance and exploitation that constitutes so much of history.

American Colleges and Universities

Ever fewer people today other than specialists or historians remember the effort to limit the presence of various ethnic groups, especially Jews, in American universities from the 1910s until the 1950s. Yet those years saw the creation of the apparatus for college admission that we now take for granted, including invention of admissions offices, detailed applications supplementing grades and test scores with essays, efforts at ethnic or racial classification, stress on "character," and even personal interviews, all of which became standard in an increasing panic to reduce the numbers of immigrant sons and daughters seeking admission to previously White, Anglo-Saxon, Protestant institutions. Such restrictions echoed European ones in modern times from the notorious Russian *numerus clausus* law of 1887 onward. That law limited the percentage of Jewish students to less than 10 percent in cities where Jews were allowed to live, 5 percent in other cities, and only 3 percent in Moscow itself. It was repealed by the revolution of 1917, just as other countries enacted formal or informal clauses of their own. For example, Hungary introduced a Numerus Clausus Act in 1920, Romania followed in 1926, and Germany in 1933 permitted only 1.5 percent Jewish enrollment. Anglophone countries preferred less formal limitations or quotas. In Britain Jews could attend the nonsectarian University College London (dubbed "that godless institution in Gower Street" by Matthew Arnold's father, Thomas) from its founding in 1828 but could not take degrees from Oxford or Cambridge until 1854 and 1856, respectively, and even then could not hold fellowships or share in university governance until passage of the Universities Tests Act in 1871, which also helped Roman Catholics. Even so, numbers remained small; by the 1890s only a dozen Jewish students attended Cambridge, and even fewer enrolled at Oxford.[1]

The growth of twentieth-century restrictions on Jewish enrollment in America coincided with sharp limitations on immigration, particularly of

Jews from Russia and Catholics from Southern Europe. In Britain and Ireland the harsh Aliens Act of 1906 had accomplished that, and further restrictions would appear in the 1930s. Turning from the melting pot ideal, the United States passed a series of such laws before the draconian limits of 1921 and 1924 succeeded in choking off most of the flow from both Russia and Southern Europe. The Immigration Act of 1921 limited immigration from any country to 3 percent of that country's population resident in the United States in 1910, and the 1924 act cut that quota from 3 to 2 percent and pushed back the source year from 1910 to 1890, with the result that combined annual immigration from Southern and Eastern Europe dwindled to just over 18,000, only 3 percent of its average prewar level. But that efficacy pertained only to fresh immigrants, not to those already here or their children. American universities responded by enacting their own restrictions on the already-arrived immigrants in parallel to the aims of the immigration acts themselves. Although Princeton had no Blacks and its rivals only a handful, the other two groups continued to climb. At Princeton, Catholics and Jews together made up only 5 percent of freshmen in 1900, at Yale just 15 percent in 1908, and at Harvard 18 percent the same year. By 1917 Jews alone constituted 9 percent of Yale and 20 percent of Harvard enrollments. Numbers of Jews would rise to 25 percent at Harvard before quotas in the 1920s reduced them to 15 percent, with parallel reductions in the smaller numbers at the other two schools. Not surprisingly, supporters of the academic restrictions also favored the national ones. For example, President A. Lawrence Lowell of Harvard, a major creator of codified limits on enrollment, became an early supporter and eventually vice president of the Immigration Restriction League, which had been founded in 1894 by Boston Brahmins to exclude "elements undesirable for citizenship or injurious to our national character." Other college presidents supporting the League included David Starr Jordan of Stanford, William DeWitt Hyde of Bowdoin, and William E. Thwing of Western Reserve. In contrast, Lowell's more liberal predecessor Charles Eliot argued for more generous enrollment policies at Harvard and became an outspoken foe of the Immigration Restriction League, working instead for its rival, the National Liberal Immigration League, to which Woodrow Wilson of Princeton also belonged.

We can get a sense of American developments through their most studied instances, admission to the "Big Three" (as they were called) of Harvard,

Yale, and Princeton in their efforts to exclude recent immigrant groups. As the sociologist Marcia Synnott concludes in her pioneering work *The Half-Opened Door,* after earlier efforts like discouragement, geographical diversity, and even acceptance of the top fraction of any high school failed to stop a growing influx as measured by academic achievement, the Big Three adopted more blatant strategies. "From the 1920s to the late 1940s, they imposed admissions quotas on Jews and, perhaps, on Catholics as well. (Concurrently, Princeton totally excluded blacks, while Harvard and Yale took only a handful each year)" (p. xviii). At the same time, the colleges categorized all three groups in line with early twentieth-century racial rhetoric, which classified Jews as a separate race. For example, Lowell of Harvard proposed to his Committee on Admissions procedures for rejecting applicants who belonged "to the Hebrew race," and Dean Wallace B. Donham worried about "racial antagonism" from admitting too many Jews; Yale president Arthur Twining Hadley passed over for a appointment to the committee for a new library one of the few Jewish professors because of "his race" and Director of Admissions Robert Nelson Corwin termed increasing Jewish enrollment a "racial problem"; and Princeton Director of Admission Radcliffe Heermance told a Harvard trustee seeking advice that the Princeton procedure "permits the racial moulding of the College pretty much as may be desired, and there is consequently no Jew question at Princeton." Such questions animated regional meetings of various administrative officers, as when Dean Randall of Brown proposed for discussion "limitation in the enrollment of Jews and Negroes" (Synnott, pp. 61, 89, 129, 154, and 16; Karabel, pp. 126). All three colleges excluded women, though they could enroll in Harvard's affiliated Radcliffe College, of which the first Jewish graduate was Gertrude Stein in 1898.

While the initial restrictions came at Columbia, which set up the nation's first substantial admissions office for that purpose in 1910, those at the Big Three received more attention and set national patterns, particularly the ones at Harvard under President A. Lawrence Lowell. His more tolerant predecessor, Eliot, still welcomed various groups, though he still believed in "racial" differences and thought it "not desirable that they more than the Irish or the Jews should lose their racial characteristics here." In contrast, Lowell argued for an outright percentage system for "any group of men who did not mingle indistinguishably with the general stream,—let us say Orientals, colored men, and perhaps . . . French Canadians. . . . This would apply to almost all, but not all, Jews" (Synnott, p. 21). Under Lowell the Harvard admissions office even developed a scheme to classify potential Jewish applicants as J1 (definitely Jewish), J2 (probably Jewish), and J3 (possibly Jewish). In contrast, Irish Catholics were the first minority group to enter Harvard in substantial numbers, with the first Irish Catholic elected a Fellow of the Harvard Corporation in 1920. "What we need is not to dominate the Irish but to absorb them," declared Lowell (p. 43). Fewer Blacks than Irish or Jews were allowed to acquire either the financial resources or the intellectual training to enter Harvard in large numbers; an illustrious early graduate was W. E. B. Du Bois, who took his BA in 1890 and his PhD in 1895. Lowell did not advocate discriminating against African Americans because so few met Harvard's standards anyway, but he did set up obstacles to their living in dormitories and limited the ability of Jews to do so as well. Ever Lowell's nemesis on such issues, the retired Eliot wrote to Professor Charles Grandgent, who chaired a committee on admissions methods, that he objected to assigning rooms "through a student committee . . . instructed to segregate Jews, and to some extent Irishmen, in certain dormitories" (p. 88). The few locations with heavy concentrations of Jewish students received mocking nicknames like "Little Jerusalem" and "Kike's Peak" from other undergraduates. Yet here as elsewhere Righteous Gentiles like Eliot and Boston's Irish Catholic mayor James Michael Curley spoke out against barriers in admission and residency. "These people seek to bar men because of an accident of birth," Curley announced at a Knights of Columbus banquet. "If the Jew is barred today, the Italian will be to-morrow . . . and at some future date the Irish" (p. 77).

Yale's restrictions were even tighter. Dean Frederick Jones displayed hysteria against both Jews and Blacks in writing to Director of Admissions Corwin in 1922: *"Too many Freshmen!* How many Jews among them? And are there any *Coons?* Pennypacker is here & much disturbed over the Jew Problem at Harvard. *Don't let any colored* transfers get *rooms* in College" (p. 142). Yet at an Association of New England Deans meeting later that year, he conceded that Jews at 10.2 percent of the college enrollment formed "not at present an *acute evil"* but fretted over continuing increases. Social restrictions reinforced the academic, more for Jews than for the few Blacks admitted in those years. The African-American football captain Levi Jackson even gained admission to the elite secret society Skull and Bones. "If my name had been reversed, I never would have made it," he observed (p. 135). Student pressure supported administrative discrimination. Mindful of the strict immigration laws of 1921 and 1924, an editorial in the *Yale Daily News* from 1926 urged that "Yale must institute an Ellis Island with immigration laws more prohibitive than those of the United States government" (p. 159). The undergraduates proposed establishment of a personnel bureau to study the character and background of applicants to the university. Although small numbers of Jews and Catholics began to appear on the faculty around 1900, Eugene Rostow wrote in his article "The Jew's Position" in 1931 that "the bald fact remains, in spite of all the official disclaimers, that there is not one Jew on the faculty of Yale college" (Karabel, p. 118).

The smallest of the Big Three, Princeton, least welcomed minorities and introduced a new variant into the restrictive repertoire. "I hope the Alumni will tip us off to any Hebrew candidates," wrote secretary of the university Varnum Lansing Collins in 1922. "As a matter of fact, however, our strongest barrier is our club system" (Synnott, p. 160). A strict hierarchy of eating and social clubs dominated the campus and discriminated blatantly against minorities, especially Jews. Princeton enrolled no Blacks at all during this period, and not until 1947 did an African American receive an undergraduate degree. When the famous muckraker Upton Sinclair visited Princeton for his book *The Goose-Step: A Study of American Education* (1923), he took note. "It is meant for gentlemen's sons, and no nonsense about it; no Negroes, few Jews or Catholics if they are known," he wrote. "The society clubs run, not merely the campus, but the faculty."[2] Ernest Hemingway, himself not overly fond of Jews, devoted the first two pages of *The Sun Also Rises* entirely to a sketch of his character Robert Cohn, who became middleweight boxing champion of Princeton to counteract the trauma he suffered as Jew there. "At the military school where he prepped for Princeton, and played a very good end on the football team, no one had made him race-conscious," observes Hemingway's narrator. "No one had ever made him feel he was a Jew, and hence any different from anybody else, until he went to Princeton." Yet Hemingway's Cohn fares better than the sole Jewish student in Scott Fitzgerald's portrait of Princeton in *This Side of Paradise*, who does not even have a name but does find his bed filled with lemon pie.

Barriers in colleges and universities provide the context for Karl Shapiro's poem "University," which sprang from his experience during a year at the University of Virginia in 1932–1933. Himself a third-generation American

Jew born in Baltimore, Shapiro scored early successes that led in 1947 to his becoming only the second Jew tenured at Johns Hopkins University before moving on to other appointments. His breaking of ethnic barriers in academia matched his breaking of them in poetry in English, still a field into which Jews rarely entered and in which they even more rarely succeeded. "Nobody in the *Oxford Book of English Verse* had been named Shapiro," he later recalled.[3] Very few at the University of Virginia were called that either. T. S. Eliot's Page-Barbour lectures there, delivered at the end of Shapiro's year and later published as *After Strange Gods: A Primer of Modern Heresy,* give some idea of the campus climate at the time. At the outset Eliot branded Jews an alien "race" and commended his audience for being "farther away from New York" and therefore "less invaded by foreign races." He went on to declare notoriously that "reasons of race and religion combine to make any large number of free-thinking Jews undesirable." No wonder that lacerated feelings pervade Shapiro's poem. Set at the beginning of a new academic year in September, "University" deliberately shocks with its blunt opening statement, "To hurt the Negro and avoid the Jew / Is the curriculum." The declaration makes clear that campus animus targets African Americans more hurtfully than it does Jews but does associate both groups with each other, just as admissions offices, social clubs, and even academic departments did. As the poem continues, the patina of Southern charm at the unnamed university renders it even worse than the "raw North." Shapiro catches, too, the importance of exclusive social organization to the system, punning on the word "club" as both weapon and social grouping: "Within the precincts of this world / Poise is a club." Alleged lack of the right kind of poise prevents Blacks and Jews from entering the club and itself becomes a kind of club to hit them with. Throughout Shapiro maintains tight control over the tone, in which deeply felt content exists within a frame of tight syllabic verse, with each of the five eight-line stanzas displaying the same varying syllabic pattern in which the shortest line is the last, giving it special emphasis. "Poise is a club" is the last line of the third stanza. Only at the very end does Shapiro's indignation escape restraint, as he denounces the school that "shows us, rotted and endowed, / Its senile pleasure."

The linkage of Blacks and Jews in Shapiro's poem reflects a long history of their joint struggle, aspects of which we have already noticed. Here solidarity in educational opportunity adds another. Yiddish newspapers arraigned

Harvard, Columbia, and Syracuse universities for discriminating against African Americans and chastised the United States Military Academy at West Point for the same reason. English-language Jewish periodicals followed suit, for example, over the expulsion of Roscoe Conklin Bruce from Harvard dormitories in 1923. Son of Mississippian Blanche Kelso Bruce, the second African American to serve in the U.S. Senate, Roscoe's case attracted widespread public attention. Periodicals like the *Jewish Tribune,* the *American Israelite,* and *American Jewish World* all denounced both Harvard and President A. Lawrence Lowell in particular. Similarly, Jewish journals protested denial of a scholarship at the Fontainebleau School of Fine Art to Black sculptor Augusta Savage because of her race.[4]

The NAACP

Jews and Blacks joined forces in the world outside of print in a variety of organizations and causes, most prominently the NAACP. There they opposed discrimination in education and politics along with the violence of lynching. The organization itself, which celebrated its centennial in 2009, grew out of response to the notorious Springfield, Illinois, riots and lynchings of August 1908 and their coverage by the Southern journalist William English Walling in articles and lectures including "The Race War in the North." The descendant of New England abolitionists Mary White Ovington heard Walling in a lecture denounce America's treatment of Negroes as worse than Russia's of Jews and convened a small meeting in her New York apartment attended by social worker Dr. Henry Moskowitz and Walling, out of which grew the famous "The Call," summoning a Lincoln Emancipation Conference and signed by sixty prominent leaders heavily represented by three groups: African Americans, including lynching opponents Ida Wells-Barnett and W. E. B. Du Bois; New England abolitionist sympathizers, including William Lloyd Garrison's grandson Oswald Garrison Villard; and Jewish activist leaders, like Rabbis Emil Hirsch of Chicago and Stephen S. Wise of New York. From the start the group proclaimed itself multiracial in both membership and issues, though of course focused on those affecting African Americans the most. Its most careful historian writes, "From the very beginning, the Association aligned itself with other oppressed minority groups. . . . The so-called Russian Resolution of the 1910 conference protested and condemned the expulsion of Jews from Kiev."[5] In 1913 the governing board reminded all branches that their inclusion in the organization required biracial membership. One of the most conspicuous Jewish recruits was the same Joel Spingarn who recruited African-American authors to Harcourt, Brace; he served first as member of the executive committee, then as chairman of the board, and from 1929 until his death in 1939 as president. Along the way he established and funded the Spingarn medal for "the highest and noblest achievement of an American Negro." The year after Spingarn died, his friend Du Bois dedicated *Dusk of Dawn: An Essay toward an Autobiography of a Race Concept* "To the memory of Joel Spingarn, scholar and knight."

In one of its longest-standing and most successful campaigns, the NAACP struggled against lynching through publicity, legal action, and mass protest, often in multiracial fashion. Indeed, the Springfield riots of 1908 sparked the founding of the organization. Early highlights included publicity in *The Crisis* from its first issue onward, formation of its Anti-Lynching Committee in 1916, the famous Silent Protest Parade in New York after the East St. Louis riots of 1917, and the *Thirty Years of Lynching* report in 1919, whose very first sentence invoked an ominous comparison to "recent outbreaks in Germany."

The Varied Victims of Lynchings

Although lynching itself eventually died out, its symbolism remains, as the recent outbreak of such incidents following the schoolyard display of nooses in Jena, Louisiana, shows. That act followed the beating of a White youth by a group of African Americans in 2006, with its subsequent trial in 2007, and spawned hundreds of copycat incidents across America. Yet hateful as such actions are, commentators erred in construing them exclusively in racial terms of Black versus White. Lynchings have targeted members of all races ever since the founding of the United States. The very term "lynching" goes back to Charles Lynch, a Virginia planter and justice of the peace. During the Revolution, he became famous for the swiftness with which he ordered Tories punished, often by fines or whipping and occasionally by hanging from a walnut tree outside his courtroom. All of his known victims were White. Indeed, most of the Americans lynched with nooses before the Civil

War were White and came from the Midwest, the West (especially California), and the South. Not until after the Civil War did lynching become a widespread means of oppressing the African-American population, especially in the former slave states, and was often led by the Ku Klux Klan.

Statistics on lynching are difficult to come by, especially before 1882 when the Tuskegee Institute began keeping records. The Tuskegee figures suggest that after that date, 3,400 African Americans were lynched by World War II, along with 1,300 Whites. But Blacks and Whites were not the only groups tyrannized by nooses. The most careful study so far, completed only three years ago, found that between 1848 and 1928 mobs lynched at least 597 Mexican Americans. Its authors explicitly called for "moving beyond the traditional limitations of the black/white paradigm." Agitation against Chinese Americans reached a peak during the years surrounding the Chinese Exclusion Act of 1882, especially in California and other western states. A particularly notorious lynching and riot erupted against Denver's "Hop Alley" Chinatown in 1880. Other lynchings aimed at groups now considered White but 100 years ago classified as separate races that also differed in religion from the American Protestant mainstream. Such feelings resulted in the infamous deaths of eleven Italians at the same time in New Orleans in 1891, one of the largest multiple lynchings in American history and one that featured the use of guns as well as nooses. When W. E. B. Du Bois began to edit *The Crisis,* the journal of the NAACP, he kept his readers well aware of such events. His very first issue contained notice of a lynching—of two Italians in Florida. The Italian government protested but the victims were found to be naturalized citizens of the United States, which led Du Bois to refer witheringly to "the inalienable right of every free American citizen to be lynched."[6] In the 1930s Du Bois hung a banner reading "A Man Was Lynched Yesterday" outside a window of the NAACP office every time a new report arrived.

One of the most notorious uses of the noose was that of the Jewish Leo Frank in Atlanta in 1915. Falsely accused of murdering his employee Mary Phagen, Frank (who managed a pencil factory) was kidnapped from his jail cell and hung from a tree in Mary Phagan's hometown of Marietta, Georgia. Ironically, the chief evidence against Frank was supplied by an African-American janitor who himself later was found to have committed the crime. The Frank case drew unusual public attention, including from the populist racist and anti-Semite senator Tom Watson and from the Ku Klux Klan. Watson inflamed crowds with his declaration that "The next Jew who does what Frank did is going to get exactly the same thing we give Negro rapists." The hullaballoo helped revive the then-languishing Klan and reinforced its triple intolerance toward African Americans, Jews, and Catholics, all of whom it lumped together. The roster of Whites, Blacks, Mexicans, Italians, and Jews does not exhaust those who suffered from the nooses of lynch mobs. A fuller listing would include Native Americans and anyone else perceived as "other." Irish violence against African Americans still attracts historical attention today, as in the 1863 Civil War draft riots in New York City. But the Irish often suffered from "racial" attacks too, both in the North and in the South. The "Chronological List of Persons Lynched" in the NAACP's own report includes among White victims such Irish names as Kelly (twice), Reilly, Connell, Sullivan, Clancy, Murphy, and Sweeny. The practice itself goes back to the first man lynched in America, John Billington. He was a White, Anglo-Saxon, Protestant Pilgrim who landed at Plymouth Rock and was hanged by an angry mob as the prime suspect in the murder of his neighbor John Newcomen. The recent spate of noose incidents should offend not just the African-American community (which has suffered the most from lynching) but everyone.

The best-known poem about lynching exemplifies its historically multiethnic nature. Made famous by Billie Holiday and then recorded by many others, "Strange Fruit" attacks lynching in its three searing stanzas on mutilated "black bodies" as the "strange fruit" hanging from Southern trees. Though sometimes misattributed to Holiday herself, both lyrics and music sprang from the pen of Abel Meeropol, who used the pseudonym Lewis Allen. A Jewish schoolteacher in New York who taught in the Bronx for twenty-seven years, Meeropol published the poem in the January 1937 issue of the *New York Teacher* and brought it to Holiday for her celebrated rendition at Café Society in Manhattan. Meeropol, a lifelong leftist, had first offered the poem to the Marxist *New Masses* and later adopted the orphaned sons of Ethel and Julius Rosenberg after their parents' conviction for spying. He later recalled, "I wrote 'Strange Fruit' because I hate lynching and I hate injustice and I hate the people who perpetuate it."[7] The scene of its rise to fame, Café Society blended the radical cabarets of Weimar Germany with the jazz clubs of Harlem to create the leading integrated nightclub in New

York City. Clientele included Nelson Rockefeller, Charlie Chaplin, Lauren Bacall, Lillian Hellman, Langston Hughes, Paul Robeson, Teddy Wilson, Sarah Vaughan, and on one occasion even Eleanor Roosevelt. Released as a recording by Commodore Records later in 1939, the song sold 50,000 copies by 1945 and rose to number sixteen on the charts. Left and liberal segments of the press praised it, but *Time* magazine branded it "a prime piece of musical propaganda for the NAACP." Though lynching had featured in fiction, theater, and art, "Strange Fruit" provided the most direct confrontation in song in English. Yiddish writers, of course, had also treated the subject, as in the poem "Lynching" from Berysh Vaynshteyn's "Negro Suite" in his 1936 volume *Brukhshtiker* (Junk), which also used the metaphor of fruit or blossoms for Black bodies dangling from trees.[8]

Klansmen and Nazis

The extreme violence of lynching helped provoke in the 1930s and 1940s the pervasive likening of Nazi oppressions in Germany to White supremacist ones in the American South. For example, it sparked the hundred-day American Crusade to End Lynching effort for a federal anti-lynching law (long sought by the NAACP) in 1946. Led by a committee chaired by Paul Robeson and including such diverse members as Albert Einstein and Lena Horne, the campaign kicked off on 22 September, the anniversary of Lincoln's Emancipation Proclamation, and Robeson led other leaders to a meeting with President Truman the next day, reported by both the mainstream and African-American press. According to the *New York Times*, Robeson urged federal legislation against lynching by asserting that it "seemed inept for the United States to take the lead in the Nuremberg trials and fall so far behind in respect to justice to Negroes in this country." The Black *Philadelphia Tribune* reported that Robeson "said it was hard to see the distinction between current lynchings and the Nuremberg war crimes trials," while in a contemporary speech over the Mutual Broadcasting System Robeson himself proclaimed that "this lynch terror . . . is not the special or exclusive concern of Negro Americans. The good Aryan who stood idly by when the German Jew was persecuted lived to learn that that was the beginning of the end of his own freedom."[9] The linkage sounds throughout the thought of Robeson and other Black leaders. A few years later, he again described the plight of

Southern African Americans as "parallel to the condition of another great people—the Jewish people of Nazi Germany," and recalled telling Truman that "the history of Nazi thought proved that they had learned much from the South." Robeson had spoken out vigorously during the 1930s themselves, telling the German-Jewish musician Hans Ernst Meier, chairman of a group of Jewish expatriates opposing Nazism, that "I as a Negro and all my fellow blacks are oppressed. . . . What Hitler is doing in Germany is the same thing—perpetuating racial hatred. We Negroes must join those who oppose racialist, warlike, and oppressive Nazism. You can always count on my help and solidarity." Robeson literally put his money where his mouth was, providing a generous and key donation to the journal *Germany Today: Inside Germany* launched by Meier's group. As he told Nathan Krems of the *Jewish Transcript* just after passage of the Nuremberg Laws in 1935, "the Negro and the Jew have the same problem."[10]

Other Black leaders struck the same dominant though not exclusive tone sounded by Robeson. For example, Langston Hughes contributed a wartime piece called "Nazi and Dixie Nordics" to the African-American *Chicago Defender* in which he likened Nazi treatment of the Jews to White Southern treatment of Blacks. "The Jewish people and the Negro people both know the meaning of Nordic supremacy," wrote Hughes. "We have both looked into the eyes of terror. Klansmen and Storm Troopers are brothers under the skin."[11] The facing cartoon, "Victory Garden Planting," showed muscular Black and White farmers collaborating to plant a seedling labeled "Better Race Relations," while the masthead carried Frederick Douglass's avowal that "I know of no rights of race superior to the rights of humanity." Comparing the Nazis to Klansmen became a recurrent trope in the Black press. Kelly Miller, the first African American admitted to Johns Hopkins University (in mathematics) and a prolific journalist who helped Du Bois on *The Crisis,* linked the two repeatedly. He entitled one of his first editorials on German anti-Semitism "Hitler—The German Ku Klux" and kept up his fire throughout the 1930s. In another piece he called Hitler "the master Ku Kluxer of Germany"; in still another he wrote, "From the way Hitler talks, one would think he is a member of the Ku Klux Klan and a native of Alabama"; and in still another he declared, "Germany is persecuting Jews, Catholics, and Negroes. Hitler is a European Ku Kluxer."[12] If African Americans connected Nazis to the Klan, they also connected Nazi laws to Jim Crow practices. An editorial in the *Afro-American* sported the title "Jim Crow for Jews

Now" and went on to compare segregation of Jews in Germany to that of Blacks in the United States. Similarly, the *Norfolk Journal* captioned an article "U.S. Swastikas Woven into Jim-Crow Institutions." And in New York City, the *Amsterdam News* captioned an editorial "Germans Adopt U.S. Jim Crow."[13] Jewish publications in both English and Yiddish had made similar comparisons, first to Russian conditions in the Pale of Settlement and later to German ones under the Nazis. Brooklyn's *Jewish Examiner,* for instance, called Southern segregation "fascism on the American domestic front" and urged Southerners to avoid contradiction in "fighting against the detestable Nazi doctrine of race superiority overseas while they fight for the right to keep it alive on these shores."[14]

Jewish-Black Animus and Alliance

Yet all was not sweetness and light between Blacks and Jews in the 1930s and during the war years. Sometimes bigotry flared on both sides, which responsible leaders sought to combat. In 1942 *Negro Quarterly* published as paired articles the Jewish scholar Louis Harap's "Anti-Negroism among Jews" and the African-American scholar L. D. Reddick's "Anti-Semitism among Negroes," both of which admitted the problem and tried to correct it. Harap quoted an editorial from the *Amsterdam Star-News* arguing that "Without reservation and camouflage Colored and Jewish Americans must unite. The wolves of intolerance are yapping savagely at the heels of both."[15] Correspondingly, the monthly *Jewish Survey* opened its columns to discussions of mutual problems by both groups. Reddick in particular pointed out that the *Survey* had pictured on its cover three recent American war heroes—Irish Colin Kelly, Jewish Meyer Levin, and African-American Doris Miller (Figure 17). Reverend Adam Powell opposed what he called "a rising tide of anti-Jewish feeling in Harlem" and urged that "we can't win any battle on the basis of hatred." Not all were so eager for cooperation, of course. The conservative Black author George Schuyler hesitated to express sympathy for German Jews, writing myopically in 1938 that "I would be able to wail a lot louder and deeper if American Jews would give more concrete evidence of being touched by the plight of Negroes." Worse yet were fringe groups like the Negro Industrial and Clerical Alliance led by Abdul Hamid with its slogan "Down with the Jews!" Close to the bottom of the scale lurked the scurrilous anti-Semitic sheet *Dynamite* in Chicago, which

JUNE, 1942 • 15c

The JEWISH SURVEY

CORP. MEYER LEVIN   CAPT. COLIN KELLY   MESSMAN DORIE MILLER

THE KLAN RIDES WITH HITLER by Frances Reich

TO OUR SOVIET BROTHERS by Dr. Nahum Goldman

MEYER LEVIN, BOMBARDIER

Figure 17. Cover of *Jewish Survey,* June 1942.

urged that "What America needs is a Hitler, and what the Chicago Black Belt needs is a purge of the exploiting Jew."[16]

Fortunately, saner and more influential voices denounced such hatred, as Du Bois did when he spoke out in the *Amsterdam News* in 1943, again tying the Nazi genocide to American lynching (though overestimating the number of Black victims):

> Of the seven and a half to eight million Jews, resident in Germany and her conquests at the beginning of this war, three million are already dead and the rest are being slowly exterminated by torture and starvation. We rightly shrieked to civilization when American Negroes were lynched and mobbed to death at the rate of 400 to 500 a year. Today in Europe and among peaceful Jews, they are killing that number each day . . . the present plight of the Jews is far worse than ours. Yet it springs from the same cause; and what is happening to Jews may happen to us in future. The United States and Great Britain could rescue from death and worse than death the three or four million surviving Jews. . . . They stand dumb, however, because many Americans and British hate Jews with the same reason and lack of reason that they hate Negroes, Indians, Chinese . . . inherited, unreasoned prejudice.

Du Bois's wrenching plea fell on deaf ears, of course, as the number of Holocaust victims climbed toward 6 million. But his exhortation reminds us not only of the congruencies between African Americans and Jews but also of the righteous people of good will who opposed all such bigotry among all groups. "Unless [race hatred] is destroyed, rooted out, absolutely suppressed, modern civilization is doomed," continued Du Bois.

Such fearful symmetries led to the "Double V" campaign among African Americans during World War II itself. Blacks had always had a complicated relationship to the American military, stretching back at least to the Revolutionary War, when Lord Dunmore's all-Black Ethiopian Regiment fought for the British with the motto "Liberty to Slaves" on the front of their uniforms. In the Civil War, the abolitionist White colonel Robert Gould Shaw famously commanded the all-Black 54th Massachusetts Volunteer Infantry and was buried in a mass grave with many of his men after the deadly battle of Charleston. But for the most part African Americans served in segregated units or else were often confined to more menial jobs as cooks and physical laborers in more integrated ones. World War II brought increased demands for equality in the armed forces. As war approached, the threat in 1941 by A. Phillip Randolph as head of the country's largest Black union and Walter White as president of the NAACP of a mass march on Washington in support of such integration resulted in President Roosevelt issuing Executive Order 8802, which established the Fair Employment Practices Commission and banned discrimination in the military and defense industries. In the event, the military then remained racially mixed but still segregated until the Truman administration after the war.

Organized initially by the important African-American newspaper, the *Pittsburgh Courier,* in 1942, the subsequent "Double V" campaign promoted victory against fascist tyranny abroad along with victory over racial injustice back home. The campaign's distinctive logo featured a double-V design with an American eagle and bright sun accompanying the slogans "Double Victory" and "Democracy at Home—Abroad" (Figure 18). Other Black newspapers quickly lent support, as did the NAACP and Urban League, among other groups fighting for social justice. So, too, did major White political figures like Eleanor Roosevelt, Wendell Willkie, Thomas E. Dewey, and several U.S. senators and representatives. One of the major patriotic drives of the war, the Double V movement included a panoply of bumper stickers, lapel buttons, and even beauty pageants, among other promotional devices. Above all, it sought to link the struggle for civil rights at home and triumph over oppression abroad in practical terms that matched the parallels invoked by writers, orators, and other leaders. African Americans remained especially sensitive, too, to Mussolini's brutal conquest of Ethiopia, the only free Black country in Africa at the time. "We have adopted the Double 'V' war cry—victory over . . . our enslavers at home and those abroad who will enslave us," trumpeted the *Courier.* "WE HAVE A STAKE IN THIS FIGHT . . . WE ARE AMERICANS TOO!"[17]

Nazi Fears of Racial Mixing

Linking the two campaigns proved easier because the Nazis themselves had done so. As Roi Ottley, the first African-American war correspondent for a major American newspaper, wrote shortly after the lynching of Emmett

Figure 18. Device for Double V campaign, from *Pittsburgh Courier,* 1942. (Courtesy, *Pittsburgh Courier* Archives.)

Till, "Few people nowadays remember that back in the 1930s Adolph Hitler sent a mission to the U.S. to study the South's treatment of Negroes, so that he could more efficiently terrorize the Jews."[18] The Nazi propaganda machine liked to twit the United States about its own racial policies even while it took them to new extremes. But first Jews had to be identified as a separate race like Blacks. The Nuremberg Laws of 1935 and their various sequels codified that status by defining a Jew as anyone with at least three Jewish grandparents (or, in the case of practicing Jews, two such grandparents) and creating two degrees of Mischlinge (mixed bloods) in line with such classifications elsewhere of other mixed-race individuals, like mulattoes. For the Nazis as for many Anglophone race theorists, the minority race, whether Jewish or Black, determined the corruption of mixed descendants. The same hysterical fear of mixture goaded Hitler himself to link Jews and Blacks repeatedly in *Mein Kampf* (1925). An often-cited passage connected the stereotype of the lustful Jew with the similar one for libidinous Blacks, especially the Black colonial troops who begat the Rhineland Negroes after World War I. Hitler saw the Black threat as part of a Jewish plot:

> With satanic joy in his face, the black-haired Jewish youth lurks in wait for the unsuspecting girl whom he defiles with his blood, thus stealing her from her people. With every means he tries to destroy the racial foundations of the people he has set out to subjugate. . . . It was and it is Jews who bring the Negroes into the Rhineland, always with the same secret thought and clear aim of ruining the hated white race by the necessarily resulting bastardization.[19]

The same point recurs fifty pages later in the denunciation of "a bastardized and niggerized world." If all this sounds like the theories of Madison Grant discussed in Chapter 1, where the mixed-race offspring always belonged to the "corrupting" race, it should. Hitler considered Grant's *The Passing of the Great Race* his "Bible." Not surprisingly, in 1937 the Nazis rounded up and sterilized hundreds of the mixed-race offspring sired by French colonial soldiers with German women in the Rhineland and of course later included the Mischlinge along with Jews in the Holocaust.

The revulsion at racial mixing in the world of politics and biology also spilled over into the realm of culture. A good place to see that is in the major

Entartete Kunst (Degenerate Art) exhibit organized by the Nazis in the late 1930s. Opening in the summer of 1937 in Munich, *Entartete Kunst* featured over 650 works of art, attracted 3 million visitors including the führer himself as it toured Germany and Austria over the next three years, and to this day exceeds in attendance all other exhibits of modern art. Soon to be banned in Germany, the artists included a dazzling galaxy of great names in modernist art to that point, including Max Beckmann, Marc Chagall, Max Ernst, George Grosz, Paul Klee, Oskar Kokoschka, Wassily Kandinsky, Franz Marc, Piet Mondrian, Emil Nolde, and Pablo Picasso. Much of the racialist theory behind the show derived from works like *Kunst und Rasse* (Art and Race) by Paul Schultze-Naumburg, who succeeded Walter Gropius as head of the Bauhaus after the dismissal of Gropius and his entire staff. The ideology of the project speaks clearly through the speech by Adolf Ziegler, president of the Reich Chamber of Visual Arts, at the opening of the exhibit. "All around us you see the monstrous offspring of insanity, impudence, ineptitude, and sheer degeneracy," declared Ziegler. "What this exhibition offers inspires horror and disgust in us all."[20]

Entartete Kunst did not limit itself to the fine arts but also surveyed music, film, radio, print media, theater, and literature. Music exemplifies the relation of each to my argument, especially in its handling of jazz. Chapter 4 explored the multiracial evolution of jazz, with African-American elements the most important but with significant contributions from Whites, particularly Jews. Black commentators like Alain Locke embraced that hybridity, seeing jazz as a "great interracial collaboration . . . a cosmopolitan affair . . . basically Negro, then, although fortunately, also human enough to be universal in appeal and expressiveness."[21] The Nazis stood the praise of hybridity on its head, damning jazz instead as another Jewish or Negro-Jewish plot to undermine the racial purity and political will of the German Reich. Richard Eichenauer's *Musik und Rasse* (Music and Race) provided a racialist ideological underpinning, following a line going back at least to Richard Wagner that saw non-German degenerate elements in music as Jewish opposites of German racial ones. The resultant hostility pervades the cover of the *Entartete Musik* division of the exhibit. It features a simianized caricature of a monkey-faced Black saxophonist wearing a tuxedo with a Star of David rather than carnation in the lapel. Invented by the nineteenth-century Belgian musician and instrument maker Adolphe Sax and praised in a famous

1842 article by the composer Hector Berlioz, the saxophone itself seemed to the Nazis a foreign import typifying the non-German corruption of Aryan music, particularly in view of its prominence in jazz. Further, this particular design itself is a distorted caricature of the first edition sheet music to Ernst Krenek's hit opera *Jonny spielt auf* ("Jonny Strikes up" or "Jonny Begins to Play"), an effort to blend jazz with classical music itself included in the *Entartete Musik* exhibit. Later banned by the Nazis, the opera premiered in Leipzig in 1927. The light allegory of its plot featured a despairing composer, an accomplished virtuoso, and an African-American jazz musician whose acquisition of an instrument of his own at the end suggests an infusion of new energy into an enervated tradition. The Nazis hated it, but the public loved it, attending 421 performances during the first season alone and even snapping up a brand of cigarette called "Jonny," still available in German-speaking countries today. Yet the Jewish star in the caricatured Jonny's lapel also points to the determination of the regime to see jazz as primarily a Jewish plot against the state. Such claims inspired mirth in the African-American press, as when the *Norfolk Journal and Guide* quoted such a German media report under the headline "Nazis 'Clear' Us of Jazz; Blame Jews."[22]

The campaign against jazz did not surface only in Germany. It turned up in the Irish Free State, which would become the Republic of Ireland after the war. But while Irish opponents of jazz used the same vocabulary of "degeneration" that marked Nazi campaigns, they meant by that primarily moral rather than racial or ethnic corruption. An alliance sprang up between the Catholic hierarchy on the one hand and nationalist groups like the Gaelic League on the other, aimed particularly at jazz dances in public halls as foreign innovations leading to sexual transgression. The *Irish Catholic Directory* branded jazz dances "importations from the vilest dens of London, Paris, and New York, direct and unmistakable incitements to evil thought and evil desires," and Reverend R. A. Devane entitled his 1931 tirade before the Criminal Law Amendment Committee "The Dance Hall, a Moral and National Menace." Popularly known as the Carrigan Committee after its chair, that panel issued a report lamenting that "degeneration in the standard of social conduct has taken place in recent years" and ascribing the decline to popular amusement, such as dance halls, moving picture houses, and—of all things—motor cars. "War against Jazz" screamed a headline on the front page of the newspaper the *Anglo-Celt* for 6 January 1934.[23] Eamon de Valera's Fianna Fail government finally yielded to the public pressure and passed the Public Dance Halls Act in 1935, which required a license for all public dancing. Such cultural repression had begun with institution of the Irish Free State itself in measures like the Censorship of Films Act of 1923. The narrow-minded nationalist Citizen who persecuted Leopold Bloom would have approved, though luminaries like W. B. Yeats did not.

The Emergency: Irish Neutrality in World War II

The partial congruence of Irish and German reactions against jazz betokened more ominous conditions that resulted in Ireland opting for neutrality during World War II, known as "The Emergency" in Ireland. Popular Catholic media began printing radically anti-Jewish articles in the 1930s, not least linking Jews with Bolshevism and the left. Diplomatically, figures like Charles Bewley, "Irish Minister Plenipotentiary and Envoy Extraordinary" in Berlin during the crucial years from 1933 to 1939, took a blatantly anti-Semitic and pro-Nazi line. He resisted issuing visas to Jews wishing to escape the Nazi terror, who in any case were not welcome to enter Ireland in significant numbers. As S. A. Roche, secretary of Ireland's Department of Justice, explained retrospectively in 1946, "Our practice has been to discourage any substantial increase in the Jewish population."[24] Despite pleas from influential Jewish Irishmen and friends of de Valera, like Robert Briscoe and Chief Rabbi Chaim Herzog, immigration may have failed to reach even the stated maximum of 500, less than 1/100th of 1 percent of the Jews who perished in the Holocaust (historian Dermot Keogh puts the number as low as sixty, which would have been 1/1000th of a percent). Meanwhile, Nazi Germany opened a radio service beamed at Ireland, first in Irish and then also in English, staffed in part by celebrated Irish émigrés, such as the author Francis Stuart, who had married Maud Gonne's daughter Iseult. Pleas from both Churchill and Roosevelt to enter the war on the Allies' side fell on deaf and even sanctimonious ears as Ireland claimed a moral superiority in remaining neutral, despite gestures like sending Dublin fire brigades to help combat fires from German bombing of Northern Ireland (which remained staunchly British) and large numbers of Irishmen serving in the British army. An Irishman who fought fascism abroad during the Spanish Civil War, Bob Doyle, recorded of his comrades that "We were Jews,

Communists, and people of various political persuasions" and noted particularly that strong backing in Dublin came from "the Jewish sections in the South Circular Road."[25] Yet Ireland also had its own homegrown fascist movement in the Blue Shirts, and on 3 January 1941 extremists bombed the main Jewish synagogue on the South Circular Road. Perhaps the nadir of this sorry chapter in Irish history came with de Valera's visit to offer condolences to the German ambassador on the death of Hitler. Even after the end of the war, Ireland was slow to recognize and deplore the scale of German atrocity.

During the war and immediately afterward many Irish voices excused Ireland's aloofness from the conflict on grounds of ignorance stemming partly from national censorship, but more recent ones have spoken louder and more clearly about shortcomings during the period, whether in fiction, drama, or poetry. In her novel *Unholy Ghosts* Ita Daly attacks even the term "Emergency" as a euphemism masking reality. As the independent schoolteacher Mona explains to her protégé Belle, "I'd have said myself that an emergency is when you run out of drink on Christmas Day. Or when you've a burst mains and you can't find a plumber. Somehow when six million people are being slaughtered you'd think that there would be a more appropriate word for it than the Emergency."[26] Martin McGuinness's play *Dolly West's Kitchen* (1919) indicts with particular bitterness Ireland's refugee policy in this exchange between Rima and Alec:

> *Rima.* And the Jews? . . . We did nothing to save them.
> *Alec.* Ireland's a neutral country.
> *Rima.* Do you believe that?
> *Alec.* No.

In poetry Thomas McCarthy's "The Dying Synagogue at South Terrace" (1989) testifies to the same moral failure, crying "David forgive us—/we who didn't believe the newsreels,/preferring hatred of England to love of you." Critic Elizabeth Cullingford points out that Louis MacNeice scathingly castigates the Irish refusal to let Allied ships use its ports for refuge and refueling when he rewrites Yeats's lines about "Mackerel-crowded seas" in addressing "the neutral island": "While to the west off your own shores the mackerel/Are fat—on the flesh of your kin."

Recovering Lost Connections

Yet even as earlier and stronger linkages of Irish and Jews yielded to separate and more isolated identities during the 1930s, some voices strove to keep the old alliances alive and to recast them in contemporary form. Those voices sounded strongly in the more open journal the *Bell,* founded by the writer Sean O'Faolain in 1940 shortly after the start of the war. As O'Faolain proclaimed at the end of his first editorial, "Whoever you are, then, O reader, Gentile or Jew, Protestant or Catholic, priest or layman, Big House or Small House—the *Bell* is yours."[27] The *Bell* kept that inclusive credo alive throughout the war and afterward, in defiance of an Irish turn inward. Its first two issues after the lifting of the censorship at the end of the war showed that in particular. The June 1945 issue featured on its title page A. J. Leventhal's article "What It Means to Be a Jew" and broached a subject normally kept under wraps during the Emergency. Friend of James Joyce and assistant to Samuel Beckett, Leventhal taught at Trinity College Dublin and participated actively in Jewish affairs in both Ireland and Palestine. An editorial headnote stated, "We must blame the Censor for the delay in publishing the following article. . . . Readers will understand that the Censorship did not allow us to mention that it even existed." Mixing autobiography and essay, the article reflected the language of the period using the Irish term "Jewman," which John Synge had inserted into a speech of Pegeen Mike in *Playboy of the Western World* ("till I'd marry a Jew-man with ten kegs of gold"). The article touches on many of the themes of this book— discrimination of groups as "racial" that we now do not think of that way, the rise of nationalist movements like Zionism, Michael Davitt's reports on the Kishineff pogrom, and the reflection of such issues in the arts. He concluded with two Whitman-like catalogues of what "does it mean to be a Jew?"—one negative and the other positive. Negatives included accusations of group guilt, of being either a financier or a Communist, of making excessive profits, of trying to take over the world, and of being a parasite on society. Against that Leventhal invoked adherence to monotheism and a great heritage, a preference for ploughshares over swords, and loyalty to one's country yet firm "resistance to tyranny and injustice." It seems incongruous now that such an article should have been silenced by government censorship until the end of the war.

The very next issue of the *Bell* turned attention to Jewish-Irish tensions across the water in its feature article "Irish versus Jew in America," by Harry Craig, then assistant editor of the magazine and later a journalist, author, and screenwriter. Focusing particularly on Boston, Craig noticed that the wave of Jewish emigrants came to the United States "as the Irish had come" and lamented that just as Yankees had rioted against the Irish, so now the Irish were attacking the Jews. He called attention to their common experience of exclusion and bigotry as in the signs "No Irish or Jews here" and their oppression along with African Americans by the Ku Klux Klan. In Craig's view, "the problem of the American Jews and the American Irish were intimately woven into each other—the K.K.K. made it so—and as such it should have led to some mutual sympathy and some understanding." He particularly lamented the rise of Michigan's Father Charles Coughlin, a right-wing American Catholic priest whose popular weekly radio program attracted as many as 10 million regular listeners. Coughlin supported first fascism and then, when war broke out, isolationism, and he fulminated against both Roosevelt and the Jews, sometimes conflating them as "Rosenfelt" and speaking with a Jewish accent. Meanwhile, his newspaper, *Social Justice,* repeatedly published the same anti-Semitic forgery, *Protocols of the Elders of Zion,* that Henry Ford had also embraced in his *Dearborn Independent.* In contrast, Craig invoked the names of Irish-American pilot Captain Colin Kelly and his Jewish-American bombardier Mayer Levin, whose Flying Fortress helped sink the Japanese battleship *Haruna* in 1941, as what Roosevelt's secretary of the interior, Harold Ickes, called "a living symbol of a unity" (see Figure 17). Craig closed with a ringing cry for interreligious cooperation by quoting the words of the Catholic philosopher Jacques Maritain: "It is certainly *possible* for Christians to be anti-semites, since one observes the phenomenon frequently enough. But it is possible for them only when they obey the spirit of the world rather than the spirit of Christianity."

The same spirit pervades another work of 1945, the American writer John Berryman's prize-winning early short story "The Imaginary Jew." Born in Oklahoma and coming to New York to study at Columbia during the era of Jewish restrictions in the 1930s, Berryman based the story on an incident that happened to him in Union Square, New York, in 1941 when a hostile Irishman mistook him for a Jew (Berryman was, in fact, Catholic, with one of his grandmothers an Irish Catholic from County Cork). John Crowe Ransom published the story in the *Kenyon Review*, where it won the Doubleday Doran first prize and subsequent translation into German by the refugee scholar Erich Kalhler. Set in the second summer of World War II, "The Imaginary Jew" chronicles the development of a young man who "tried not to think about Europe" to an identification with its victims, especially Jews. The narrator describes himself as born in a part of the South without Jews and not knowing any until college, when he irritates his Gentile teammates on the rowing team by befriending its Jewish members without at first realizing that they were Jewish. He comes to recognize the discrimination around him and that "certain Houses existed *only* for Jews, who were excluded from the rest."[28] Tellingly, Berryman sets that remark in 1933, the year that the Nazis came to power, and has the narrator recognize word of German persecution filtering into the country later.

Although the narrator describes himself as "spectacularly unable to identify Jews as Jews," he ironically ends up mistaken for one in a dispute with an older Irishman in the political wrangling of Union Square. Accused of being Jewish, he repeatedly denies it in the vain hope that "if *once* this evil for which we have not even a name could be exposed . . . it would fall to the ground." Unable to convince the Irishman, even though like Berryman the narrator himself is part Irish, he has no reply to the query "Are you cut?"— meaning is he circumcised. A few days later he realizes the point of the upsetting incident in a closing, humane vision of broad human identification: "My persecutors were right: I was a Jew. The imaginary Jew I was was as real as the imaginary Jew hunted down, on other nights and days, in a real Jew . . . the real and the imaginary blood flow down together." Through imagination the young narrator comes to realize a common element in all humanity and to identify with the persecuted of all groups, one of which enters the story briefly and the mind of its creator more pervasively—African Americans. The narrator briefly mentions that the language has no insulting term for liking Jews (like "kike-lover") parallel to the offensive "nigger-lover." Berryman himself, of course, famously identified with Blacks as well as with Jews. Responding to an interviewer's question about the influence of blues and minstrel songs on his *Dream Songs* sequence, Berryman immediately invoked "The Imaginary Jew" as parallel. "I wrote a story once called 'The Imaginary Jew,'" he said. "Well, the Negro business—the blackface—is related to that."

John Berryman was not the only writer who saw this relation during the 1930s and the war years. Zora Neale Hurston joined the many authors who detected links between the treatment of Jews in Nazi Germany and that of African Americans in the Jim Crow South. Born in the all-Black town of Eatonville, Florida, Hurston's checkered education brought her eventually to the attention of leading African-American intellectual Alain Locke at Howard University and then, at Columbia, to that of anthropologist Franz Boas, himself a German-Jewish immigrant and a leading opponent of racialist theory. Boas's theories of cultural relativism and anti-racism jibed with her own tendencies and gave them a formal framework. Papa Franz, as she called him, presided over her graduate studies in anthropology, encouraging and supporting her research into Southern Black folklore. He wrote a flattering preface for her resultant account, *Mules and Men* (1935), in which he praised "the great merit of Miss Hurston's work" and noted "the amalgamation of African and European tradition" in Negro life. Just as her Jewish mentor supported the cause of African Americans, so did his leading African-American student favor that of Jews, especially during the 1930s and World War II, which brought anti-Semitism to the forefront. More neglected today than in its own time, her 1939 novel *Moses, Man of the Mountain* provides the most extended and powerful linkage of the anti-Nazi cause abroad and anti-Jim Crow one at home in American fiction. She creates there a stunning triple analogy among the plight of the Israelites in ancient Egypt, Blacks in the slave and then Jim Crow South, and Jews in Nazi Germany.

Generally positive about Jews, Hurston did not wholly escape the pervasive prejudice of her time. For example, in a letter apropos of the Gentile Southern liberal Lillian Smith's best-selling novel *Strange Fruit* about miscegenation between an educated Black woman and a White man, Hurston veered into an attack on leftist agitation for reform. "The money is put up by Jews for the Negro to carry the ball for them," she wrote. But more often she took brave and clear-sighted stands against bigotry, both in print and in private letters. When fellow anthropologist Jane Belo complained in 1940 of family opposition to her marrying the Austrian-Jewish immigrant Frank Tannenbaum, a fellow social scientist at Columbia, Hurston quickly offered support. "So far as your family ganging up on you on the Jewish question, you can point with pride to Secretary of State Cordell Hull. His wife is a Jew from an old Virginia family," she wrote. "I opened a window in my soul and sent out my spirit to help you safely into Frank's arms." She stood up even more vehemently against anti-Semitism when it surfaced against Fred Irvine, the captain of a small boat she thought of chartering for a research trip. "One man who envies Fred in several ways came on board my boat and whispered to me that Fred is part English Jew," Hurston wrote to Carl Van Vechten. "I knew that the bastard had race prejudice that must include Negroes as well as Jews, so I booted his hips right off my boat." Her expressions of solidarity could include the positive as well as the negative. Near the end of her ironic wartime essay "The Pet Negro System," Hurston testified to the power of friendship and love to overcome barriers of separation, choosing examples from the early days of the NAACP. "So you see how this friendship business makes a sorry mess of all the rules made and provided James Weldon Johnson, the crusader for Negro rights, was bogged to his neck in white friends whom he loved and who loved him," she wrote in H. L. Mencken's *American Mercury.* "Dr. William E. Burkhardt DuBois [*sic*], the bitterest opponent of the white race that America has ever known, loved [Jewish] Joel Spingarn and was certainly loved in turn by him. The thing doesn't make sense. It just makes beauty."[29]

Just as James Joyce drew on J. F. Taylor's use of Moses and the Exodus to draw parallels between ancient Jews and modern Irish in *Ulysses,* so did Hurston turn to the biblical Jewish story to dramatize those between the Jews in Egypt and African Americans in the South, whether under slavery or under Jim Crow. These parallels begin in the opening chapter of *Moses, Man of the Mountain,* with its list of lashings for "working slow" or "sassing the bossman," and run right through to the cry of the Jewish people upon Pharaoh's capitulation. For that Hurston conscripts the same Negro spiritual that Martin Luther King Jr. used in his famous "I Have a Dream" speech: "Free at last! Free at last! Thank God Almighty I'm free at last!"[30] Her use of the Exodus story takes a distinguished place in other African-American adaptations, ranging from folk spirituals like "Go Down, Moses" to the distinguished cadences of Frederick Douglass, W. E. B. Du Bois, and others. But as she does with gender, Hurston gives the tale a distinctive twist by adding a third term to the evolving parallels—the condition of Jews in Nazi Germany. Because the modern reader may pass by those parallels,[31] I stress them here. They burst out in the two-page first chapter, whose first paragraph announces that "a ruler great in his newness and new in his greatness had arisen in Egypt." They continue through the fivefold penalties for Israel defying imperial authority and the proscription of male children, culminating in the revelation that "Hebrews were disarmed and prevented from becoming citizens of Egypt, they found out that they were aliens, and from one decree to the next they sank lower and lower" (p. 2). The parallels to the Nuremberg Laws and other edicts stripping Jews of citizenship, taking away other rights, and eventually promoting genocide come through clearly. Like Hitler, Pharaoh famously refuses to let the Jews go. Domestically, he maintains control by authoritarian means, as the insistent invocations of the Gestapo as Pharaoh's "secret police" suggest: "some place like that the secret police don't know about yet"; "Pharaoh's secret police don't never stop prowling"; and "that's to keep them secret police all fuddled up," for example (pp. 4, 8, 134). The racial laws at home go with a xenophobia on both domestic and foreign fronts. "Pharaoh was not interested in the ways of other peoples" but instead "was interested in winning wars at home and abroad" (p. 55).

Favoring hybridity and its open acknowledgement, Hurston had little use for Nazi doctrines of racial purity in her writings of this time. In her most famous novel, *Their Eyes Were Watching God* (1937), published only two years before *Moses,* the heroine Janie firmly rejects the social-climbing Mrs. Turner's suggestion that light-skinned mulattoes like herself and Janie should split off from darker Blacks. "Us can't *do* it," exclaims Janie. "We'se uh mingled people and all of us got black kinfolks as well as yaller kinfolks." Hurston advances such racial mixing as a general principle in her autobiographical *Dust Tracks on a Road* (1942), only three years after *Moses.* "It is a well-known fact that no matter where two sets of people come together, there are bound to be some in-betweens," she maintains in a paragraph that ends by invoking Adolf Hitler.[32] She mounts a more extended attack in *Moses,* beginning with her opening invocation of the Nuremberg Laws and running throughout the novel. She dramatizes her contention by continually alluding to the mixed blood of Moses and even of Pharaoh himself in ways that echo the persistent rumor that Hitler himself had a Jewish grandparent. After Jochobed tells Miriam that "we is kinfolks to the Pharaohs now," an elder points out, "There is plenty of Hebrew blood in that family already. That is why that Pharaoh wants to kill us all off. He is scared somebody will come along and tell him who his real folks are." Another elder responds, "the higher-ups who got Hebrew blood in 'em is always the ones to persecute us. . . . The grandmother of Pharaoh was a Hebrew woman" (pp. 33–34). The sustained assault on imputed Egyptian doctrines of racial purity and eugenics creates an extended parallel to the racialist theories that underpinned discrimination against African Americans in the United States and Jews in contemporary Germany.

Hurston's sympathy for the plight of European Jewry prompted her to contemplate an extended history of the Jews, which morphed into her unpublished book on Herod the Great. "I want to write the story of the 3000 years struggle of the Jewish *people* for democracy and the rights of man," she wrote in the letter to Van Vechten. "In the book I plan to set the struggle in Judea against like things in Greece, the Roman Empire, England, Europe and show that instead of the Jewish people being a peculiarly evil and hard-headed race of people, doomed by God to suffer and be hated, that they were just people, fighting for all those things which other people hold sacred and conducing to the rights and dignity of man. . . . They have fought the good fight longer than anyone else in the world" (pp. 529–531). The Herod project did not come to fruition during Hurston's lifetime, but she continued to argue for sympathy between African Americans and Jews and to link their causes. In her 1950 article "What White Publishers Won't Print," she creates the satiric American Museum of Unnatural History replete with stereotypical displays of different ethnic and racial types. Deploring publishers who "shy away from romantic stories about Negroes and Jews," Hurston sees such aversion as reinforcing notions of separation and apartness, and even of lack of humanity in minority groups. "Argue all you will about injustice, but as long as the majority cannot conceive of a Negro or a Jew feeling and reacting inside just as they do, the majority will keep right on believing" in fundamental differences between races as surely as Pharaoh led the Egyptians and Hitler the Germans to think that way about the Jews (*I Love Myself*, pp. 170–171).

Opposed to such literal and metaphoric ghettoizing stand notions of common humanity, as Leopold Bloom recognized in his famous response to the bigoted Citizen's query about his country and its ensuing invocation of love as the "opposite of hatred." Bloom's way leads to empathy and even identification with other groups, as Joyce himself displayed toward Jews and

Jewish issues. So, too, did the Jewish artist Isac Friedlander and the African-American artist Wilmer Angier Jennings. I regret that copyright restrictions prevent me from reproducing their reciprocal works; Friedlander's 1931 "Exodus" and Jennings's 1946 "Sanctuary" were first paired in a 1992 exhibition in New York at the Jewish Museum and reproduced in the resultant book, *Bridges and Boundaries*. Friedlander emigrated from his native Latvia, then part of the Russian Empire, to Canada and then New York City. Struck by the African-American life he encountered in Harlem, Friedlander in 1931 began a series of woodcuts including "Negro Revue," "Negro Head," and "Revival" that often stressed affinities with other groups. Anticipating Hurston's *Moses*, his "Exodus" depicts the going out of the Jews from Egypt in terms of Black slaves leaving bondage for freedom. Barefoot and with clearly African features, they trudge from darkness on the right to light and liberty on the left, carrying belongings and children with them. Correspondingly, the African-American painter and printmaker Wilmer Angier Jennings produced immediately after the war his linocut "Sanctuary." That work depicts light and dark faces seeking refuge in a manner that would befit both the Underground Railroad and the World War II underground that smuggled Jews from continental Europe; Jennings heightened the parallel by including himself and family members among the crowd. Both prints testify to an empathy for others going well beyond the barriers of one's own group. Significantly, both Friedlander and Jennings worked extensively for the Works Progress Administration during the Depression. As African-American artist Hughie Lee Smith recalled of interracial mingling during those years, "We artists got along . . . as human beings creating art. There were no black projects or white projects, and that was one of the good things about that whole period."[33]

Reaching beyond the limits of one's own group pervades Arthur Miller's sometimes-neglected minor masterpiece *Incident at Vichy*, as it does other works in this study. One of Miller's few overtly Jewish efforts, the play renders an oblique but increasingly horrifying look at the Holocaust through a provincial police station in Vichy France, where French and German authorities jointly sift through a group of ten prisoners (nine men and a boy) to determine which are Jewish. All three of our groups underwent a key catastrophe central to their identity in the modern era—for Irish the Famine of the 1840s, for African Americans the horrors of the Middle Passage to slavery in the Americas, and for Jews of course the genocide of 6 million of their brethren by the Nazis. As we have seen, each group not only mourned its own suffering but sympathized with the sorrow of others. Frederick Douglass, for example, sent back dispatches to the *Liberator* from Famine Ireland and thought the suffering there matched or even exceeded that of the Black South, while both Paul Robeson and Jean Toomer, among many others, responded to the suffering in the voices of Jewish cantors and Du Bois himself wrote movingly about the Holocaust. Correspondingly, Daniel O'Connell denounced the horrors of the slave trade, and although some Irish supported slavery, others joined him in vehemently opposing it. Sympathy for Blacks surfaces repeatedly, too, whether head-on in Harriet Beecher Stowe's hugely influential *Uncle Tom's Cabin* or more obliquely in James Joyce's *Ulysses*. Writers like F. Scott Fitzgerald in *The Great Gatsby* went out of their way to include African Americans in a plot that did not demand them, as did Israel Zangwill in *The Melting Pot*. So, too, does Miller in *Incident at Vichy*, where one character remarks that "every nation has condemned somebody because of his race, including the Americans and what they do to Negroes."[34]

Far from peripheral, the linkage between Jews and Blacks, among others, proved as central to Miller's conception of the play as Hurston's connection did to her novel. In his 1965 essay "Guilt and *Incident at Vichy*" Miller linked "the jumble of emotions surrounding the Negro in this country and the whole unsettled moral problem of the destruction of the Jews in Europe." He emphasized that the play "is not 'about Nazism' or a wartime horror tale . . . the underlying issue . . . has to do with our individual relationships with injustice and violence."[35] For Miller moral responsibility resided with the individual, not the group, and involved concern for others, including those from other races and ethnicities. Hence in the 1965 essay he praised the trio of slain civil rights workers Michael Schwerner, James Chaney, and Andrew Goodman, murdered the previous year in Mississippi, during the Freedom Summer of 1964. Miller saw them as transforming guilt into responsibility and so opening the way to a vision beyond remorse or helplessness. Significantly for our purposes, Chaney was an African American from Mississippi, while Schwerner and Goodman were White Jews from New York. By connecting his Holocaust drama to the struggle for Black civil rights, Miller mounts a sort of reverse Double V campaign that continues the connections forged by Langston Hughes and so many others in the 1930s and 1940s. Miller's strategy has come to seem common usage today: as with other terms like "ghetto" and "diaspora" that originally applied only to Jews, the word "Holocaust" itself now attracts a wide range of applications, some of them vigorously contested.

Whatever its wider implications, *Incident at Vichy* itself focuses on the Holocaust. Yet Miller carefully includes a Gypsy and a Gentile Austrian prince along with his detained Jews; in fact, the Gypsy attracts stereotyped disapproval from one of the other prisoners and the officials question him first. By keeping the Holocaust offstage, Miller intensifies its horror. The strategy derives from Greek drama, where appalling events like the blinding of Oedipus usually take place offstage. This hybrid work written in English by a second-generation Jewish American that even preserves the Aristotelian unities of time, place, and action in a play set in France about German and Polish mass murder thus enacts its own advocacy of connection even in its form. And besides including other groups, Miller deconstructs the notion of group homogeneity by representing a varying array of Jews—the bohemian painter Lebeau, socialist electrician Bayard, bourgeois businessman Marchand, actor Monceau, psychiatrist and underground member Leduc, and the anonymous Waiter, Boy, and Old Jew. Each strikes a pose as the truth of their situation breaks in—Lebeau frets, Bayard blusters, Marchand manipulates, Monceau postures, and Leduc veers between understanding and defiance, while among the nameless characters the Waiter frankly fears, the Boy worries about his mother, and the Old Jew silently endures. They move from denial through Bayard's description of the locked freight cars and Polish engineer in the railway yards to von Berg's disruptive query about whether they have been detained because they are Jews, and at last to the Waiter's report of furnaces in Poland. Along the way they studiously avoid Jewish identification with phrases like "some racial . . . implication" and the euphemism "Peruvian" for "Jewish." The term "Peruvian" often appeared in the slang of the time. The man of letters John Gross recalls in his memoir *A Double Thread: Growing Up English and Jewish in London* that "the nickname we used for them [immigrant Hassidim] was 'Peruvians.'"[36]

When Leduc observes that "Jews are not a race, you know. They can look like anybody" (p. 26), he evokes the social construction of racial categories and their changes over time that were noted in Chapters 1 and 3. Jews particularly trouble such constructions because their appearance varies so much and they can belong to any "race," as Zangwill among many others noted. Hence the obsession of the authority figures in *Incident at Vichy* about identifying Jews. The German major, the French police captain, and especially the German Professor Hoffman of the Race Institute ring the changes of such pseudoscientific efforts ranging from measuring noses and skulls to inspecting penises for circumcision. Such efforts derive from the racialist science of the nineteenth century developed in the wake of Darwin by Robert Knox, George Gliddon, and Josiah Nott, and particularly from the French doctor Paul Broca and his contributions to physical anthropology. Convinced that mental and cultural racial differences derived from physical factors, Broca devised over forty instruments for measuring parts of the human body, including calipers, pelvimeters, craniostats, and torsiometers. Such thinking led eventually to Francis Galton and the eugenics movement and eventually to the perverted eugenic laws of the Nazi regime, including the Law for the Prevention of Genetically Diseased Offspring and its consequent Genetic Health Courts. In the play, Miller's professor comes from the Race Institute, apparently based on the Kaiser Wilhelm Institute for Anthropology, Human Genetics, and Eugenics, established in Weimar Germany in 1927 for the study of *Rassenhygiene,* or racial hygiene.[37] Boasting that "my degree is in racial anthropology," he oversees the measuring of noses and inspection of penises to carry out the regime's "Racial Program" (pp. 41–42). The horrifying consequences of such thought in the Nazi regime led to widespread revulsion and discrediting among all but fringe elements after the war.

At the heart of such racialist thinking lies a mad quest for otherness than can affect victims as well as victimizers. "Part of knowing who we are is knowing we are not someone else," exclaims the doctor Leduc to the prince von Berg in their confrontation near the end of the play. "And Jew is only the name we give to that stranger, that agony we cannot feel, that death we look at like a cold abstraction. Each man has his Jew; it is the other. And the Jews have their Jews. And now, now above all, you must see that you have yours" (p. 66). Leduc's speech begins from the now widely accepted point about victimized groups as others but then proceeds to finer nuance than such thinking often entails. Obviously, Jews function as primary others in a play about the Holocaust. The play's insistence that "Jew is only the name we give to that stranger" enables the linkages that we have seen Miller making to other groups and situations, especially those of African Americans. Yet the passage goes a step further in arguing that even victims create others to themselves, in this case that "the Jews have their Jews." So, too, can the Irish have their Irish and the Blacks their Blacks, as the Citizen in Joyce's *Ulysses* or the anti-Semitism among some African Americans demonstrates. That is what both the Jewish Leduc and the Gentile prince come to learn.

But learning is not enough: justice demands action as well. That divide separates those like the German army major who despises Nazi policies and the Austrian prince who actively opposes them at the end. Despite misgivings, the major caves in to the demands of the professor from the Race Institute, particularly when threatened with consequences of refusing to carry out his assignment. In contrast, the prince moves from the opening naïveté revealed in his query to his fellow detainees about whether they are Jews to an increasingly complex understanding that results in his handing his pass to Leduc rather than using it for his own release at the end. "Take it! Go!" he whispers fiercely. In that act the prince not only risks his own life to save another but also faces his own complicity in not opposing the regime sooner. He becomes a fully realized human being. That is one reason why the prince has a name—von Berg—in contrast to the nameless major who can claim only the identity of his office. Lest we miss the importance of the contrast between the two men and their choices, Miller ends the play with the major and von Berg wordlessly confronting each other. "They stand there, forever incomprehensible to one another, looking into each other's eyes," says the stage direction. The play then ends with the silent entrance of a new group of four new prisoners, whose situation stands as synecdoche for the necessity of continual choice as history progresses. As Miller observed in an interview at the time of the play's first production, "The occasion of the play is the occupation of France but it's about today."[38]

Two figures who would have understood the play's call to action for groups other than one's own were the author and wit Dorothy Parker and the rabbi Joachim Prinz, both of whom behaved righteously toward groups other than their own. Born Dorothy Rothschild, Parker became a drama critic and writer for *Vogue, Vanity Fair,* and the *New Yorker* as well as a member of the celebrated Algonquin Round Table in the 1920s and eventually published volumes of short stories and poetry as well. She also became a fierce civil rights advocate and during the 1930s a supporter of leftist causes, including the Spanish Civil War and Anti-Nazi League. Dying three years after the premiere of *Incident at Vichy,* she left her entire estate to the Martin Luther King Jr. Foundation and, after King's death, the NAACP. That organization buried her remains in a memorial garden at its national headquarters, where a plaque reads in part: "Defender of human and civil rights. For her epitaph she suggested, 'Excuse my Dust.' This memorial garden is dedicated to her noble spirit which celebrated the oneness of humankind and to the bonds of everlasting friendship between Black and Jewish people. Dedicated by the National Association for the Advancement of Colored People." Joachim Prinz also understood the necessity for speech and action. Born in Germany, he became the youngest rabbi in Berlin before emigrating to the United States in 1937. He turned into not only a major American rabbi but also, mindful of his experiences in Germany, a leading figure in the civil rights movement, for which he marched and spoke on numerous occasions. As president of the American Jewish Congress, he helped plan the 1963 March on Washington with Bayard Rustin and others. There he spoke immediately after a stirring spiritual by folk singer Odetta and shortly before Martin Luther King delivered his "I Have a Dream" speech. "When I was the rabbi of the Jewish community in Berlin under the Hitler regime, I learned many things. The most important thing that I learned under those tragic circumstances was that bigotry and hatred are not the most urgent problem," he told the crowd. "The most urgent, the most disgraceful, the most shameful and the most tragic problem is silence."[39]

Righteous Gentiles

If Miller's Prince von Berg had lived in real life rather than in a fictional play, he might have earned recognition as one of the Righteous Gentiles, or Righteous among the Nations, honored at the Israeli Holocaust memorial Yad Vashem. Established in 1953, Yad Vashem takes its name from Isaiah 56.5: "And to them will I give in my house and within my walls a memorial and a name [a "yad vashem"] . . . that shall not be cut off." The end of the first paragraph of the "Martyrs and Heroes Remembrance Law" setting it up mandates recognition of the Righteous among the Nations (*Chasidei Umot HaOlam*), a term taken from Jewish tradition and redefined as non-Jews who risked their lives to save Jews during the Holocaust. The law makes such recognition a duty; Yad Vashem believes that "Israel has an ethical obligation to acknowledge, honor, and salute, on behalf of the Jewish people, those non-Jews who helped Jews in the hour of their greatest need, despite great risk to themselves," and that "They prove that one can and should oppose evil, that resistance is possible, not only as part of a group, but as an individual."[40] Recognition of Righteous Gentiles thus repudiates demonization of the other even in the darkest of times and instead insists upon recognition of the humanity and heroism displayed by those outside the group. As the medal awarded to the Righteous explains in words from the Talmud: "Whosoever preserves one life—it is as though he has preserved the entire world." By 2008 over 22,000 individuals had received such recognition by the commission established in 1963. They represent a variety of faiths, races, and ethnicities, ranging from Abdul Abdelwahhab who became in 2007 the first Arab to receive such recognition (for hiding several Jewish families on his estate in Tunisia) to the still-pending award for Monsignor Hugh O'Flaherty, an Irish Catholic official who served in the Vatican during World War II and himself saved thousands of Roman Jews from annihilation. Yad Vashem even erected a granite sculpture honoring the many unknown Righteous Gentiles of the time. It depicts one bystander covering his or her eyes while a second defiantly gazes at the evil and shelters a woman and baby (Figure 19). The fact that the sculptor, Shelomo Selinger, himself survived Holocaust camps intensifies the work's power.

But in a larger sense, we can think of any of the many men and women who served and saved groups other than their own as among the righteous with a small "r," whether they risked their lives or only their reputations. Frederick Douglass stood among them when he exposed the horrors of Famine Ireland for an American audience; Franz Boas stood among them when he led the twentieth-century fight against racialist science; nationalists like Edward Blyden, J. F. Taylor, and Theodor Herzl, who took heart from each other's struggles, stood among them; Israel Zangwill stood among them when he championed African Americans in *The Melting Pot* and *Old Newland*, as did George Eliot when she wrote *Daniel Deronda* and Harriet Beecher Stowe when she penned *Uncle Tom's Cabin*; Al Jolson stood among them when he defended the right of Eubie Blake and Noble Sisle to eat in public restaurants; Alfred Knopf, Horace Liveright, and the Boni brothers

Figure 19. Shelomo Selinger (sculptor, b. 1928), *The Unknown Righteous among the Nations*, 1987. (Collection of the Yad Vashem Art Museum, Jerusalem. Gift of Alexander Bronowski, Haifa.)

stood among them when they published books by our three groups; Joel Spingarn and W. E. B. Du Bois stood among them in their friendship and devotion working for the NAACP and other institutions; and James Joyce, Zora Neale Hurston, and Arthur Miller stood among them in creating common cause among Jews, Blacks, and Irish. This book is dedicated to my wife and children, but it is also dedicated to the righteous of whatever race, religion, or other group who stood bravely for the values it embraces. May their names be for a blessing.

NOTES

INDEX

Notes

Introduction

1. L. P. Hartley, *The Go-Between* (London: Hamish Hamilton, 1953), p. 9.

2. Benedict Anderson, *Imagined Communities*, rev. ed. (London: Verso, 1991)

3. *The Life and Writings of Frederick Douglass*, vol. 1, ed. Philip S. Foner (New York: International Publishers, 1950), pp. 139–141, reprinted from *The Liberator*, 27 March 1846, pp. 2–3.

4. *Narrative of the Life of Frederick Douglass, an American Slave* (New York: Viking Penguin, 1986), pp. 73, 83–84.

5. *The Norton Anthology of American Literature*, 5th ed. (New York: Norton, 1998), p. 2064.

6. Daniel O'Connell, *Daniel O'Connell upon American Slavery* (New York: American Anti-Slavery Society, 1860), p. 9; Frederick Douglass, *The Frederick Douglass Papers*, vol. 1, ed. John W. Blassingame (New Haven, Conn.: Yale University Press, 1979), p. 44.

7. W. E. B. Du Bois, "The Negro and the Warsaw Ghetto," in *The Oxford W. E. B. Du Bois Reader*, ed. Eric J. Sundquist (New York: Oxford University Press, 1996), p. 472.

8. Claude McKay, "How Black Sees Green and Red," in *The Passion of Claude McKay: Selected Poetry and Prose*, ed. Wayne Cooper (New York: Schocken Books, 1973), p. 59.

9. Frederick Douglass, *Life and Times of Frederick Douglass*, in *Autobiographies*, ed. Henry Louis Gates Jr. (New York: Library of America, 1996), p. 1000. The quotation comes from the expanded 1892 edition of *Life and Times*, the third version of his autobiography.

10. Elizabeth Butler Cullingford, *Ireland's Others: Gender and Ethnicity in Irish Literature and Popular Culture* (Notre Dame, Ind.: University of Notre Dame Press, in association with Field Day, 2001). I have also profited from Tracy Mishkin's comparison of the Irish and Harlem Renaissances in her book *The Harlem and Irish Renaissances: Language, Identity, and Representation* (Gainesville: University Press of Florida, 1998), and C. L. Innes's study of Irish-African interactions

in her book *The Devil's Own Mirror: The Irishman and the African in Modern Literature* (Washington, D.C.: Three Continents Press, 1990). See, too, my own article, "Afro-Celtic Connections," in *Literary Influence and African-American Writers,* ed. Tracy Mishkin (New York: Garland, 1996), pp. 171–188.

11. Eric J. Sundquist, *Strangers in the Land: Blacks, Jews, Post-Holocaust America* (Cambridge, Mass.: Harvard University Press, 2005). Hasia Diner's *In the Almost Promised Land: American Jews and Blacks, 1915–1935* (Baltimore: Johns Hopkins University Press, 1995) and Eric L. Goldstein's *The Price of Whiteness: Jews, Race, and American Identity* (Princeton, N.J.: Princeton University Press, 2006) have also proven repeatedly helpful.

12. Paul Gilroy, *The Black Atlantic: Modernity and Double Consciousness* (Cambridge, Mass.: Harvard University Press, 1993). For an interesting study of what might be called the "White Atlantic," see Robert Weisbuch, *Atlantic Double-Cross: American Literature and British Influence in the Age of Emerson* (Chicago: University of Chicago Press, 1986).

13. Cornel West, *Beyond Eurocentrism and Multiculturalism,* vol. 1: *Prophetic Thought in Postmodern Times* (Monroe, Me.: Common Courage Press, 1993), p. 4. For other works related to this approach and pertinent to this study, see, among others, Declan Kiberd, *Inventing Ireland: The Literature of the Modern Nation* (Cambridge, Mass.: Harvard University Press, 1966); Anthony Appiah, *In My Father's House: Africa in the Philosophy of Culture* (New York: Oxford University Press, 1992); Henry Louis Gates Jr., *The Signifying Monkey: A Theory of Afro-American Literary Criticism* (New York: Oxford University Press, 1988); and Ross Posnock, *Color and Culture: Black Writers and the Making of the Modern Intellectual* (Cambridge, Mass.: Harvard University Press, 1998).

14. Among whiteness scholars, the work of Michael Rogin, David Roediger, Noel Ignatiev, and Matthew Frye Jacobson has been particularly helpful to me. See especially Jacobson's *Whiteness of a Different Color: European Immigrants and the Alchemy of Race* (Cambridge, Mass.: Harvard University Press, 1998).

15. George M. Fredrickson, *Racism: A Short History* (Princeton, N.J.: Princeton University Press, 2002); David A. Hollinger, *Postethnic America: Beyond Multiculturalism,* rev. ed. (New York: Basic Books, 2005).

16. F. James Davis, *Who Is Black?* 10th anniversary ed. (University Park: Penn State University Press, 2001).

17. Matheus's piece received additional exposure when Alain Locke reprinted it in *The New Negro;* see p. 90 for the passage quoted.

18. H. S. Constable, *Ireland from One or Two Neglected Points of View* (London: Liberty Review Publishing Co., 1899). The quotation from Fitzgerald in the following paragraph comes from F. Scott Fitzgerald, *The Great Gatsby,* preface and notes by Matthew J. Bruccoli (New York: Scribner, 1995), p. 14.

19. *New York Amsterdam News,* 2 May 1928, p. 7, and 9 July 1930, p. 9.

20. See George Shepperson, "African Diaspora: Concept and Context," in *Global Dimensions of the African Diaspora,* ed. Joseph E. Harris (Washington, D.C.: Howard University Press, 1982), pp. 46–53; and Gilroy, *Black Atlantic,* pp. 205–216.

21. *The Oxford Companion to African American Literature,* ed. William Andrews, Frances Smith Foster, and Trudier Harris (New York: Oxford University Press, 1997), p. 90; Edward Blyden, *The Jewish Question* (Liverpool: Lionel Hart, 1898), p. 7; Theodor Herzl, *Old New Land,* trans. Lotta Levensohn (New York: Markus Wiener Publishing and The Herzl Press, 1987), p. 170.

22. Amos Elon, *Herzl* (New York: Holt, Rinehart, and Winston, 1975), p. 168; Douglas Hyde, "The Necessity for De-Anglicising Ireland," in *Irish Literature: A Reader,* ed. Maureen Murphy and James MacKillop (Syracuse, N.Y.: Syracuse University Press, 1987), pp. 146–147; R. Nathaniel Dett, ed., *Religious Folk-Songs of the Negro* (Hampton, Va.: Hampton Institute Press, 1927), p. xii; George Eliot, *Letters,* vol. 6, ed. Gordon S. Haight (New Haven, Conn.: Yale University Press, 1956), p. 438.

23. Israel Zangwill, *The Melting-Pot* (New York: Macmillan, 1932, rpt., Manchester, N.H.: Ayer, 1994), pp. 203–204.

24. Henry Pratt Fairchild, *The Melting Pot Mistake* (Boston: Little, Brown, 1926), p. 113; Lothrop Stoddard, *The Rising Tide of Color against White World Supremacy* (New York: Scribner, 1920), p. 165; Franz Boas, "The Great Melting Pot and Its Problem," *New York Times Book Review,* 6 February 1921, p. 3.

25. Melvin B. Tolson, *"Harlem Gallery" and Other Poems,* ed. Raymond Nelson (Charlottesville: University Press of Virginia, 1999), pp. 4, 217.

26. West, *Beyond Multiculturalism and Eurocentrism,* p. 4; Davis quoted in Peter Pettinger, *Bill Evans: How My Heart Sings* (New Haven, Conn.: Yale University Press, 1998), p. 63.

27. William Faulkner, *Selected Letters* (New York: Viking, 1978), p. 41; Louis Harup, *The Image of the Jew in American Literature* (Philadelphia: Jewish Publication Society, 1974), p. 495.

28. Marcia Graham Synnott, *The Half-Opened Door: Discrimination and Admissions at Harvard, Yale, and Princeton, 1900–1970* (Westport, Conn.: Greenwood Press, 1979), p. 142.

29. Langston Hughes, "Nazi and Dixie Nordics," *Chicago Defender,* 10 March 1945, p. 1; *Paul Robeson Speaks: Writings, Speeches, Interviews, 1918–1974* (New York: Citadel Press, 1998), p. 90.

30. Harry Craig, "Irish versus Jew in America," *The Bell* 10.4 (July 1945): 299.

31. Arthur Miller, *Incident at Vichy* (New York: Penguin, 1985), pp. 51, 66; Robert Hayden, *Collected Poems,* ed. Frederick Glaysher, introduction by Arnold Rampersad (New York: Liveright, 1996), p. 98.

1. Races

1. *Selected Letters of James Joyce,* ed. Richard Ellmann (London: Faber and Faber, 1975, rpt. 1992), p. 271.

2. James Joyce, *A Portrait of the Artist as a Young Man,* ed. Hans Walter Gabler (New York: Vintage, 1993), passim. (*Note:* throughout the text, further references to cited works will be made parenthetically by page number.) Vincent J. Cheng, *Joyce, Race, and Empire* (Cambridge: Cambridge University Press, 1995), p. 17, comments illuminatingly on the term in *Portrait.*

3. James Joyce, *Ulysses: The Corrected Text,* ed. Hans Walter Gabler et al. (New York: Random House, 1986), 12.1467, p. 273, and 17.403, p. 554.

4. Quoted in Dermot Keogh, *Jews in Twentieth-Century Ireland* (Cork: Cork University Press, 1998), pp. 7, 20. Of Davitt's many defenses of Irish Jews, Keogh here cites a letter to the *Freeman's Journal,* 13 July 1893.

5. William Rothenstein, *Since Fifty: Men and Memories, 1922–38,* 3 vols. (New York: Macmillan Company, 1940), 3:283.

6. Sidney Webb, *The Decline in the Birth Rate* (London: Fabian Society, March 1907), p. 17.

7. George Bernard Shaw, *John Bull's Other Island* (Harmondsworth: Penguin Books, 1984), p. 80.

8. Ralph Waldo Emerson, "Race," chapter 4 of *English Traits,* in *Essays and Lectures* (New York: Library of America, 1983), p. 792.

9. Both passages appear in Michael B. Oren's illuminating *Power, Faith, and Fantasy: America in the Middle East, 1776 to the Present* (New York: Norton, 2007), pp. 282–284.

10. *The World's Work* 6 (1903): 3612. I first came across this work in Eric L. Goldstein's helpful *The Price of Whiteness: Jews, Race, and American Identity* (Princeton, N.J.: Princeton University Press, 2006), which I have drawn on elsewhere in this study.

11. Booker T. Washington, *The Future of the American Negro* (Boston: Small Maynard & Company, 1900), p. 183.

12. Paul Robeson, "I Want to Be African," in *Paul Robeson Speaks,* ed. Philip S. Foner (New York: Brunner/Mazel, 1978), p. 90.

13. James Weldon Johnson, *Along This Way: The Autobiography of James Weldon Johnson* (New York: Viking, 1933), p. 136.

14. James Alan McPherson, "Indivisible Man," in *Conversations with Ralph Ellison,* ed. Maryemma Graham and Amritjit Singh (Jackson: University Press of Mississippi, 1995), p. 180. I first came across this remark in Eric Sundquist, *Strangers in the Land: Blacks, Jews, Post-Holocaust America* (Cambridge, Mass.: Harvard University Press, 2005), p. 96.

15. *Oxford English Dictionary,* 2nd ed. (1989, online edition updated 1996), accessed through the University of Michigan Library.

16. Raymond Williams, *Keywords: A Vocabulary of Culture and Society,* rev. ed. (New York: Oxford University Press, 1985), p. 250.

17. Ivan Hannaford, *Race: The History of an Idea in the West* (Baltimore: Johns Hopkins University Press, 1996), pp. 20–21; George M. Fredrickson, *Racism: A Short History* (Princeton, N.J.: Princeton University Press, 2002), p. 17. Fredrickson also sees the "conversos" or underground Jews of Spain as playing a key role in the development of postmedieval racism: see his chapter 1, esp. pp. 31–32, where he writes, "Closer to modern racism, arguably its first real anticipation, was the treatment of Jewish converts to Christianity in fifteenth- and sixteenth-century Spain."

18. Frank M. Snowden Jr., *Before Color Prejudice: The Ancient View of Blacks* (Cambridge, Mass.: Harvard University Press, 1983), p. 63. For the following quotation from the encyclopedia, see *Encylopedia Judaica,* 2nd ed., ed. Michael Berenbaum and Fred Skolnik (Detroit: Macmillan Reference, 2007), p. 45.

19. For two of the many good accounts of the rise of racialist science, see Thomas F. Gossett, *The History of Race in America* (New York: Oxford University Press, 1963, new ed. 1997), and John P. Jackson Jr. and Nadine M. Weidman, *Race, Racism, and Science: Social Impact and Interaction* (New Brunswick, N.J.: Rutgers University Press, 2006).

20. Robert Knox, *The Races of Men: A Philosophical Enquiry into the Influence of Race over the Destinies of Nations* (London: Henry Renshaw, 1862), p. v.

21. Kenneth R. H. Mackenzie, "The Life and Anthropological Labours of Dr. Nott of Mobile," *Journal of the Anthropological Society of London* 6 (1868): lxxx.

22. J. C. Nott, "The Mulatto a Hybrid," *American Journal of the Medical Sciences* 6 (1843): 252–256.

23. J. C. Nott and George R. Gliddon, *Types of Mankind: Or, Ethnological Researches,* 6th ed. (Philadelphia: Lippincott, Grambo; London: Trubner, 1854), pp. 111, 115, 122, 454.

24. John Beddoe, *The Races of Britain: A Contribution to the Anthropology of Western Europe* (London: Hutchinson, 1971), facsimile edition of 1885 ed. with introduction, pp. 5, 11.

25. William Z. Ripley, *The Races of Europe: A Sociological Study* (New York: D. Appleton, 1910), p. 400 for remark on Jews and p. 318 for map of "Relative Brunetness."

26. Katharine Morrison McClinton, *The Chromolithographs of Louis Prang* (New York: Clarkson N. Potter, distributed by Crown Publishers, 1973), p. 37.

27. *Journal des Débats,* as quoted in L. Perry Curtis, *Apes and Angels: The Irishman in Victorian Caricature,* rev. ed. (Washington, D.C.: Smithsonian Institution, 1997), p. 1.

28. *Charles Kingsley, His Letters and Memories of His Life,* ed. by his wife (London: Henry S. King, 1877), pp. ii, 107.

29. George Washington Williams, "A Report on the Proposed Congo Railway," in Joseph Conrad, *Heart of Darkness*, 3rd ed., ed. Robert Kimbrough (New York: Norton, 1988), p. 118.

30. T. S. Eliot, *After Strange Gods: A Primer of Modern Heresy* (New York: Harcourt, Brace, 1934), pp. 18, 20.

31. T. S. Eliot, *Ara Vos Prec* (London: Ovid Press, printed by John Rodker, 1920), pp. 16–17; reprinted in the United States with some changes as *Poems* (New York: Alfred A. Knopf, 1920). The two following quotations come from pp. 18 and 14, respectively. Eliot's scurrilous and long-unpublished King Bolo poems feature the African Bolo and his Bantu queen in comic conflict with the Italian Columbo but still manage to work in a rhyme on "Passover" and "assover" to connect Africans and Jews.

32. Henry James, *The American Scene* (Bloomington: Indiana University Press, 1968), pp. 123, 132–134.

33. Gossett, *Race,* p. 82.

34. Campbell Gibson and Kay Jung, "Historical Census Statistics on Population Totals by Race, 1790 to 1900," Working Paper Series No. 56 (Washington, D.C.: U.S. Census Bureau, Population Division), available at http://www.census.gov/population/www/documentation/twps0056.html (accessed 11 May 2010).

35. Melissa Nobles, *Shades of Citizenship: Race and the Census in Modern Politics* (Stanford, Calif.: Stanford University Press, 2000), pp. 1–3. See also her helpful charts on pp. 28 and 44.

36. "Guidance on Aggregation and Allocation of Multiple Race Responses," http://www.whitehouse.gov/omb/bulletins/b00-02.html (accessed 11 May 2010). Helpful books on the census, and on Statistical Directive No. 15, include David Hollinger, *Postethnic America: Beyond Multiculturalism* (New York: Basic Books, 2000); Melissa Nobles, *Shades of Citizenship: Race and the Census in Modern Politics* (Stanford, Calif.: Stanford University Press, 2000); and Margo J. Anderson and Stephen E. Fienberg, *Who Counts? The Politics of Census-Taking in Contemporary America* (New York: Russell Sage Foundation, 1999), esp. chapter 8.

37. Jennifer Lee and Frank D. Bean, "America's Changing Color Lines: Immigration, Race/Ethnicity, and Multiracial Identification," *Annual Review of Sociology* 30 (2004): 221–242, p. 228. For two excellent if more popular accounts, see Lawrence Wright, "One Drop of Blood," *The New Yorker,* 28 July 1994, pp. 46–55; and Tamar Jacoby, "An End to Counting by Race?" *Commentary,* June 2001, pp. 37–40.

38. The list appeared on the back of all ship passenger manifest forms. For a reproduction, see Marian L. Smith's helpful article "INS Administration of Racial Provisions in U.S. Immigration and Nationality Law since 1898," *Prologue: Quarterly of the National Archives and Records Administration* 34.1 (Spring 2002): 91–105, p. 93.

39. *Dictionary of Races and Peoples* (Washington, D.C.: Government Printing Office, 1911), p. 3.

40. Ibid., pp. 100–101. For an account of Jewish opposition to this category in the context of immigration and other racial debates of the time, see Eric L. Goldstein, *The Price of Whiteness: Jews, Race, and American Identity* (Princeton, N.J.: Princeton University Press, 2006), pp. 102–115.

41. F. James Davis, *Who Is Black? One Nation's Definition*, 10th anniversary ed. (University Park: Penn State University Press, 2001), p. 13.

42. Bryan Cheyette, *Constructions of "The Jew" in English Literature and Society: Racial Representations, 1875–1945* (New York: Cambridge University Press, 1993, rpt. 1995), pp. 8, 12.

43. Arthur T. Abernethy, *The Jew a Negro: Being a Study of the Jewish Ancestry from an Impartial Standpoint* (Moravian Falls, N.C.: Dixie Publishing Company, 1910), p. 11. Helpful information can be found in Leonard Rogoff's "Is the Jew White? The Racial Place of the Southern Jew," *American Jewish History* 85.3 (1997): 195–230, which contains on p. 215 the quotation from Ripley.

44. Lothrop Stoddard, "The Pedigree of Judah," reprinted from *The Forum*, March 1926, in *A Gallery of Jewish Types* (Marietta, Ga.: The Thunderbolt, n.d.), *Forum*, p. 326.

45. F. Scott Fitzgerald, *The Great Gatsby*, preface and notes by Matthew J. Bruccoli (New York: Scribner, 1995), p. 11. Tom Buchanan's tirade comes from pp. 17–18.

46. Madison Grant, *The Passing of the Great Race, or the Racial Basis of European History*, rev. ed. (New York: Scribner, 1918), pp. vii, 16–17.

47. Lothrop Stoddard, *The Rising Tide of Color against White World-Supremacy* (New York: Scribner, 1920), p. 5.

48. See, for example, Carlyle Van Thompson's *The Tragic Black Buck: Racial Masquerading in the American Literary Imagination* (New York: Peter Lang, 2004), chapter 4. For a more moderate view stressing Gatsby's ambiguous ethnic origins, see Meredith Goldsmith, "White Skin, White Mask: Passing, Posing, and Performing in *The Great Gatsby*," *MFS: Modern Fiction Studies* 49.3 (Fall 2003): 443–468.

49. F. Scott Fitzgerald, *Trimalchio: An Early Version of The Great Gatsby*, ed. James L. W. West III (Cambridge: Cambridge University Press, 2000), p. 103.

50. James Joyce, *The Critical Writings*, ed. Ellsworth Mason and Richard Ellmann (Ithaca, N.Y.: Cornell University Press, 1989), pp. 165–166; James Joyce, *Finnegans Wake* (New York: Penguin, 1976), p. 18.

51. See Ira B. Nadel, *Joyce and the Jews* (Gainesville: University Press of Florida, 1996), pp. 49–51. The following quotation comes from Maurice Fishberg, *The Jews: A Study of Race and Environment* (London: Walter Scott, 1911), p. 474; James Joyce, *Ulysses*, ed. Hans Walter Gabler (New York: Random House, 1986), p. 400.

52. Elizabeth Butler Cullingford, *Ireland's Others: Ethnicity and Gender in Irish Literature and Popular Culture* (Notre Dame, Ind.: University of Notre Dame Press in association with Field Day, 2001), p. 134.

53. For sheet music containing the original words and score, see the University of Colorado at Boulder library Web site, http://ucblibraries.colorado.edu/cgi-bin/ sheetmusic.pl?RagIfTheMan&Rag&main (accessed 18 February 2008). For "The Boys of Wexford," see http://www.traditionalmusic.co.uk/song-midis/Boys_of_ Wexford_(2).htm (accessed 18 February 2008).

54. James Joyce, *Ulysses: A Critical and Synoptic Edition,* 3 vols., ed. Hans Walter Gabler (New York: Garland, 1986), 1:362. I have discussed the uses of this edition for interpretation at greater length in *Material Modernism: The Politics of the Page* (Cambridge: Cambridge University Press, 2001), chapter 6 ("Joyce and the Colonial Archive").

55. *Dubliners: Text and Criticism,* ed. Robert Scholes and A. Walton Litz (New York: Penguin, 1996), p. 198.

56. Alain Locke, ed., *The New Negro* (New York: Atheneum, 1992), p. 7.

57. Alain Locke, "Harlem," *Survey Graphic* 6.6 (March 1925): 629.

58. Gossett, *Race,* p. 418. Stoddard's remark is cited by Matthew Frye Jacobson, *Whiteness of a Different Color: European Immigrants and the Alchemy of Race* (Cambridge, Mass.: Harvard University Press, 1998), p. 184; and Michael Rogin, *Blackface, White Noise: Jewish Immigrants in the Hollywood Melting Pot* (Berkeley: University of California Press, 1996), p. 89.

59. W. E. B. Du Bois, *Black Folk Then and Now: An Essay in the History and Sociology of the Negro Race* (New York: Henry Holt, 1939), p. vii.

60. *The New Negro, an Interpretation,* ed. Alain Locke (New York: Albert and Charles Boni, 1925), title page. For the paperback reprint, see note 56 above.

61. Aaron Douglas, 1973 speech quoted in George Hutchinson, *The Harlem Renaissance in Black and White* (Cambridge, Mass.: Harvard University Press, 1995), p. 398. I am indebted to Hutchinson's wonderful scholarship and also to two other books on *The New Negro* and its milieu: Anne Elizabeth Carroll, *Word, Image, and the New Negro* (Bloomington: Indiana University Press, 2005); and Martha Jane Nadell, *Enter the New Negroes: Images of Race in American Culture* (Cambridge, Mass.: Harvard University Press, 2004), both of which I reviewed in "'New Negroes' and Lost Connections: Re-Viewing the Text," *Michigan Quarterly Review,* 45.4 (Fall 2006): 713–721.

62. For an account of the meeting and responses to it, see Jeffrey C. Stewart, *To Color American: Portraits by Winold Reiss* (Washington, D.C.: National Portrait Gallery, 1989). The quotations come from pp. 50 and 54.

63. Jean Toomer, *Cane,* Introduction by Arna Bontemps (New York: Harper & Row, 1969), p. viii. See Charles T. Davis, "Jean Toomer and the South," *Studies in the Literary Imagination* 7.2 (Fall 1974): 23–37, for a good general discussion of the subject. The second remark is quoted in George Hutchinson, "Jean Toomer and American Racial Discourse," *Texas Studies in Literature and Language,* 35.2 (Summer 1993): 230. The Toomer papers are now in the Beinecke Library at Yale University.

64. *The Philosophy of Alain Locke,* ed. Leonard Harris (Philadelphia: Temple University Press, 1989), p. 206.

65. *American Hebrew,* 14 October 1927, as cited in Robert L. Carringer, *The Jazz Singer* (Madison: University of Wisconsin Press, 1979), p. 11.

66. Samson Raphaelson, *The Jazz Singer* (New York: Brentano's, 1925), p. 115. In the preface Raphaelson remarks that "jazz is prayer" and repeats the odd interpretation of Arnold's lines.

67. Irving Howe, *World of Our Fathers: The Journey of the East European Jews to America and the Life They Found and Made* (New York: Simon and Schuster, 1976), p. 563.

68. Michael Rogin, *Blackface, White Noise,* pp. 100, 116. Rogin's point of view reappears in the work of several "whiteness historians," even in that of Matthew Frye Jacobson, whom I have found valuable elsewhere.

69. Michael Alexander, *Jazz Age Jews* (Princeton, N.J.: Princeton University Press, 2001), p. 173.

70. Al Jolson, "The Art of Minstrelsy," *Theatre* 27.207 (May 1918): 290–292. All other quotes from Jolson about minstrelsy in this paragraph come from the same brief article.

71. For material in this paragraph, see Herbert G. Goldman, *Jolson: The Legend Comes to Life* (New York: Oxford University Press, 1988), pp. 57–58, 170–171, 304–305, and passim; and Joseph Ciolino, "Al Jolson Wasn't Racist," *Black Star News,* 22 May 2007, available at http://www.blackstarnews.com (accessed 13 March 2008). See also Jim Haskins and N. R. Mitgang, *Mr. Bojangles: The Biography of Bill Robinson* (New York: William Morrow, 1988).

72. See, in order, the reviews in *Variety,* 12 October 1927, p. 16; *New York Times,* 7 October 1927, p. 24; *Moving Picture World,* 22 October 1927, p. 514; and *Film Daily,* 23 October 1927, p. 6.

73. Hasia Diner, *In the Almost Promised Land: American Jews and Blacks, 1915–1935* (Baltimore: Johns Hopkins University Press, 1977, rpt. 1995), pp. 68–69.

74. *New York Amsterdam News,* 2 May 1928, p. 7. For other quotations from African-American papers in this paragraph, see *New York Amsterdam News,* 9 July 1930, p. 9; *The Afro-American* (Baltimore), 12 May 1928, p. 8; and *Pittsburgh Courier,* 25 June 1927, section 2, p. 2. I am grateful to the superb second chapter of Lisa Naomi Silberman Brenner's doctoral dissertation "The Jazz Singer's Legacy: The Racial Role-Play of African-Americans and Jews in Twentieth Century American Performances" (PhD diss., Columbia University, 2004), for its illumination of *The Jazz Singer'*s reception in its own time.

75. Sheila Tully Boyle and Andrew Bunie, *Paul Robeson: The Years of Promise and Achievement* (Amherst: University of Massachusetts Press, 2001), pp. 55, 356.

76. *Paul Robeson Speaks,* pp. 73, 85.

77. Diner, *In the Almost Promised Land,* p. 68.

78. *Paul Robeson Speaks,* p. 393. For more information on Robeson and the chant, see Jonathan Karp's excellent article "Performing Black-Jewish Symbiosis: The 'Hassidic Chant' of Paul Robeson," *American Jewish History* 91.1 (2003): 53–81.

2. Diasporas and Nationalisms

1. Franz Boas's article originally appeared in *Everybody's Magazine* 31 (November 1914): 671–674, and then in revised form in *Race and Nationality,* Special Bulletin of the American Association for International Conciliation (New York: American Association for International Conciliation, January 1915). It is most easily accessible under the title "National Groupings" in Boas's *Race and Democratic Society* (New York: J. J. Augustin, 1945); see p. 109 for the remark quoted.

2. *Oxford English Dictionary,* 2nd ed. (1989, online edition updated 1996), accessed through the University of Michigan Library.

3. Michael Galchinsky, "Scattered Seeds: A Dialogue of Diasporas," in *Insider/ Outsider: American Jews and Multiculturalism,* ed. David Biale, Michael Galchinsky, and Susan Heschel (Berkeley: University of California Press, 1998), p. 194. Among the vast literature on Jewish diaspora, I have found the recent articles of Galchinsky particularly helpful for this project; see also his "Africans, Indians, Arabs, and Scots: Jewish and Other Questions in the Age of Empire," *Jewish Culture and History* 6.1 (Summer 2003): 46–60. Daniel and Jonathan Boyarin's "Diaspora: Generation and the Ground of Jewish Identity," *Critical Inquiry* 19.4 (Summer 1993): 693–725, has been both influential and controversial in its effort to reverse the valences of diaspora and Israeli nationhood.

4. George Shepperson, "African Diaspora: Concept and Context," in *Global Dimensions of the African Diaspora,* ed. Joseph E. Harris (Washington, D.C.: Howard University Press, 1982), pp. 46–53, esp. pp. 46 and 51; Paul Gilroy, *The Black Atlantic: Modernity and Double Consciousness* (Cambridge, Mass.: Harvard University Press, 1993), p. 205, cf. p. 208; Mary J. Hickman, "Migration and Diaspora," in *The Cambridge Companion to Modern Irish Culture,* ed. Joe Cleary and Claire Connolly (Cambridge: Cambridge University Press, 2005), pp. 118–119.

5. William Safran, "Diasporas in Modern Societies: Myths of Homeland and Return," *Diaspora* 1.1 (1991): 83–99, esp. pp. 83–84. For a good survey of more hybridity-based theories of diaspora, see James Clifford, "Diasporas," *Cultural Anthropology* 9.3 (1994): 302–338.

6. For Douglass's usage, generally following the King James Version, see *The Norton Anthology of American Literature,* 5th ed. (New York: Norton, 1998), p. 2064.

7. Byron, "By the Rivers of Babylon We Sat Down and Wept," in *Byron's Hebrew Melodies,* ed. Thomas L. Ashton (Austin: University of Texas Press, 1972), p. 163. For Lincoln, see Daniel J. Elazar, *The Covenant Tradition in Politics,* vol. 3 (New Brunswick, N.J.: Transaction Publishers, 1998), chap. 1; Christina Rossetti,

"By the Waters of Babylon, B.C. 570," *Macmillan's Magazine* 14 (May–October 1866): 424.

8. Katharine Tynan, *The Wandering Years* (Boston: Houghton Mifflin, 1922), p. 287; James Joyce, *Ulysses,* ed. Hans Walter Gabler (New York: Random House, 1986), p. 37; James Joyce, *Finnegans Wake* (New York: Viking Penguin, 1959), p. 103.

9. Sinéad O'Connor, *Theology* (New York: Koch Records, 2007); The Melodians, *Rivers of Babylon: The Best of the Melodians* (New York: Sanctuary Records, 1997); Matisyahu, *Youth* (New York: Sony/Columbia, 2006).

10. Alexander Crummell, *Africa and America: Addresses and Discourses* (New York: Negro Universities Press, 1969), pp. 409–410; John Cromwell, *The Negro in American History* (Washington, D.C.: American Negro Academy, 1914), p. 137; Crummell, *Africa and America,* p. 39.

11. Albert Allson Whitman, *Not a Man and Yet a Man* (Springfield, Ohio: Republic Printing Co., 1877), p. 222; Mary Weston Fordham, *Magnolia Leaves* (Charleston, S.C.: Walker, Evans, and Cogswell, 1897), p. 60; Arna Wendell Bontemps, *Personals* (London: Paul Breman, 1973), pp. 28–29.

12. *The Poems of Charles Reznikoff,* ed. Seamus Cooney (Boston: Black Sparrow, 2005), p. 112.

13. *The Poetical Works of Henry Wadsworth Longfellow,* Riverside ed., vol. 3 (Boston: Houghton, Mifflin, 1890), pp. 33–36; Emma Lazarus, *Selected Poems and Other Writings,* ed. Gregory Eiselein (Peterborough, Canada: Broadview, 2002), p. 50.

14. Lazarus, *Selected Poems,* pp. 110, 263, 267, and appendix D. For the picture of Eliot on Lazarus's desk, see H. E. Jacob, *The World of Emma Lazarus* (New York: Shocken Books, 1940), pp. 119–120. For information on Lazarus, I am indebted to Esther Schor's excellent biography *Emma Lazarus* (New York: Schocken, 2006), and articles by Max Cavitch, "Emma Lazarus and the Golem of Liberty," *American Literary History* 18.1 (2006): 1–28; Ranen Omer-Sherman, "'Thy People Are My People': Emma Lazarus, *Daniel Deronda,* and the Ambivalence of Jewish Modernity," *Journal of Modern Jewish Studies* 1.1 (2002): 49–72; and Michael Weingrad, "Jewish Identity and Poetic Form in 'By the Waters of Babylon,'" *Jewish Social Studies,* n.s., 9.3 (2003): 107–120.

15. Eliezar Ben-Yehuda, *A Dream Come True,* trans T. Muraoka and ed. George Mandel (Boulder, Colo.: Westview Press, 1993), p. 27. *A Dream Come True* was originally published as a series of articles in the Hebrew magazine *Ha-Toren* from December 1917 to December 1918. *The Complete Diaries of Theodor Herzl,* vol. 1, ed. Raphael Patai, trans. Harry Zohn (New York: Herzl Press, 1960), p. 72.

16. *The George Eliot Letters,* vol. 6, ed. Gordon S. Haight (New Haven, Conn.: Yale University Press, 1955), p. 301. I owe the previous point about the Goldsmids to Michael Galchinsky's fine article "Africans, Indians, Arabs, and Scots," p. 55.

17. George Eliot, *Daniel Deronda* (New York: Random House, 2002), p. 216. Further quotations from the novel refer to this edition and are cited parenthetically by page number within the text.

18. Harriet Beecher Stowe, *The Annotated Uncle Tom's Cabin,* ed. Henry Louis Gates Jr. and Hollis Robbins (New York: Norton, 2007), pp. 35, 131, 213.

19. George Eliot, *Impressions of Theophrastus Such,* ed. Nancy Henry (Iowa City: University of Iowa Press, 1994), pp. 151–152, 155.

20. Bryan Cheyette, *Constructions of "the Jew" in English Literature and Society: Racial Representations, 1875–1945* (Cambridge: Cambridge University Press, 1993), p. 268. That thread runs throughout Cheyette's study, which notes in its introduction that "'The Jew', like all 'doubles', is inherently ambivalent and can represent both the 'best' and the 'worst' of selves" (p. 12).

21. Joyce, *Ulysses,* pp. 116–117 (emphasis in original). All further quotations from that novel are from this text (i.e., the Gabler edition) and are cited parenthetically by page number within the text.

22. *United Ireland,* 10 October 1891, p. 4, reprinted in W. B. Yeats, *The Poems* (revised), ed. Richard J. Finneran (New York: Macmillan, 1989), p. 531.

23. Quoted in Karin Margaret Strand, "W. B. Yeats's American Lecture Tours" (PhD diss., Northwestern University, 1978), pp. 187–188.

24. Douglas Hyde, "The Necessity for De-Anglicising Ireland," in *Irish Literature: A Reader,* ed. Maureen Murphy and James MacKillop (Syracuse, N.Y.: Syracuse University Press, 1987), pp. 146–147; Geoffrey Keating, *The General History of Ireland* (London: B. Creake, 1732), pp. 339–340.

25. Walter Laqueur, *A History of Zionism* (New York: Holt, Rinehart and Winston, 1972), p. xiii.

26. Amos Elon, *Herzl* (New York: Holt, Rinehart, and Winston, 1975), pp. 130, 168.

27. Theodor Herzl, *The Jewish State* (New York: Dover, 1988), pp. 76, 153.

28. The Hamas charter is available at http://www.mideastweb.org/hamas.htm (accessed 18 May 2010).

29. Theodor Herzl, *Old New Land,* trans. Lotta Levensohn (New York: Markus Wiener Publishing and The Herzl Press, 1987), p. 170.

30. Sarah H. Bradford, *Harriet Tubman: The Moses of Her People,* 2nd ed. (1886; rpt., Gloucester, Mass.: Peter Smith, 1981), pp. 3, 37. Cf. the fuller text of "Go Down, Moses" in *The Norton Anthology of African American Literature,* ed. Henry Louis Gates Jr. and Nellie Y. McKay (New York: Norton, 1997), p. 14. Howard Sage, "An Interview with Ralph Ellison: Visible Man," *Pulp* 2 (1976): 10–12, p. 10.

31. Alain Locke, ed., *The New Negro: An Interpretation* (New York: Albert and Charles Boni, 1925), p. 7. Later in the essay Locke adds that "As with the Jew, persecution is making the Negro international" (p. 14). James Weldon Johnson and J. Rosamond Johnson, *The Books of American Negro Spirituals,* 2 vols. (1925; rpt., New York: Da Capo Press, 1969), 1:20–21.

32. *The Book of American Negro Poetry,* rev. ed., ed. James Weldon Johnson (New York: Harcourt, Brace, Jovanovich, 1969, rpt. 1983), pp. 41, 210.

33. *The Oxford Companion to African American Literature,* ed. William Andrews, Frances Smith Foster, and Trudier Harris (New York: Oxford University Press, 1997), p. 90; Hollis R. Lynch, "A Black Nineteenth-Century Response to Jews and Zionism: The Case of Edward Wilmot Blyden," in *Jews in Black Perspectives: A Dialogue,* ed. Joseph R. Washington Jr. (Cranbury, N.J.: Associated University Presses, 1984), p. 48.

34. Edward Blyden, *The Jewish Question* (Liverpool: Lionel Hart, 1898), p. 7.

35. Israel Zangwill, *The Melting Pot* (New York: Macmillan, 1932), pp. 203, 204. Given continual immigration into the United States, that "final type" remains in process rather than reaching a fixed stasis.

36. W. E. B. Du Bois, "Not 'Separatism,'" *Crisis* 17 (February 1919): 166, as quoted in "Jews and the Enigma of the Pan-African Congress of 1919," in *Jews in Black Perspective,* p. 63.

37. Robert A. Hill, "Black Zionism: Marcus Garvey and the Jewish Question," in *African Americans and Jews in the Twentieth Century,* ed. V. P. Franklin, Nancy L. Grant, Harold M. Kletnick, and Genna Rae McNeil (Columbia: University of Missouri Press, 1998), p. 41. The quotation about "the initiators of the Pan-African movement" in the previous paragraph comes from Hill, p. 70. *The Marcus Garvey and Universal Negro Improvement Association Papers,* vol. 2, ed. Robert A. Hill (Berkeley: University of California Press, 1983), p. 58.

38. Yitzhak Shamir, *Summing Up: An Autobiography* (Boston: Little, Brown, 1994), p. 8.

39. Robert Briscoe, with Alden Hatch, *For the Life of Me* (Boston: Little, Brown, 1958), p. 325. For later quotations in this paragraph, see pp. 264–265 and 307. Unpublished typescript, Jabotinsky Institute (Tel Aviv), folder 253, no. 1.

40. Joyce, *Ulysses,* p. 280.

41. See Martin Gilbert, *The Atlas of Jewish History,* rev. ed. (New York: William Morrow, 1993), pp. 80, 93, 94, 113, 69, 116; and Mitchell G. Bard, *Myths and Facts: A Guide to the Arab-Israeli Conflict* (Chevy Chase, Md.: American-Israeli Cooperative Enterprise, 2002), pp. 163, 157, 161, 168, and 158, respectively.

3. Melting Pots

1. Israel Zangwill, *The Melting Pot* (New York: Macmillan, 1932), p. 203.

2. Emma Lazarus, *Selected Poems and Other Writings,* ed. Gregory Eiselein (Peterborough, Canada: Broadview, 2002), p. 176.

3. Ibid., p. 233.

4. This paragraph is based on information in Marvin Trachtenberg, *The Statue of Liberty* (New York: Viking Penguin, 1986), chapter 1 and passim; and in Oscar Handlin, *The Statue of Liberty* (New York: Newsweek Book Division, 1977). For the Lowell remark, see his letter to Lazarus, 17 December 1883, in *Letters to Emma Lazarus in the Columbia University Library,* ed. Ralph L. Rusk (New York:

New York Public Library, 1949), p. 74. For other information on publication, see Bette Roth Young's *Emma Lazarus in Her World* (Philadelphia: Jewish Publication Society, 1995), chapter 1.

5. I cannot bring myself to forsake the public inscriptions of this poem without mentioning the recent granite plaque in the International Arrivals Building of John F. Kennedy Airport in New York, which we might call the "PC version" of the poem. Now that immigrants arrive by airplane perhaps even more often than by boat, someone had the good idea of affixing Lazarus's poem to welcome them at the air terminal just as earlier the Statue of Liberty had welcomed immigrants to New York harbor. But a crucial line has been left out, even though its omission destroys the rhythm and rhyme scheme. The large gold letters now proclaim:

> Give me your tired, your poor,
> Your huddled masses yearning to breathe free . . .
> Send these, the homeless, tempest-tost to me.
> I lift my lamp beside the golden door!

The omitted line read: "The wretched refuse of your teeming shore." Presumably, the powers that be thought that line would be insulting to new immigrants, perhaps even destructive of their self-esteem. Like most efforts of the language police, this one backfires, and to anyone who knows the original, the censored form of the inscription reveals chiefly the extraordinary condescension of the censors toward those whom they think that they are protecting. As the noted naturalist Stephen Jay Gould wrote in an indignant Op-Ed piece in the *New York Times* in 1995, "The language police triumph, and integrity bleeds. . . . Did these particular police ever hear of metaphor? Did they consider that Lazarus might have been describing the attitudes of ruling classes in foreign lands toward their potential emigrants? Play it safe and destroy poetry." See Stephen Jay Gould, "No More 'Wretched Refuse,'" *New York Times,* Op-Ed page, 7 June 1995.

6. *Historical Statistics of the United States,* ed. Susan B. Carter et al., 5 vols. (New York: Cambridge University Press, 2006), 1:1–523 and tables Ad25–79. For statistics in the following sentence, see pp. 1–524, corrected for the anomalous spike created by the Immigration Reform and Control Act of 1986. For the figures for the twelve years ending in 1910, see *Dictionary of Races or Peoples* (Washington, D.C.: Government Printing Office, 1911), p. 8.

7. J. Hector St. John de Crevecoeur, *Letters from an American Farmer,* ed. Susan Manning (New York: Oxford University Press, 1997), pp. 43–44.

8. Ralph Waldo Emerson, *Journals: 1845–1848,* ed. Edward Waldo Emerson and Waldo Emerson Forbes (Boston: Houghton Mifflin, 1912), p. 115.

9. Frederick Jackson Turner, *The Frontier in American History* (New York: Henry Holt, 1921), p. 29. The best tracing of the shifting significance of the "melting pot" image is Philip Gleason, "The Melting Pot: Symbol of Fusion or Confusion?" *American Quarterly* 16.1 (Spring 1964): 20–46; and Gleason, "Confusion

Compounded: The Melting Pot in the 1960s and 1970s," *Ethnicity* 6.1 (March 1979): 10–20. For two other particularly helpful works, see also Arthur Mann, *The One and the Many: Reflections on the American Identity* (Chicago: University of Chicago Press, 1979), chapter 5; and Werner Sollors, *Beyond Ethnicity: Consent and Descent in American Culture* (New York: Oxford University Press, 1986), chapter 3. On the evolution of the title, see Edna Nashon, *From the Ghetto to the Melting Pot: Israel Zangwill's Jewish Plays* (Detroit: Wayne State University Press, 2006), pp. 213–214. Nashon's edition contains a wealth of information about the play, which I have found very helpful.

10. *Dictionary of Races or Peoples*, p. 2. See Chapter 1 of this volume for discussion of this document.

11. *Complete Diaries of Theodor Herzl*, 5 vols., ed. Raphael Patai (New York: Herzl Press, 1960), 1:276 and 2:517.

12. Israel Zangwill, *Speeches, Articles and Letters*, ed. Maurice Simon (London: Soncino Press, 1937), p. 93.

13. Letter of 7 October 1908, Annie Russell MS Collection, New York Public Library, as quoted in Maurice Wohlgelernter, *Israel Zangwill: A Study* (New York: Columbia University Press, 1964), p. 177.

14. *Letters of Theodore Roosevelt*, vol. 6, ed. Elting E. Morison et al. (Cambridge, Mass.: Harvard University Press 1952), p. 1289. The following unpublished letter, Roosevelt to Zangwill, n.d. [1911], is quoted in Nashon, *From the Ghetto to the Melting Pot*, p. 242. Information about annual reprinting comes from Mann, *The One and the Many*, p. 101.

15. *Chicago Daily Tribune*, 20 October 1908; *Unity*, 29 October 1908, p. 133; and *Chicago Daily News*, 21 October 1908. See, too, Joe Kraus, "How the Melting Pot Stirred America: The Reception of Zangwill's Play," *Melus* 24.3 (Fall 1999): 3–19; and Gary Szuberla, "Zangwill's *The Melting Pot* Plays Chicago," *Melus* 20:3 (Fall 1995): 3–20.

16. *New York Times*, 7 September 1909; *Evening Sun*, 10 September 1909; *New York Press*, 7 September 1909. Quotations from London reviews come from Zangwill's afterword (for London *Times*); *The English Review*, 17.65 (April 1914): 130; and *The Athenaeum*, 31 January 1914, p. 171.

17. Horace Kallen, "Democracy versus the Melting-Pot," *The Nation*, 18 January 1915, p. 220; Randolph Bourne, "Trans-National America" (1916), in *The American Intellectual Tradition: A Source Book*, ed. David A. Hollinger and Charles Capper (New York: Oxford University Press, 1977), p. 171; and "The Jew and Trans-National America," *Menorah Journal* 2.5 (December 1916): 277.

18. See the seminal account of the Ford English School, Jonathan Schwartz's "Henry Ford's Melting Pot," in *Ethnic Groups in the City: Culture, Institutions, and Power* (Lexington, Mass.: D. C. Heath, 1971), pp. 191–198, from which the remark by the Ford spokesman also comes. The quote from Henry Ford is on p. 191 and the spokesman on p. 192. For Lawrence W. Levine, see his chapter "From the Melting Pot to the Pluralist Vision," in *The Opening of the American Mind* (Boston:

Beacon Press, 1996). Levine borrowed the term "Anglo-conformity" from sociologists Stewart and Mildred Cole. See also the account in Neil Baldwin, *Henry Ford and the Jews* (New York: Public Affairs, 2001), pp. 41–42.

19. Henry Pratt Fairchild, *The Melting-Pot Mistake* (Boston: Little, Brown, 1926), p. 10.

20. Michael Davitt, *Within the Pale: The True Story of Anti-Semitic Persecutions in Russia* (London: Hurst and Blackett, 1903), p. v.

21. "Jews Mourn Davitt," *New York Times,* 4 June 1906.

22. See Cormac Ó Gráda, *Jewish Ireland in the Age of Joyce: A Socioeconomic History* (Princeton, N.J.: Princeton University Press, 2006), chapter 1. Most Irish Jews of the time had immigrated from a few nearby villages in Lithuania.

23. Dermot Keogh, *Jews in Twentieth-Century Ireland* (Cork: Cork University Press, 1998), p. 20. I am indebted to Keogh for the quotations from Davitt and Redmond later in this paragraph.

24. Typescript letter from Israel Zangwill, 28 September 1906, in Central Zionist Archive, Jerusalem, file A120/463.

25. Hasia R. Diner, *In the Almost Promised Land: American Jews and Blacks, 1915–1935* (Baltimore: Johns Hopkins University Press, 1995), p. 97. For the two following quotations from the *Forward,* see Diner, *In the Almost Promised Land,* pp. 75–76; and for those later in the paragraph, see Eric. L. Goldstein, *The Price of Whiteness: Jews, Race, and American Identity* (Princeton, N.J.: Princeton University Press, 2006), pp. 80–81.

26. W. E. B. Du Bois, "Editorial: East St. Louis," *The Crisis* 14.5 (September 1917): 216; Booker T. Washington, *The Man Farthest Down* (Garden City, N.Y.: Doubleday, 1912), pp. 246, 263.

27. *Cleveland Gazette,* 18 February 1911 and 29 April 1911; Baltimore *Afro-American,* 25 June 1910; St. Louis *Argus,* 30 March 1917; and New York *Age,* 22 March 1917. For analysis of these and other quotations, see Arnold Shankman's useful article "Brothers across the Sea: Afro-Americans on the Persecution of Russian Jews, 1881–1917," *Jewish Social Studies* 37:2 (Spring 1975): 114–121.

28. James Weldon Johnson, ed., *The Book of American Negro Poetry* (New York: Harcourt, Brace and Co., 1922, rev. 1931; rpt. n.d.), p. 41. Quotations from the novel come from James Weldon Johnson, *Autobiography of an Ex-Colored Man,* ed. William L. Andrews (New York: Penguin, 1990).

29. James Weldon Johnson, *Writings* (New York: Library of America, 2004), p. 811.

4. Popular and Institutional Cultures

1. Cornel West, *Beyond Eurocentrism and Multiculturalism,* vol. 1: *Prophetic Thought in Postmodern Times* (Monroe, Me.: Common Courage Press, 1993), p. 4.

2. Edward Said, *Musical Elaborations* (New York: Columbia University Press, 1991), p. 53; Gary Gerstle, *American Crucible: Race and Nation in the Twentieth Century* (Princeton, N.J.: Princeton University Press, 2001), p. 164.

3. Alain Locke, "The Contribution of Race to Culture," in *The Philosophy of Alain Locke,* ed. Leonard Harris (Philadelphia: Temple University Press, 1989), p. 203. In a later essay Locke urged that groups did not posses "proprietary rights" to culture (p. 233).

4. For the Armstrong remark, see Gene Lees, *Cats of Any Color: Jazz Black and White* (New York: Oxford University Press, 1994), p. 2; for the Ellington one, see Terry Teachout, "The Color of Jazz," in *A Terry Teachout Reader* (New Haven, Conn.: Yale University Press, 2004), p. 254.

5. James Weldon Johnson, *The Book of American Negro Spirituals,* with musical arrangements by J. Rosamond Johnson (New York: Viking, 1925), p. 28.

6. Herb Snitzer, *Jazz: A Visual Journey* (Clearwater, Fla.: Notables, 1999), p. 7. The other version of the portrait discussed in this paragraph appeared on the cover of *Metronome* for December 1960.

7. Louis Armstrong, *Louis Armstrong—a Self-Portrait: The Interview by Richard Meryman* (New York: Eakins Press, 1971), p. 24.

8. Louis Armstrong, *Louis Armstrong in His Own Words,* ed. Thomas Brothers (New York: Oxford University Press, 1999), p. 5. Further references to this work will be cited parenthetically by page number within the text.

9. *The Louis Armstrong Companion: Eight Decades of Commentary,* ed. Joshua Berrett (New York: Schirmer Books, 1999), pp. 173–174.

10. Willie the Lion Smith with George Hoefer, *Music on My Mind: The Memoirs of an American Pianist* (New York: Doubleday, 1964), p. 5 (hereafter cited parenthetically by page number within the text).

11. Milton "Mezz" Mezzrow and Bernard Wolfe, *Really the Blues* (London: Jazz Book Club by arrangement with Secker and Warburg, 1959), p. 18.

12. John White, *Artie Shaw: His Life and Music* (New York: Continuum, 2004), pp. 61–62. All Shaw and Holiday quotations in this paragraph come from pp. 60–64 of this source.

13. David Yaffe, *Fascinating Rhythm: Reading Jazz in American Writing* (Princeton, N.J.: Princeton University Press, 2006), p. 16. I am indebted to Yaffe's powerful arguments in support of a positive view of melting-pot interactions in jazz. For the following quotation, see Yaffe, p. 19.

14. Many Jewish-American writers changed their names, too: Nathan Weinstein became Nathaniel West, Itzok Isaac Gronich became Mike Gold, Julian Shapiro became John Sanford, and Nelson Ahlgren Abraham became Nelson Algren. The quotation from Ethel Waters comes from Jeffrey Melnick, *A Right to Sing the Blues: African Americans, Jews, and American Popular Song* (Cambridge, Mass.: Harvard University Press, 1999), p. 180. I have found Melnick's work as

useful as Yaffe's, though Melnick's approach comes closer to that of the "white-ness" historians than to Yaffe's stance.

15. Jenna Weissman Joselit, "Gershwin's American 'Rhapsody,'" *Forward,* 10 November 2006. See Howard Pollack's recent and authoritative biography, *George Gershwin: His Life and Work* (Berkeley: University of California Press, 2006), for a longer account, esp. p. 297. See also Charles Hamm, *Yesterdays: Popular Song in American* (New York: Norton, 1979), p. 350; *Opportunity* 3.29 (May 1926): 132–133.

16. Yaffe, *Fascinating Rhythm,* p. 16. The additional list draws on Pollack, *George Gershwin,* p. 480.

17. Pollack, *George Gershwin,* p. 573. Quotations from Pollack in this discussion will be cited parenthetically by page number within the text.

18. Isaac Goldberg, *George Gershwin: A Study in American Music* (New York: Frederick Ungar, 1958; originally published by Simon and Schuster in 1931), p. 40. Cf. Goldberg's *Tin Pan Alley* (New York: John Day, 1930), p. 293.

19. Jerome Kern, *The Jerome Kern Song Book,* ed. with introduction by Oscar Hammerstein II (New York: Simon and Schuster, 1955), p. 3.

20. Bernard A. Bergman, "He Says It with Music," *American Israelite* 68.44 (4 May 1922): 1; Michael Alexander, *Jazz Age Jews* (Princeton, N.J.: Princeton University Press, 2001), p. 164.

21. Melnick, *A Right to Sing the Blues,* pp. 25–26; *New York Times,* 14 December 1924, p. X8.

22. Virgil Thomson, "Gershwin," in *Virgil Thomson: A Reader,* ed. Richard Kostelanetz (New York: Routledge, 2002), pp. 150, 152.

23. Charles Hamm, *Irving Berlin: Songs from the Melting Pot: The Formative Years, 1907–1914* (New York: Oxford University Press, 1977), p. 107; Edward Jablonski, *Harold Arlen: Happy with the Blues* (New York: Doubleday, 1961), p. 68.

24. Robert F. Moss, "Side by Side: Irish and Jews in American Theater," *Jewish Daily Forward,* 2 July 2008, available at http://www.forward.com/articles/12372 (accessed 1 June 2010).

25. William H. A. Williams, *'Twas Only an Irishman's Dream: The Image of Ireland and the Irish in American Popular Song Lyrics, 1800–1920* (Urbana: University of Illinois Press, 1996), p. 192. The lyrics of "If It Wasn't for the Irish and the Jews" that follow are my transcription from the original recording.

26. Edward T. O'Donnell, "Abie's Irish Rose," *Irish Echo,* 19 May 2004; available at www.edwardtodonnell.com/hibchronabiesirishrose.html (accessed 7 July 2008).

27. Anne Nichols, *Abie's Irish Rose* (New York: Samuel French, 1938), pp. 4, 113, 118, 122, 123.

28. *Film Daily and Weekly Film Digest,* 26 September 1926, p. 6; Eric L. Goldstein, *The Price of Whiteness: Jews, Race, and American Identity* (Princeton, N.J.: Princeton University Press, 2006), p. 134. See also Lily Carthew, *The American Idea* (Boston: Walter H. Baker, 1918), p. 14.

29. Wallace Stevens, *Collected Poems* (New York: Alfred A. Knopf, 1968), p. 215.

30. Robert Kimball, ed., *The Complete Lyrics of Ira Gershwin* (New York: Da Capo Press, 1998), p. 29. Becoming popular in the early twentieth century, the terms "highbrow" and "lowbrow" derive from nineteenth-century racial science, particularly phrenology.

31. Ralph Ellison, "Change the Joke and Slip the Yoke," in his *Shadow and Act* (New York: Vintage Books, 1972), p. 58.

32. Cited by David E. Chinitz in his very helpful *T. S. Eliot and the Cultural Divide* (Chicago: University of Chicago Press, 2003), p. 29, which argues at length for Eliot's involvement with popular culture. I have also profited particularly from Michael North's discussion of African-American dialect in his *The Dialect of Modernism: Race, Language, and Twentieth Century Literature* (New York: Oxford University Press, 1994), esp. chapters 1 and 4. The most provocative and debated recent text on Eliot and Jews is Anthony Julius's *T. S. Eliot, Anti-Semitism, and Literary Form* (Cambridge: Cambridge University Press, 1995).

33. For a transcription of the lyrics and music of "Shakespearian Rag," see Lawrence Rainey, *The Annotated Waste Land with Eliot's Contemporary Prose* (New Haven, Conn.: Yale University Press, 2005), pp. 96–99; for the deleted opening, see T. S. Eliot, *The Waste Land: A Facsimile and Transcript of the Original Drafts*, ed. Valerie Eliot (New York: Harcourt Brace Jovanovich, 1971), p. 5.

34. Ezra Pound, *The Cantos* (New York: New Directions, 1970; 10th printing 1986), p. 433.

35. Ezra Pound, *The Confucian Odes: The Classic Anthology Defined by Confucius* (New York: New Directions, 1959), p. 100.

36. Ezra Pound, *Translations* (New York: New Directions, 1963), pp. 286, 288. "Yiddische Charleston Band" appeared in *An Objectivist's Anthology*, ed. Louis Zukofsky (Le Beausset, France: To Publishers, 1932), p. 45. Pound told Robert Duncan that the first line should have begun "Jazzin' Jhesus." See Donald Gallup, *Ezra Pound: A Bibliography* (Charlottesville: University Press of Virginia, 1983), p. 155.

37. Russell Sanjek, *American Popular Music and Its Business: The First Four Hundred Years*, vol. 2 (New York: Oxford University Press, 1988), p. 279. See p. 414 for a list of songs selling over a million copies by 1908, which also included Bob Cole and the Johnsons' "Under the Bamboo Tree."

38. William Jerome and Jean Schwartz, "Bedelia" (New York: Shapiro Remick and Company, 1903), inside front cover.

39. Charles A. Madison, *Jewish Publishing in America: The Impact of Jewish Writing on American Culture* (New York: Sanhedrin Press, 1976), p. 251.

40. Alfred Harcourt, "Publishing in New York," in *Publishers on Publishing*, ed. Gerald Gross (New York: R. R. Bowker and Grosset & Dunlap, 1961), p. 255.

41. For the Christopher Morley remark, see John Tebbel's authoritative *A History of Book Publishing in the United States*, vol. 3 (New York: R. R. Bowker, 1978), p. 117. For Huebsch's own comment, see *Publishers on Publishing*, pp. 298–299.

42. Langston Hughes, *The Big Sea: An Autobiography* (New York: Knopf, 1940), pp. 254–255.

43. Pound's contract with Liveright is quoted in Noel Stock, *The Life of Ezra Pound* (New York: Pantheon Books, 1970), p. 246. For Faulkner's remark, see William Faulkner, *Selected Letters* (New York: Viking, 1978), p. 41.

44. Waldo Frank, *Our America* (New York: Boni and Liveright, 1919), pp. 8–9.

5. The Gathering Storm

1. For more on matters covered in this and the following paragraph, see Marcia Graham Synnott, *The Half-Opened Door: Discrimination and Admissions at Harvard, Yale, and Princeton, 1900–1970* (Westport, Conn.: Greenwood Press, 1979); Jerome Karabel, *The Chosen: The Hidden History of Admission and Exclusion at Harvard, Yale, and Princeton* (Boston: Houghton Mifflin, 2005); Richard S. Levy, ed., *Antisemitism: A Historical Encyclopedia of Prejudice and Persecution* (Santa Barbara, Calif.: ABC-CLIO, 2005); and Todd M. Endelman, *The Jews of Britain, 1656–2000* (Berkeley: University of California Press, 2002).

2. Upton Sinclair, *The Goose-Step: A Study of American Education* (Pasadena, Calif.: Upton Sinclair, 1923), p. 112.

3. Karl Shapiro, *The Poetry Wreck: Selected Essays* (New York: Random House, 1975), p. 210. The poem "University" is quoted from Karl Shapiro, *New and Selected Poems, 1940–1986* (Chicago: University of Chicago Press, 1987), pp. 13–14. Eliot's remarks come from *After Strange Gods: A Primer of Modern Heresy* (London: Faber and Faber, 1934), pp. 20, 16.

4. See Hasia Diner, *In the Almost Promised Land: American Jews and Blacks, 1915–1935* (Baltimore: Johns Hopkins University Press, 1995), pp. 49, 99–100.

5. Charles Flint Kellogg, *NAACP: A History of the National Association for the Advancement of Colored People*, vol. 1: *1909–1920* (Baltimore: Johns Hopkins University Pres, 1967), p. 44; for a briefer account of the role of Jews in the early days of the NAACP, see Diner, *In the Almost Promised Land*, 119–142.

6. Many books deal with aspects of the history of lynching. For a good brief overview, see the review article by David Levering Lewis, "An American Pastime," *New York Review of Books*, 24 November 2002, pp. 27–30. For partial data, see the NAACP report *Thirty Years of Lynching in the United States, 1889–1918* (New York: NAACP, 1919); the reference to Germany appears in the first sentence on p. 5. The report missed the last recorded public lynching in Michigan, of the Irish immigrant William Sullivan in 1893. William C. Carrigan and Clive Webb provide supplementary data in "The Lynching of Persons of Mexican Origin or Descent in the United States, 1848 to 1928," *Journal of Social History* 37.2 (Winter 2003): 411–438; the quotation in my text comes from their abstract. The Du Bois quotation appears in *The Crisis: A Record of the Darker Races* 1.1 (November 1910): 11. An earlier version of my remarks here appeared in "Nooses at Central

Mich. Should Offend Everyone," the lead Op-Ed piece in the *Detroit News*, 29 November 2007, p. 19A. For the quotation from Tom Watson, see Steve Oney, *And the Dead Shall Rise: The Murder of Mary Phagan and the Lynching of Leo Frank* (New York: Pantheon, 2003), p. 558.

7. David Margolick, *Strange Fruit: The Biography of a Song* (New York: HarperCollins, 2001), p. 13. I have drawn on Margolick for much of the information in this paragraph; the later quote from *Time* magazine is on p. 55.

8. Berysh Vaynshteyn, "Lynching," in *American Yiddish Poetry: A Bilingual Anthology*, ed. Benjamin and Barbara Harshav (Stanford, Calif.: Stanford University Press, 2007), pp. 647–648. Among other Yiddish works dealing with lynching, Joseph Opatoshu's *Lintsheray un andere dertsaylungen* [Lynching and other stories] (Vilna: B. Kletskin, 1927) deserves special mention. As Eric Sundquist points out, its title story likens a small-town Southern lynching to a pogrom in Russia and contends that "If today they lynch a black, tomorrow it will be a Jew." See Sundquist, *Strangers in the Land: Blacks, Jews, Post Holocaust America* (Cambridge, Mass.: Harvard University Press, 2005), p. 27.

9. See the reprinted press reports in "American Crusade to End Lynching," in *Paul Robeson Speaks: Writings, Speeches, Interviews, 1918–1974*, ed. Philip S. Foner (New York: Kensington, 1978), pp. 173–178. The next remark quoted appears on p. 309 of the same source.

10. Sheila Tully Boyle and Andrew Bunie, *Paul Robeson: The Years of Promise and Achievement* (Amherst: University of Massachusetts Press, 2001), pp. 357–358.

11. Langston Hughes, "Nazi and Dixie Nordics," *Chicago Defender*, 10 March 1945, p. 1.

12. As quoted in the closest study of the subject, Lunabelle Wedlock's *The Reaction of Negro Publications and Organizations to German Anti-Semitism* (Washington, D.C.: The Graduate School, Howard University, 1942), pp. 48, 105. I am indebted generally to Wedlock's study, which originated as a PhD dissertation chaired by Alain Locke.

13. *Afro-American*, 14 October 1933, p. 16; *Washington Tribune*, 10 June 1939, p. 5; and *Amsterdam News*, 31 December 1938, p. 1.

14. Quoted in Eric L. Goldstein, *The Price of Whiteness: Jews, Race, and American Identity* (Princeton, N.J.: Princeton University Press, 2006), p. 196, along with other examples. See, too, Deborah Dash Moore, *GI Jews: How World War II Changed a Generation* (Cambridge, Mass.: Harvard University Press, 2004), for more detail.

15. Both articles are conveniently reprinted in *Bridges and Boundaries: African Americans and American Jews*, ed. Jack Salzman, Adina Back, and Gretchen Sullivan Sorin (New York: George Braziller in association with the Jewish Museum, 1992), pp. 74–85.

16. See Wedlock, *The Reaction of Negro Publications*, pp. 72–77. For the following quotation from Du Bois, see "As the Crow Flies," *New York Amsterdam News*,

18 September 1943, reprinted in *Newspaper Columns by W. E. B. Du Bois,* ed. Herbert Aptheker, 2 vols. (White Plains, N.Y.: Kraus-Thomson Organization, 1986), 1:554. For a valuable overview of Du Bois and the Holocaust, see "'A Calamity Almost beyond Comprehension': Nazi Anti-Semitism and the Holocaust in the Thought of W. E. B. Du Bois," *American Jewish History* 88.1 (2000): 53–93.

17. For information in this and the preceding paragraph, I have drawn on Michael L. Cooper, *The Double V Campaign: African Americans in World War II* (New York: Dutton, 1998); Gary Donaldson, *The History of African-Americans in the Military* (Malabar, Fla.: Krieger Publishing, 1991); Lawrence P. Scott, *Double V: The Civil Rights Struggle of the Tuskegee Airmen* (East Lansing: Michigan State University Press, 1994); and the online files of the *Pittsburgh Courier,* including especially its explanation of the campaign in the issue for 14 February 1942, from which the quotation comes; see http://bsc.chadwyck.com (accessed 3 June 2010).

18. Ottley's column from the *Chicago Defender* is reprinted in Christopher Metress, *The Lynching of Emmett Till* (Charlottesville: University of Virginia Press, 2002), p. 132.

19. For an accessible short summary, see "The Nuremberg Race Laws" and related links on the Web site of the United States Holocaust Memorial Museum and its *Holocaust Encyclopedia,* available at http://www.ushmm.org/outreach/nlaw .htm. For the quotations from Hitler, see Adolf Hitler, *Mein Kampf,* trans. Ralph Manheim (Boston: Houghton Mifflin, 1999), p. 325. Cf. pp. 383 and 624. For Grant's book as Hitler's "Bible," see Sundquist, *Strangers in the Land,* p. 187. I have also profited from George M. Frederickson's discussion of Nazis and Jews in *Racism: A Short History* (Princeton, N.J.: Princeton University Press, 2002), esp. pp. 117–129.

20. The best source of information on *Entartete Kunst* is Stephanie Barron, *"Degenerate Art": The Fate of the Avant-Garde in Nazi Germany* (Los Angeles: Los Angeles County Museum of Art, 1991), in which the quotation from Ziegler appears on p. 45. See also Michael H. Kater, *Different Drummers: Jazz in the Culture of Nazi Germany* (New York: Oxford University Press, 1992).

21. Alain Locke, *The Negro and His Music,* Bronze Booklet no. 2 (Washington, D.C.: Associates in Negro Folk Education, 1936), p. 72, quoted in Paul Gilroy, *Against Race: Imagining Political Culture beyond the Color Line* (Cambridge, Mass.: Harvard University Press, 2000), p. 296.

22. The report appeared on 21 December 1935, p. 9, as quoted in Gilroy, *Against Race,* p. 294.

23. For quotations in this paragraph, see Gearóid Ó hAllmhuráin, "Dancing on the Hobs of Hell: Rural Communities in Clare and the Dance Halls Act of 1935," *New Hibernia Review* 9.4 (Winter 2005): 9–18, esp. p. 11; and Jim Smyth, "Dancing, Depravity, and All That Jazz," *History Ireland* 1.2 (Summer 1993): 51–54.

24. For this quotation and other information in this paragraph, see especially Dermot Keogh, *Jews in Twentieth-Century Ireland: Refugees, Anti-Semitism, and*

the Holocaust (Cork: Cork University Press, 1998); the quotation is on p. 161, and the lowest estimate on p. 192.

25. Bob Doyle, *Brigadista: An Irishman's Fight against Fascism* (Blackrock, Ireland: Currach Press, 1976), pp. 45, 66.

26. Ita Daly, *Unholy Ghosts* (London: Bloomsbury, 1996), p. 81, quoted in Keogh, *Jews in Twentieth-Century Ireland*, p. 192. The quotations from McGuinness, McCarthy, and MacNeice are reproduced in Elizabeth Cullingford, *Ireland's Others: Ethnicity and Gender in Irish Literature and Culture* (Notre Dame, Ind.: University of Notre Dame Press in association with Field Day, 2001), pp. 68–70.

27. Quotations from the *Bell* come from 1.1 (October 1940): 9; 10.3 (June 1945): 207–216; and 10.4 (July 1945): 293–303.

28. John Berryman, "The Imaginary Jew," in *The Freedom of the Poet* (New York: Farrar, Straus & Giroux, 1976), p. 361. All other quotations from the story come from this source. For the quotation from the interview cited at the end of the next paragraph, see Peter Stitt, "Excerpts from Interviews with John Berryman," available at http://www.english.illinois.edu/Maps/poets/a_f/berryman/interviews.htm (accessed 13 March 2009).

29. *Zora Neale Hurston: A Life in Letters*, ed. Carla Kaplan (New York: Doubleday, 2003), pp. 538, 457, 526; and *I Love Myself When I Am Laughing*, ed. Alice Walker (Old Westbury, N.Y.: Feminist Press, 1979), p. 162.

30. Zora Neale Hurston, *Moses, Man of the Mountain* (New York: Harper, 1991), pp. 2, 180. Further quotations from the novel will be cited parenthetically by page number within the text.

31. The parallels to Nazi Germany have received some attention in scholarship. See particularly Deborah E. McDowell, "Foreword," in *Moses, Man of the Mountain* (New York: Harper, 1991), esp. pp. xv–xx; Robert E. Hemenway, *Zora Neale Hurston: A Literary Biography* (Urbana: University of Illinois Pres, 1977), chapter 10; Melanie J. Wright, *Moses in America: The Cultural Uses of Biblical Narrative* (New York: Oxford University Press, 2003), pp. 59–69; and Mark Christian Thompson, "National Socialism and Blood-Sacrifice in Zora Neale Hurston's *Moses, Man of the Mountain*," *African American Review* 38.3 (2004): 395–415.

32. Zora Neale Hurston, *Their Eyes Were Watching God* (Urbana: University of Illinois Press, 1978), p. 210, and *Dust Tracks on a Road* (New York: Harper, 1991), pp. 171–172.

33. Quoted in Halima Taha, *Collecting African American Art Works on Paper and Canvas*, rev. 2nd printing (Burlington, Vt.: Verve Editions, 2008), p. 184.

34. Arthur Miller, *Incident at Vichy* (New York: Penguin, 1985), p. 51. Further quotations from the play will be cited parenthetically by page number within the text.

35. Arthur Miller, "Guilt and *Incident at Vichy*," in *Echoes Down the Corridor: Collected Essays, 1944–2000*, ed. Steven R. Centola (New York: Viking, 2000), p. 70.

36. John Gross, *A Double Thread: Growing Up English and Jewish in London* (Chicago: Ivan R. Dee, 2002), p. 29.

37. See John P. Jackson Jr. and Nadine M. Weidman, *Race, Racism, and Science: Social Impact and Interaction* (New Brunswick, N.J.: Rutgers University Press, 2006), pp. 44–45, 55, 72, 74, and 81 for Broca, and pp. 122–123 for the Kaiser Wilhelm Institute. Stephen Jay Gould's *The Mismeasure of Man* (New York: Norton, 1996) provides a useful overview, especially the chapter on Broca and his followers.

38. Quoted in Janet N. Balakian, "The Holocaust, the Depression, and McCarthyism: Miller in the Sixties," in *The Cambridge Companion to Arthur Miller*, ed. Christopher Bigsby (New York: Cambridge University Press, 1997), p. 126.

39. For Dorothy Parker, see http://www.naacp.org/about/history/dparker; and for Joachim Prinz see http://www.joachimprinz.com, which under "Civil Rights" reprints Prinz's 1964 address (both accessed 16 April 2009).

40. See the Web site of the Israel Ministry of Foreign Affairs, http://www.mfa.gov.il/MFA/MFAArchive/2000_2009/2003/6/The%20Righteous%20Among%20the%20Nations (accessed 17 April 2009), and of Yad Vashem itself, http://www.yadvashem.org.il/ (accessed 2 June 2010). The wording in translation of the Talmudic inscription on the medal awarded to the Righteous comes from the first site.

Index